CONGRESS AND THE POLITICS OF NATIONAL SECURITY

In the wake of 9/11, a growing number of observers and practitioners have called for a reexamination of our national security system. Central to any such reform effort is an evaluation of Congress. Is Congress adequately organized to deal with national security issues in an integrated and coordinated manner? How have developments in Congress over the past few decades, such as heightened partisanship, message politics, party-committee relationships, and bicameral relations, affected topical security issues? This volume examines variation in the ways Congress has engaged those federal agencies overseeing our nation's national security as well as various domestic political determinants of security policy.

David P. Auerswald is professor of security studies at the National War College. Before joining the National War College, he was an assistant professor of political science at George Washington University; served on the Senate Foreign Relations Committee Staff, working for then-Senator Joseph Biden of Delaware; and was a staff assistant for U.S. Senator Timothy Wirth of Colorado. He has worked on the congressional reform team of the Project on National Security Reform, the U.S. Central Command's 2008–2009 Assessment Team, and the 2008 "Alternative Futures" project for the Office of the Secretary of Defense. He is the author and co-author, respectively of *Disarmed Democracies: Domestic Institutions and the Use of Force* and *The Kosovo Conflict: A Diplomatic History through Documents*.

Colton C. Campbell is professor of national security strategy at the National War College. Prior to joining the National War College, he was a Legislative Aide to U.S. Representative Mike Thompson of California, where he handled Appropriations, Defense, and Trade matters. Before that, he was an Analyst in American National Government at the Congressional Research Service, an associate professor of political science at Florida International University, and an APSA Congressional Fellow in the office of Senator Bob Graham of Florida. He is the author, co-author, and co-editor of several books on Congress, including *Discharging Congress: Government by Commission* and *Impeaching Clinton: Partisan Strife on Capitol Hill*.

T0349758

Congress and the Politics of National Security

Editors

DAVID P. AUERSWALD

National War College, National Defense University

COLTON C. CAMPBELL

National War College, National Defense University

CAMBRIDGE
UNIVERSITY PRESS

CAMBRIDGE UNIVERSITY PRESS
Cambridge, New York, Melbourne, Madrid, Cape Town,
Singapore, São Paulo, Delhi, Tokyo, Mexico City

Cambridge University Press
32 Avenue of the Americas, New York, NY 10013-2473, USA

www.cambridge.org
Information on this title: www.cambridge.org/9780521187268

First published 2012

Printed in the United States of America

A catalog record for this publication is available from the British Library.

Library of Congress Cataloging in Publication data
Congress and the politics of national security / [edited by] David P. Auerswald,
Colton C. Campbell.
    p.   cm.
Includes bibliographical references and index.
ISBN 978-1-107-00686-7 (hardback) – ISBN 978-0-521-18726-8 (paperback)
1. National security – Law and legislation – United States.   2. National security – Political
aspects – United States.   I. Auerswald, David P.   II. Campbell, Colton C., 1965–
KF4850.C66   2012
343.73′01–dc23   2011030486

ISBN 978-1-107-00686-7 Hardback
ISBN 978-0-521-18726-8 Paperback

For Jen, Robin, and Katie, with all my love
–DPA

For Marilyn and Caden, with all my love
– CCC

Contents

Contents

Figures and Tables

FIGURES

TABLES

Contributors

David P. Auerswald is professor of security studies at the National War College. Before joining the National War College, he was an assistant professor of political science at George Washington University; served on the Senate Foreign Relations Committee Staff, working for then-Senator Joseph Biden of Delaware; and was a staff assistant for U.S. Senator Timothy Wirth of Colorado. He has worked on the congressional reform team of the Project on National Security Reform, the U.S. Central Command's 2008–2009 Assessment Team, and the 2008 "Alternative Futures" project for the Office of the Secretary of Defense. He has published books and articles on a variety of foreign policy topics, including the treaty advice and consent process in the Senate, the politics of U.S. missile defense policy, the War Powers Act, the evolution of the National Security Council system, domestic and intra-alliance debates during military interventions, and deterrence of terrorist attacks.

Timothy Balunis is a lieutenant commander in the United States Coast Guard and assistant professor of public policy at the U.S. Coast Guard Academy. He graduated from the U.S. Coast Guard Academy, earned an M.A. in National Security and Strategic Studies from the U.S. Naval War College, attended the John F. Kennedy School of Government at Harvard University, and earned a Master's in Public Policy.

Colton C. Campbell is professor of national security strategy at the National War College. Prior to joining the National War College, he was a Legislative Aide to U.S. Representative Mike Thompson of California, where he handled Appropriations, Defense, and Trade matters. Before that, he was an analyst in American National Government at the Congressional Research Service, an associate professor of political science at Florida International University, and an APSA Congressional Fellow in the office of Senator Bob Graham of Florida. He is the author, co-author, and co-editor of several books on

Congress, including *Discharging Congress: Government by Commission* and *Impeaching Clinton: Partisan Strife on Capitol Hill.*

Susan B. Epstein is a specialist in foreign policy at the Congressional Research Service. She has written on a variety of foreign policy topics, including foreign relations authorization, foreign policy agency reorganization, foreign aid reform, democracy promotion, U.S. public diplomacy, and embassy security.

Louis Fisher is scholar in residence at the Constitution Project and author of more than a dozen books, including *Constitutional Conflicts Between Congress and the President, Presidential War Power, In the Name of National Security,* and *Military Tribunals and Presidential Power.*

William Hemphill is a major in the U.S. Army and former assistant professor in the Department of Social Sciences at the United States Military Academy, teaching international relations and comparative politics. He earned his undergraduate degree from Princeton University and a Master's degree in public policy from Harvard University's John F. Kennedy School of Government.

Bernard Horowitz is a research Fellow with the American Bar Association's Standing Committee on Law and National Security. He is co-editor of a forthcoming book, *Patriot Debates II: Contemporary Issues in National Security.*

Loch K. Johnson is regents professor of international affairs at the University of Georgia, senior editor of the international journal *Intelligence and National Security,* and author most recently of *The Threat on the Horizon: America's Search for Security after the Cold War.*

Robert David Johnson is professor of history at Brooklyn College. He is the author and editor of several books on Congress and the presidency, including *All the Way with LBJ: The 1964 Presidential Election; Congress and the Cold War; The Presidential Recordings: Lyndon B. Johnson,* vols. 2–5; and *The Peace Progressives and American Foreign Relations.*

Mark J. Oleszek is assistant professor of political science at Albright College, where he teaches courses on American politics and public policy. His research examines the dynamics of personal interaction and collegial collaboration in congressional lawmaking, an interest borne from previous work on Capitol Hill with the Senate Democratic Policy Committee. A recent graduate of the University of California, Berkeley, his doctoral dissertation is titled "Collaboration and Lawmaking in the United States Senate."

Walter J. Oleszek is senior specialist in American National Government at the Congressional Research Service, where he has worked since 1968. He has served as either a full-time professional staff aide or consultant to a number of House and Senate legislative reform efforts, such as the House Select Committee on Committees (1973–1975). In 1993, he was policy director of the Joint Committee on the Organization of Congress. He is the author or co-author of several books on Congress, including *Congress and Its Members*, 13th ed.; *Congressional Procedures and the Policy Process*, 7th ed.; and *Congress under Fire: Reform Politics and the Republican Majority*.

Harvey Rishikof is chair of the American Bar Association Standing Committee on Law and a former professor of law and national security studies at the National War College, where he chaired the department of national security strategy. He is a lifetime member of the American Law Institute and the Council on Foreign Relations. He was a federal law clerk in the Third Circuit for the Honorable Leonard I. Garth, a Social Studies Tutor at Harvard University, attorney at Hale and Dorr, Administrative Assistant to the Chief Justice of the United States, legal counsel for the deputy director of the Federal Bureau of Investigation, and Dean of Roger Williams School of Law. He has written numerous articles, law reviews, and book chapters. His book, co-edited with Roger George, is *The National Security Enterprise: Navigating the Labyrinth*.

Pat Towell is a specialist in U.S. defense policy and budgets at the Congressional Research Service. Prior to joining CRS he was a Senior Fellow at the Center for Strategic and Budgetary Assessments. He also covered defense policy for *Congressional Quarterly* for more than 25 years. During that time, he covered the defense budget process each year from presidential submission through final congressional and presidential action. Prior to joining *CQ*, he was a Political Science lecturer at California State University, Bakersfield.

PART ONE

Historical and Institutional Challenges

1

Congress and National Security

David P. Auerswald and Colton C. Campbell

Over the last decade, a growing number of scholars and practitioners have called for a reexamination of our national security system, with much attention devoted to interagency reform (Davidson 2009, Smith 2009, Project on National Security Reform 2008). The structures and processes set in place more than a half-century ago by the National Security Act of 1947, they argue, are outdated, designed to meet the security challenges of the Cold War era instead of those of the 21st century. This can have potentially sobering outcomes, as the Project on National Security Reform noted in its 2008 study. Accordingly, the U.S. government is unable to "integrate adequately the military and nonmilitary dimensions of a complex war on terror" or to "integrate properly the external and homeland dimensions of post-9/11 national security strategy" (Project on National Security Reform 2008, ii).

Any major reform of the nation's national security system will require congressional action. Indeed, Congress has a constitutional responsibility to weigh issues of national security concerns. Congress has the authority to raise an army and a navy, to regulate the armed forces, and to declare war. It must authorize new federal policies and determine the scope of agency actions and portfolios. It is Congress that must appropriate the money for the federal government. In addition, Congress may influence military strategy directly by legislating war aims or military regulations, or indirectly by altering the end-strength and weapons systems of the different services. If no major reform can occur without congressional action, the obvious question is whether Congress is willing and/or able to execute such a major national security undertaking.

Having the constitutional authority is a necessary, but not sufficient, condition for congressional influence in national security policy. Congressional

The views expressed in this chapter are those of the authors and not the National Defense University, the Department of Defense, or any other entity of the United States Government.

influence depends on Congress having the ability and the will to become involved in national security debates. The jury is still out on both fronts. Is the "first branch" of government adequately organized to deal with national security issues in an integrated and coordinated manner? And how have developments in Congress over the past few decades, such as heightened partisanship, message politics, party-committee relationships, and bicameral relations, affected topical security issues? These are important questions, as the United States cannot form alliances, agree to strategic arms control accords, procure weapons systems, or create new programs vital to national security matters without the explicit approval of Congress.

What explains the ebb and flow of congressional involvement? Theories of presidential-congressional interaction during military conflicts offer some clues. Scholars usually invoke at least one of three related arguments: that Congress lacks the means of restraining the president, that Congress lacks the will to do so, or some combination of the two. The first school of thought argues that for structural reasons Congress is usually ineffective at challenging the president once the president begins using force abroad. That is, Congress lacks the means to constrain presidents. The president is able to act in foreign conflicts due to his constitutional powers and the accrued prerogatives of his office while Congress must often pass veto-proof legislation to constrain him. The executive branch, speaking with one voice, can articulate unified positions while Congress speaks with a multitude of voices, making agreement on executive constraints unlikely. The executive can respond to international conflicts in a timely manner, but Congress often takes months or longer to respond to a president's initiatives (Lindsay 1994, Hilsman 1987, Krasner 1978, Dahl 1950). Congress is better suited to indirectly affect presidential behavior by manipulating public opinion, but even that gives Congress relatively little influence during military conflicts due to the rally-around-the-flag phenomenon or the president's ability to take his case to the people directly (Levy 1989, Kernell 1986).

These executive powers, combined with past failures of congressional policy making and a more complex international world, led Congress to abdicate conflict policy-making authority to the president (Kellerman and Barilleaux 1991). Attempts at congressional resurgence, begun between the mid-1960s and 1970s, have continually failed to redress the balance between Congress and the president (Blechman 1992, Destler 1985, Sundquist 1981). From a structural perspective then, U.S. presidents retain substantial autonomy from legislative control in the realm of conflict decision making.

A second argument is that Congress lacks the will to act during military conflicts (Hinckley 1994, Koh 1990a). Presidents have powerful incentives to take charge during military conflicts, incentives that Congress does not share. The president represents a national constituency, giving him an electoral motivation to confront international threats to the nation. Congressional districts have parochial interests that provide disincentives for congressional criticism. Members instead focus their energies on policies that more directly affect their districts (Mayhew 1974). At best, Congress engages in symbolic criticism of the president's performance in military conflicts without making a concerted effort to change national security policy.

A third and related school combines the first two arguments. Congress and the president compete for control over national security policy, but who wins control depends on the characteristics of the issue area under dispute (Rosner 1995). Borrowing from structural arguments, this school claims that Congress has greater direct influence over U.S. foreign policy when it has time to react to international events. Presidents thus have the most control over foreign policy during military crises and other time-sensitive negotiations. Borrowing from the motivations argument, this school of thought also argues that Congress will never realize its potential to act during military conflicts because action forces it either to support the troops in the field or to appear unpatriotic. The crux of this school of thought, as well as the other two arguments it is based on, is thus that Congress "cannot compel [the president] to follow any of the advice that members might care to offer" (Lindsay 1994, 151). Analysts of U.S. foreign policy conclude that the president's foreign policy tools and motivations simply overwhelm the efforts of Congress to control security policy (Schlesinger 1973, Kellerman and Barilleaux 1991).

CONGRESSIONAL WILL

Most foreign policy experts argue that Congress has little direct influence over foreign affairs and national security issues. Lawmakers' preoccupation with domestic issues, especially constituency concerns and business, has traditionally been the cause for selective congressional intervention, often precipitated by crises abroad or by a widely publicized foreign policy debacle (Burgin 1991, Clausen 1973). As a consequence, the typical congressional attention span for national security is episodic and lacks an overall strategy (Crabb 1995).

Congress has at times empowered the president, and at other times set conditions and limits to presidential action (Stevenson 2007, Sundquist 1981). Until recently, Congress had been relatively silent on questions of national security in the post-9/11 world. Through 2006, the continuing post-9/11 threat environment and Republican control of the legislative and executive branches reinforced historical congressional deference to the president on national security (Ornstein and Mann 2006, Rudalevige 2006, Fisher 2000). Republican-controlled congresses gave only a cursory examination to the administration's creation of Northern Command and the Department of Homeland Security (DHS), two of the largest changes to U.S. security policy in decades. Similarly, these congresses argued over the distribution of the foreign aid budget rather than the need for a whole-scale change in our nation-building capability. Yet this pattern started to change in the 110th Congress (2007–2009), when Democratic majorities in each chamber became more assertive on Iraq and Afghanistan, military tribunals, detainee policy, extraordinary rendition, and electronic surveillance of American citizens (Friel 2007).

Whether members of Congress choose to become involved in national security matters, especially those involving conflicts, is problematic. If Congress is concerned with reelection, then electoral calculations are crucial to a lawmaker's decision about becoming involved in national security policy making. When members of Congress take positions on security budgets or military procurement, or during foreign policy crises or military conflicts, these actions may help the electorate distinguish between political parties, and partisan identification is a very strong determinant of voting behavior (Campbell et al. 1976). Members may also care about the national interest irrespective of electoral gains. National security in general, and military conflicts in particular, are also important issues for a broad range of constituencies, such as friends or family of the military, military contractors, industries affected by the outcome of international crises, and those concerned with human rights, just to name a few. The involved constituencies may demand a legislator's participation in security debates to help protect their threatened interests. In sum, legislators participate in security policy if some portion of their core reelection constituency is concerned with the policy outcome (Lindsay 1994, Burgin 1991).

Involvement is not without its risks, particularly if the national security policy is placed under the umbrella of a consensus issue. Such instances create electoral disincentives for congressional engagement. To label a military conflict as consistent with Containment or the Monroe Doctrine, for instance, is one way for a president to ensure congressional support. In such instances, a member of Congress who speaks out against consensus goals risks electoral punishment. Being labeled as soft on communism for taking a position contrary to Containment was something most elected officials avoided. That reluctance has often extended to the means used by the president to reach a consensus goal, at least if criticizing the means used could be equated with having dissimilar policy goals. For example, speaking out against military intervention in Iraq or Afghanistan might lead to being labeled soft on terrorism. Finally, the individual lawmaker may also share many of the president's goals during the conflict and thus see no need to speak out.

The 1958 U.S. intervention in Lebanon illustrates how presidents use consensus issues to avoid congressional restraints, even when faced with opposition majorities on Capitol Hill. President Eisenhower asked the Democratically controlled Congress for the statutory authority to use U.S. armed forces in the Middle East, should that use become necessary to combat a communist invasion. Congress responded by passing the Middle East Resolution, granting the president limited discretion to use force.[1] Before the president could do so, he was required to certify that the country being helped was facing armed aggression from a communist state, and he could use force only "consistent with the Constitution of the United States." Most important, Congress reserved the right to terminate the president's authority to use force in the Middle East (and thus end any deployment) by passing a concurrent resolution. Congress included these provisions because it was unwilling to give the president a blank check to use force (Fisher 1995, Congressional *Quarterly Almanac 1957*, 573).

Yet Eisenhower faced little congressional resistance when he deployed approximately 15,000 troops to Lebanon in 1958, after the fall of the Iraqi monarchy. While Eisenhower did not share partisan affiliation with a majority in Congress, he threatened the Democratic leadership with publicly calling the deployment an effort to combat communism in the Middle East should the Democrats protest his actions (Memorandum of a Conversation with the President, 221). This explicit, calculated threat to use the anti-communism rallying cry linked the deployment to the Cold War consensus, greatly decreasing the chances of successful congressional action to reverse the deployment. Had Congress acted against President Eisenhower, and had Eisenhower carried out his domestic threat, the Democratic majority would have been seen as sympathizing with the communist movement. Not surprisingly, House Speaker Sam Rayburn (D-TX) publicly supported the president, even going so far as to halt debate on the House floor when the subject of the Lebanon conflict arose (*Congressional Record* 1958, 13978).

Shared partisanship with the president is a second reason for congressional acquiescence during conflicts. The greater the number of presidential partisans in Congress, the less likely Congress will be to act collectively to halt a

---

[1] PL 85–7 (H. J. Res. 117, enacted March 9, 1957). The legislative history made clear that the law did not "delegate or diminish" the congressional power to declare war, or enlarge the president's power as commander in chief. See *House Report No. 2*, 85th Congress, 1st Session, January 25, 1957, p. 7. For a slightly different interpretation, see also James L. Sundquist, *The Decline and Resurgence of Congress* (Washington, DC: Brookings Institution, 1981), p. 116.

presidential initiative. Just as confronting a president from the opposing party
might help a member get reelected, confronting a president of one's own party
might decrease one's chances of reelection. First, helping overturn the policies of one's own president cannot but hurt that president's chances for reelection. By extension, losing the presidency hurts the member's chances of riding
the president's coattails into office. Second, overturning one's own president
weakens the party image in the minds of the voters, either in terms of its unity
or its record of accomplishments. Third, challenging one's own president in
all likelihood means that party leaders will not help the member of Congress
with fund-raising and campaigning. Fourth and related, the insurgent member might face sanctions from his or her party leadership in Congress, ranging
from losing a coveted committee assignment to being excluded from deliberations on appropriation bills.

At the end of World War II, for example, Congress was wary of making an
open-ended military commitment to the United Nations (UN). Congressional
members of the American delegation to the UN Charter negotiations ensured
that participation in UN military operations would be in accordance with
each member-nation's constitutional processes. The 1945 UN Participation
Act codified that sentiment into law, stipulating that the president could not
commit substantial U.S. forces to UN missions without expressed congressional consent. Five years later President Harry Truman ignored both the letter
and the spirit of the law when deploying U.S. forces to the Korean peninsula.[2]
Truman disregarded the *ex-ante* constraint because he faced little chance of
domestic penalties from a Congress controlled by his own party.[3]

Finally, the duration of a military conflict or national security concern may
also affect levels of congressional opposition. Congressional inaction during
short-term crises, for instance, holds few electoral risks or rewards. Should

[2]   The Senate responded by passing (69–21) in 1951 a non-binding Senate resolution (S. Res. 99)
      asking that future troop commitments to bilateral or multilateral treaty partners be subjected
      to a congressional vote before being undertaken (section 6). Consideration of this legisla-
      tion became known as the Great Debate of 1951. For a legislative history, see *Congressional
      Quarterly Almanac, 1951*, vol. VII, pp. 220–232. See also *Senate Report 175*, 82nd Congress, 1st
      Session, pp. 2–3; Fisher, pp. 97–101. President Truman's disdain for the resolution is appar-
      ent in "The President's News Conference of January 11, 1951," *Public Papers of the President,
      Harry S. Truman, 1951* (Washington, DC: Government Printing Office, 1965), pp. 18–22.
[3]   Most Democratic congressional leaders spoke in favor of the president's actions. See *Foreign
      Relations of the United State, 1950*, vol. VII, pp. 200–202; *Congressional Record*, 81st Congress,
      2nd Session (June 1950), pp. 9154–9160, 9268–9269, 9319–9329, 9537–9540. Indeed, these
      same congressional leaders advised Truman against requesting a congressional vote on the
      intervention, warning that Republican members would use that opportunity to criticize
      the administration. See Dean Acheson, *The Korean War* (New York: W. W. Norton, 1971),
      pp. 32–33; and *Foreign Relations of the United States, 1950*, vol. VII, pp. 286–291.

the crisis end badly, Congress can always blame the president and avoid the blame themselves. Success, on the other hand, rarely reflects on Congress. Instead, either the military or the president receives all the praise. Inactivity during longer crises poses more significant electoral risks. Congress may suffer an electoral backlash for taking no action should the crisis result in defeat. Taking action during long-term initiatives is far less risky, in that Congress can justify its actions in terms of reining in a reckless president or avoiding another Vietnam.

CONGRESSIONAL ABILITY

Congress is often dubbed powerless to directly affect presidential power in the areas associated with national security. What is clear, pursuant to the Constitution, is that the underlying relationship between Congress and the executive in national security issues is one of shared agenda control. Each branch has the power to affect U.S. policy. While contemporary presidents generally direct this agenda, control occasionally shifts toward Congress, as it did in the inter-war period, in the absence of consensus over American grand strategy, and given that absence, during divided government or prolonged military conflicts.

One reason is that today's legislative branch is armed with resources to actively engage in national security matters. The proliferation of congressional support staff and news media have facilitated congressional activism and provided individual members an incentive to be involved in major national security legislation. That is a dramatic change from 50 years ago. In the 1950s, national security decisions essentially were made by a handful of powerful committee chairmen. In the late 1960s and early 1970s, in reaction to Vietnam and Watergate and the growth and complexity of the federal government, Congress increased the number of congressional oversight panels and their associated staffs, as well as created various legislative branch research entities. These resources gave members of Congress the means to become assertive on security issues. At the same time, the proliferation of media outlets and the explosion of interest groups gave members of Congress an incentive to speak out. Today's members are adept at harnessing television coverage and interacting with interest groups to get their points across. In short, individual members now have both the means and an incentive to challenge the president's security priorities. Indeed, virtually every member of Congress can now become involved to some degree in national security debates.

It is unclear, however, whether these trends can overcome structural biases toward congressional inaction. Consider that there are inevitably differences between the majority and minority parties on major security issues, to say nothing of the often-heated negotiations between the two congressional chambers. Within each chamber, there are jurisdictional disputes between the authorizing and appropriating committees, and between different authorizing committees. Moreover, a large number of committees are involved in complex issues like national and homeland security, requiring consensus from each committee before legislation can be sent to the president. And initiatives challenging presidential priorities often must be passed with veto-proof majorities, which raises the bar to effective action even higher.

So while members' constituency interests, policy preferences and ideological dispositions as well as public opinion influence congressional will to engage in national security matters, Congress's institutional structures and processes frequently bias that body toward legislative inaction. The hyperpartisanship that characterizes the current climate on Capitol Hill, for instance, has made congressional parties much more active in agenda formation, elevated inter-party tensions (Forgette 2004), and impacted the working relationship in Congress (*Congressional Record* 2005, 10547). Additionally, some question whether Congress's proclivity toward tradition, embodied in many of its anticipated rules and procedures, hinders the legislative process. Is an institution designed in the 18th-century adequately prepared to adapt to the realities of 21st-century government?

Partisan Divides

These two factors – Congress's willingness and ability to influence national security policy – intersect when we consider partisan divides in each chamber. There is an oft-quoted adage when discussing national security that "politics stops at the water's edge." That is, members of Congress and other elected officials are apt to set aside their partisan differences in the interest of common defense. Yet the politics of national security are no more immune to the increasing partisan atmosphere in Washington than any other area of public policy (Zelizer 2010, Wirls 2008). Some members, particularly those departing the institution and reflecting on their congressional careers, readily comment about the steady march by both parties toward ever more partisan and personal attacks. Partisanship has worn away the comity that normally encourages the flow of legislation, as negotiating with those on the opposite side of a debate is "vilified by the hard-liners on both sides of the aisle" (Collins 2010, B4). Moreover, such partisanship has "infused the rhetoric surrounding national security discussions" and obstructed Congress's critical role of oversight (*Congressional Record*, April 29, 2010, E705).

For many congressional observers of the different forms of political strife on Capitol Hill – from committee turf battles over jurisdiction within a congressional chamber to conference committee tug-of-war struggles between members of the House and Senate – the real conflict stems from the distinctly partisan alignment between Democrats and Republicans and their subsequent battle for majority status. The two parties have become increasingly polarized over time (Ahuja 2008), often finding that partisan politics win elections, despite the costs to governing (Rae and Campbell 2001). Congressional parties have allowed their extreme wings to dominate decision making, at the expense of the middle (Fleisher and Bond 2004, Binder 2001) and, for some, have "broken" Congress as a branch of government (Mann and Ornstein 2006).

Partisanship has entered the legislative arena through the electoral process. Constituency changes have led to the election of representatives and senators who are more ideologically compatible with their party colleagues than with the rest of the country (Cooper and Young 2002, Erickson and Wright 2001). This has been especially evident in the Senate (Sinclair 2012), an institution long steeped in the tradition of individualism. By contrast with the impersonal, hierarchical, and disciplined House, the Senate long tolerated and even promoted individualism, reciprocity, and mutual accommodation. For the past several decades, however, rising partisanship has worked to reverse the senatorial tradition toward individualism. Nearly half the Senate in the 111th Congress (2009–2011) was made up of members who had previously served in the House, a good number of whom were schooled in relentless and combative partisanship.

One implication of such heightened partisan polarization has been less legislative productivity, especially in the Senate. In the last 50 years the percentage of major legislation before the Senate that has encountered problems related to extended-debate has risen from 8 percent to 70 percent (Sinclair 2010). When in the minority, senators of both parties increasingly exploit dilatory devices, such as the filibuster and secret "holds," to bring the chamber to a standstill. Defenders say this protects minority rights, permits thorough consideration of bills, and dramatizes contentious issues. Critics contend that filibusters and holds enable minorities to extort unwanted concessions and has caused the Senate to descend into complete dysfunction (Bennett 2010). In response to such increased minority obstructionism, the majority party leadership or rank-and-file members routinely file cloture motions rather than agreeing to allow amendments to be debated, or employ other procedural tactics, such as "filling up the amendment tree" to prevent consideration of alternative amendments by minority members (Rybicki 2010, Smith and Gamm 2009).

Antiquated Architecture

There is no doubt that Congress is an institution rooted in history, embracing many vestiges from bygone eras. But some question whether the legislative branch can adequately manage today's national security concerns, especially at a time when new and delicate challenges minimize the margin of error. Critics contend that Congress is too slow to change and is poorly organized to deal with the security needs of the 21st century. By most accounts, the intent to involve Congress in the most extreme matters of national security, such as making war, was a calculated attempt to purposely slow down the process (Alstyne 1972). A large, deliberative body like Congress naturally moves slowly. When faced with problems of monumental dimensions, Congress often approaches solutions in small discrete steps, building agreement from the bottom up, reflecting the institution's decentralized structure. Even following the harsh terrorist attacks of September 11, the Senate's unabashed historian, the late Senator Robert C. Byrd (D-WV) cautioned against the president's excessive authority and use of force. "But in the heat of the moment, in the crush of recent events, I fear we may be losing sight of the larger obligations of the Senate," he said. He continued, "Our responsibility as Senators is to carefully consider and fully debate major policy matters, to air all sides of a given issue, and to act after full deliberation. Yes, we want to respond quickly to urgent needs, but a speedy response should not be used as an excuse to trample full and free debate" (*Congressional Record* 2001, S9948).

OVERVIEW OF THE BOOK

Few works on Congress specifically explore the first branch's role in foreign policy, and those that do tend not to consider the changed 21st-century security environment, with the United States engaged in two wars, facing the threat of global terrorism and accelerated proliferation of weapons of mass destruction (WMD). Moreover, these works typically address general foreign policy and the issues associated with policy formation (Lindsay 1994), everything from lobbyists to the media to the National Security Council system (Wittkopf and McCormick 2004), rather than the more focused, and relatively unexplored, question of the congressional role in national security. In short, they are very broad rather than detailed. A similar pattern exists with volumes on congressional decision making. Whether edited collections of essays or single-authored works, most devote no more than a chapter to Congress and foreign policy, and almost none touch on the national security affairs beyond a discussion of the War Powers Act. Finally, there are extended case studies that examine the role of Congress on a particular instance of policy making or that go into great detail as to congressional deliberations on a particular issue (Locher 2002), but they are not generalizable across time or to other national security issues.

This volume focuses on the role of Congress in national security policy, both across time and a variety of topical security issues. The chapters that follow examine variation in the ways Congress has engaged those federal agencies overseeing national security as well as various domestic political determinants of security policy. The volume is divided into three parts. The first part includes chapters on the historical context of congressional power in the national security arena and an examination of whether, as currently organized, Congress is capable of dealing with national security issues in an integrated manner. As Robert David "KC" Johnson writes in Chapter 2, before the post–Cold War era, Congress's role in foreign affairs was marked by four distinct periods. From the nation's founding through the 1820s, lawmakers devoted much attention to translating the Constitution's often vague clauses into the actual making of foreign policy. For the remainder of the 19th century, Congress generally staved off challenges from presidents who sought greater executive freedom of action. From 1899 through the Second World War, Congress engaged the executive in a series of battles over war making and treaty making, which became less important during the Cold War, when members of Congress found other ways to influence foreign affairs, such as procedure, power of the purse, and oversight.

Chapter 3 explores the institutional challenges facing Congress in the post-9/11 era. Confronted with historically high levels of partisan polarization on Capitol Hill, Congress, in the view of Mark and Walter Oleszek, has experienced great difficulty keeping pace with the president in matters of national security decision making. One of Congress's most fundamental challenges, they argue, is to effectively supervise and hold accountable the dramatic expansion of the homeland security, defense, and intelligence establishment. The authors consider a variety of reform proposals aimed at rectifying the imbalance between Congress and the president in national security affairs – including a review of several oversight recommendations offered by the 9/11 Commission – and conclude by assessing the prospects for collaboration and coordination between Congress and the president moving forward.

Part two contains various chapters on current oversight challenges facing Congress, with particular emphasis on defense, homeland security, intelligence, and foreign affairs. This section opens by examining the relationship between Congress and the Department of Defense in Chapter 3. Congressional oversight and direction of U.S. defense policy is too often underappreciated for its impact on the country's security. Frequently Congress is derided either for micromanaging defense policy in a way that advantages constituency interests at the expense of the national interest, or for allowing the Defense Department unfettered access to the nation's coffers. Both views are off the mark, according to Pat Towell. He argues that there is a raft of issues – highly consequential for the U.S. national security posture, but engaging relatively few political interests outside the defense community – concerning which the defense committees have asserted themselves. Moreover, on the face of it, these committee initiatives have been sufficiently significant in their intended impact that they deserve more attention than they have received from students of the defense policy-making process. The defense authorizing committees are never going to be able to single-handedly dictate the size of the defense budget – too many other members of Congress have a stake in that fight to defer to any one committee – but there is a host of other important defense issues over which the Armed Services committees are likely to exercise significant influence.

Homeland security has become a central component of national security strategy in the aftermath of the 9/11 terrorist attacks. Yet the merging of more than 20 agencies and departments into the Department of Homeland Security has not been without controversy. Critics have argued that the agency is inefficient; that it lacks a common culture, personnel system, and mission; and that it has never had dedicated leadership. Supporters point out that such major reorganizations take time, and they note that there has not been a terrorist attack on U.S. soil since the department's creation. And many on Capitol Hill wonder if it is not time to reorganize the new department, or at least split off selected agencies like the Coast Guard or the Federal Emergency Management Agency (FEMA). As Timm Balunis and Bill Hemphill discuss in Chapter 5, creating the DHS involved a series of negotiations between the White House and the Congress and might never have happened had it not been for the pressure of the 9/11 families and the 9/11 Commission itself. The Bush (43) administration initially resisted creating a new department, instead preferring to coordinate existing departments through a Homeland Security Advisor (HSA) and a Homeland Security Council. Such a council was not sufficient for some members of Congress, however, and met with resistance from parts of the executive branch, in large part because the HSA had no control over agency budgets, portfolios, or personnel. The administration eventually accepted the idea of a new, permanent department but argued that such a department could be created at little or no additional expense. Indeed, the administration believed that the new department could remain revenue neutral and accomplish its new missions, all while fulfilling the original duties of its constituent parts. However, congressional oversight of homeland security is quite fragmented compared to oversight of other executive departments, and this diminishes the overall clarity and coherence of homeland security policy. This, in turn, has presented the DHS leadership with a significant opportunity cost.

Chapter 6 looks at the relationship between Congress and intelligence agencies. Sixteen federal intelligence agencies comprise America's intelligence community. These agencies are vital as a first line of defense for the United States against threats from at home and abroad. Yet, like other government organizations, according to Loch Johnson, they can fall prey to Lord Acton's well-known prophecy that power tends to corrupt. History reveals that a nation's secret agencies have sometimes turned their surveillance capabilities against the very citizens they were meant to shield. Efforts by Congress to maintain accountability over the intelligence agencies have been uneven, with some lawmakers displaying a strong interest in carrying out "oversight" but most engaging in overlook. An ongoing vibrant democracy in the United States will depend, in part, on more members of Congress dedicating themselves to the task of ensuring intelligence accountability.

The section concludes with a discussion by Sue Epstein of U.S. foreign aid. Going back to the post–World War II era, the United States has used foreign aid as a foreign policy and national security tool to prevent the spread of communism, reward peace agreement participants, and combat terrorism, among other objectives. Most administrations, including both the George W. Bush and Obama administrations, have spoken in favor of supporting and bolstering development to become a stronger weapon in America's arsenal. However, finding a coherent foreign aid policy in Congress has become increasingly challenging given that there are 535 members of Congress with differing views, strained budgets, relationships with multiple committees, and constituents who urge Congress to reduce its funding because they do not see foreign aid benefiting them. This chapter discusses some of those challenges.

The final portion of the book, Part three, includes chapters on various domestic policy determinants of security policy, including enemy combatant detainees, arms control, and national security surveillance. Chapter 8 reviews the history and current debates surrounding due process for detainees suspected of engaging in terrorist activities. Harvey Rishikof and Bernard Horowitz argue that Congress has largely deferred to the president and the courts on detainee policy. Due to congressional inaction, or at best sporadic and incomplete attempts at legislative solutions to the questions of detainees, detention policy remains largely undefined. Instead, we have a series of Supreme Court, court of appeals, and district court opinions, executive orders and military commissions, and weak, incomplete legislation. Four big questions raised by the process of detention – who is subject to detention, what is the appropriate due process for detainees, when should detention end, and what are state responsibilities for repatriating detainees – remain unresolved. As a result, we have detainees but no agreement among the three branches of government to collectively define U.S. policy.

Chapter 9 explores the Senate's role in the general treaty advice process and in the specific 2010 consideration of the New START arms control treaty. In this chapter David Auerswald argues that the constitutional requirement for advice and consent gives the Senate the means to influence national security policy during consideration of treaties. A variety of factors – to include the time period of the treaty's consideration, the ideological distance between the president and the treaty pivot, and the type of treaty being considered – help determine the extent to which individual senators choose to add policy initiatives to treaty ratification documents. In the case of New START, the Senate included policy guidance on missile defense, the modernization of the nuclear stockpile and infrastructure, global strike capabilities, tactical nuclear weapons and mobile missiles, among others. If the record from the past 60 years and recent debate over New START are a guide, policy making via advice and consent will continue to have an important impact on U.S. foreign policy in the years ahead. As a result, presidents who want the country to speak with a single voice would be wise to clear the national script with the Senate, because the Senate is likely to use the advice and consent process, when available, to shape long-term U.S. foreign policy in ways that may conflict with presidential initiatives.

The volume concludes by exploring national security surveillance, one facet of the intelligence programs introduced earlier in Chapter 6. In Chapter 10, Lou Fisher explores the interplay between law enforcement and intelligence surveillance technology, court interpretations of the constitutionality of using that technology, and the episodic congressional reactions to both. Historically, the debate over national security surveillance is a proxy for the continued struggle between the three branches of government. Presidents continually push the bounds, at times aided and encouraged by Congress. The courts respond. Congress occasionally takes action when forced to by the courts or when presidents overstep their authority. Fisher traces how this inter-branch dance plays out in post-9/11 debates over electronic eavesdropping. He argues that the Bush (43) administration engaged in a widespread surveillance program based on an assertion of inherent executive authority, Congress took few concrete actions in response (other than to give telecommunications firms immunity from prosecution), leaving the courts to challenge the president in the Al-Haramin case. The result has been less than hoped for by proponents of a strong legislature.

Returning to where we started, these chapters demonstrate that Congress has the capability and at times the will to significantly influence national security policy. Congressional tools vary depending on the issue area under scrutiny, but they do exist. Congress is strongest on issues dealing with the power of the purse or its inherent Article I powers. Congress is weakest during crises or on issues that rely on presidential initiatives for their generation. Congressional will seems to depend on the time period, partisan configuration of government, and the electoral payoffs associated with taking action. Finally, the chapters in this volume point out that the courts have a significant role to play in national security policy, particularly when Congress specifically enfranchised the courts into the policy process or when Congress refuses to take action.

2

Congress and U.S. Foreign Policy before 9/11

Robert David Johnson

Paul Kennedy has written of the need to "reconcile the 'structuralist' and the 'individualist' approaches to understanding the making of foreign policy." National ideology, he argued, results "from the fusion of two elements: the individual perceptions and insights of thinkers about the nature of politics and the institutional means by which those perceptions are transmitted to a wider audience" (Kennedy 1982, 144, 148). This admonition especially assists in explaining U.S. foreign policy, since the structure of the U.S. government has exercised an unusually significant role on the U.S. response to world affairs. Given a constitutional structure that features a complex intersection of executive with various types of legislative powers, understanding the U.S. position in international affairs requires including the congressional perspective.

Before the post–Cold War period, the congressional role in U.S. foreign policy divided into four distinct eras. The first extended from the Constitutional Convention through the 1820s and featured a series of precedents translating the Constitution's often vague clauses into the actual making of foreign policy. The second lasted for the remainder of the 19th century, with a generally dominant Congress debating and (at least after the 1840s) ultimately rejecting territorial expansion – all while staving off challenges from presidents such as James Polk and James Buchanan who sought greater executive freedom of action. The period from 1899 through World War II was characterized by a series of battles between Congress and the executive over the two primary foreign policy powers shared between the two branches – war making and treaty making. Those two congressional functions became less important during the Cold War, but ambitious members of Congress found other ways – procedure, power of the purse, oversight – to influence foreign affairs.

In the hyper-partisanship that has characterized recent congressional history, it remains unclear how much these past precedents can help in an analysis of the ways the contemporary Congress approaches international questions.

PRECEDENTS

In an 18th-century environment of nation-states in which executives controlled foreign policy, the United States stood out. Among the most revolutionary aspects of the Constitution was its assigning most foreign policy powers to the legislature rather than to the president. Congress received the power to declare war, and military appropriations were limited to two years, to provide a check against militaristic legislators. The power of the purse, and authority to regulate foreign commerce, also were assigned to Congress.

Yet, in the end, the framers created a document that one noted scholars has described as representing an "invitation to struggle" in foreign affairs (Crabb 1992). In the final stages of the Constitutional Convention, modifications to the document limited the congressional role in foreign policy, with the delegates perhaps remembering the national security dangers of a weak executive from the Articles of Confederation period. The function of Congress to "make" war became the power to "declare" war, while the Committee on Style transferred the power to negotiate treaties from the Senate to the president (subject to advice and consent from two-thirds of the Senate), as part of a compromise that created the Electoral College as the method for choosing the chief executive (Rakove 1984; Banks and Raven-Hansen 1994).

In a system designed with an invitation to struggle and a Constitution filled with vague clauses dealing with foreign policy, events in the nation's early legislative sessions established precedents. And so, on August 22, 1789, when senators declined to advise George Washington after the president suddenly arrived in the upper chamber – sitting in the presiding officer's chair – and requested input about negotiations for an Indian treaty, the "advise" portion of the "advise and consent" treaty-making clause was weakened.[1] Debate over Jay's Treaty in 1794 performed a similar limiting function for the House's role in treaty matters. Despite the Senate's narrow approval, the treaty remained controversial in the South and among some opposition legislators. James Madison, then serving in the House, tried to block funds to implement the treaty; Washington successfully resisted, arguing that such a move would violate the spirit of the Constitution's assigning treaty-related matters exclusively to the president and the Senate (Elkins and McKitrick 1994).

---

[1] Senators said they needed time to study relevant documents before advising Washington formally; the president, frustrated, exclaimed, "This defeats every purpose of my being here!" See U.S. Senate, Office of the Historian, "August 5, 1789: Irritating the President," http://www.senate.gov/artandhistory/history/minute/The_Senate_Irritates_President_George_Washington.htm.

Early 19th-century events, meanwhile, suggested that Congress's war-making power might not be as robust as promised in the ratification debates. Although the letters of marque clause implied that Congress, not the executive, would have primary power to wage undeclared wars, the reverse held true in practice (Lofgren 1972). Even Thomas Jefferson, who campaigned on a platform of strict construction of the Constitution, waged an undeclared naval conflict with the Barbary States (Jefferson's action provided a precedent for future chief executives, including those of the 21st century, to exercise national security powers that seemed to go beyond the bounds of the Constitution). Meanwhile, the failure of the House "War Hawks" to pressure then-president James Madison into a premature declaration of war against England showed that even a relatively weak chief executive could resist congressional efforts to dominate the war-making power (Stuart 1982; Fritz 1976).

The U.S. response to the Spanish-American revolutions showed the strengths and limitations of Congress's foreign policy powers in other ways. A setback for legislative power came in 1818, after Representative Henry Clay (Democratic Republican-KY) sponsored a resolution demanding that the United States extend diplomatic recognition to the several South American states. Citing Emer de Vattel as his authority, Clay contended that "an oppressed people were authorized, wherever they could, to rise and break their fetters," and that the United States, unless it wanted to "pass sentence of condemnation on the founders of our liberty," needed to support such ventures (*Annals of Congress* 1818; Hoskins 1927). Then-Secretary of State John Quincy Adams denounced the resolution, which ultimately failed, as a measure intended "to control or overthrow the executive," and deadpanned that its mere introduction suggested that "the present session will stand remarkable in the annals of the Union for showing how a legislature can keep itself employed when having nothing to do" (Weeks 1992, 103).

But while even a master legislator such as Clay struggled to mobilize congressional power to initiate foreign policy ventures, Adams – as president – discovered to his chagrin that the constitutional structure gave Congress more than enough power to block executive initiatives. In 1826, as part of an effort to drive Spain from the Western Hemisphere once and for all, delegates from several newly independent Latin American states met in Panama to discuss a joint military effort to liberate Cuba. Adams proposed sending diplomatic representatives to the Panama Congress, with an implicit promise that the United States would assist the venture. Adams's efforts, however, encountered a combination of partisan fallout from the disputed election of 1824 and ill-concealed hostility to aiding Latin American revolutions. Representative William Rives (Jacksonian-VA) addressed the latter issue bluntly, asking,

"Sir, is there to be no limit to our benevolence for these People? There is a point, beyond which, even parental bounty and natural affection cease to impose an obligation. That point has been attained with the States of Spanish America" (Gleijeses 1992). Congressional delay blocked funding for the delegates until after the Panama Congress had concluded its gathering.

CONGRESSIONAL POWER AND 19TH-CENTURY IMPERIALISM

Anti-imperialism in the United States dated back to the Revolution: a belief that the United States should promote international revolution, regardless of the short-term strategic consequences, infused the writings of Anti-Federalists such as Brutus during the debate over the Constitution. Clay's 1818 resolution showed how the concept appealed to more mainstream figures. But by the time of the Second Party System, anti-imperialism had moved to the fringes and was chiefly employed by anti-slavery activists, for whom protecting weaker nations abroad supplemented their domestic beliefs. For instance, abolitionists flooded Congress with petitions demanding the recognition of Haiti in the hopes of building support for racial equality – and the House responded by instituting a "gag rule," which prohibited the reading of these petitions on the House floor (Jenkins 2002).

The intersection between slavery, anti-imperialism, and congressional power in foreign affairs became more pronounced in the 1840s. In 1846, James Polk's launching the Mexican War exposed him to charges of usurping legislative prerogatives, thereby reopening debates about executive authority in foreign affairs that had been dormant since the early 19th century. Meanwhile, the introduction of the Wilmot Proviso (which sought to forbid slavery in any territories acquired from Mexico) eradicated any demarcation between international affairs and domestic matters by establishing a clear link between slavery and expansion. House Abolitionists made the case against expansionism the most aggressively: led by John Quincy Adams (at this point concluding his career, as a Whig congressman from Massachusetts) and Joshua Giddings (Whig-OH), they transferred their opposition to slavery to the international arena and used the war to illustrate Slave Power's dominance over the nation's political structures. Ironically, Southerners strengthened the abolitionists' hand by touting the need for more slave states as a justification in and of itself for embracing imperialism (Howe 1991; Hietala 1985).

Partisan gridlock accompanied this ideological polarization. In what Joel Silbey (1967) has described as a political system oriented toward the "shrine of party," the changing context of foreign policy issues splintered Polk's coalition, diluting support for the president's bid to annex all of Mexico and to intervene in the Yucatecan civil war. With Polk complaining privately about the "troublesome obstacle" of Congress having "greatly paralyzed" his diplomacy, his term ended with Latin American policy immobilized by growing sectional tensions, institutional conflict between the legislative and executive branches, intense partisan attacks, and sharp disagreement between pro-slavery expansionists and abolitionist anti-imperialists (May 1989; Hietala 1985; Langley 1976; Potter 1976; Schroeder 1973).

The following decade also featured an institutional change, largely unrelated to the era's political tumult, in how Congress approached international issues. By the time of Andrew Jackson's administration, the Senate had replaced the House as the more significant branch of the legislature on domestic matters; Alexis de Tocqueville, during his tour of the United States, celebrated the upper chamber as a body "of eloquent advocates, distinguished generals, wise magistrates, and statesmen of note, whose language would at times do honor to the most remarkable parliamentary debates in Europe" (de Tocqueville 2003). Indeed, the likes of Thomas Hart Benton, Daniel Webster, Henry Clay, and John Calhoun ushered in a "golden age" in which the Senate dominated Washington's political life. On foreign policy matters, however, the Senate's emergence occurred more gradually; opposition to Polk's foreign policy was sustained by anti-imperialists in the House. But by the 1850s, most major international initiatives – such as approving the Clayton-Bulwer Treaty (which conditioned construction of a Central American canal upon agreement with the British) and the Gadsden Treaty (to acquire a sliver of land from Mexico), and confirming Franklin Pierce's minister to the pro-slavery usurper William Walker's government in Nicaragua – involved powers assigned to the Senate alone rather than both houses of Congress. In addition, the emergence of the Republican Party created a well-organized dissenting bloc in a body that, unlike the more centralized House of Representatives, sported a culture hospitable to those with alternative viewpoints (Swift 1996, Peterson 1987, Potter 1976, Holt 1933).

In the late 1850s, the increased prominence of the Senate and the tendency for debates over imperialism to assume constitutional implications produced a series of institutional showdowns about Congress's proper role in foreign policy. With previous service as secretary of state, U.S. senator, and minister to Britain, James Buchanan appeared to have more qualifications to address international matters than any chief executive since John Quincy Adams. His experience had convinced Buchanan that the American constitutional structure was poorly suited to the mid-19th century diplomatic environment, and that foreign powers would take his international assertiveness seriously only if he could prove that – unlike the five presidents who had preceded him – his actions would not later be repudiated by Congress. As a result, the most aggressive attempt to redefine the foreign policy relationship between Congress and the executive during the 19th century occurred under a president whom historians almost universally (and correctly) regard a failure (Binder 1994; Moore 1910, 165; *New York Herald* 1859).

Buchanan first exhibited his agenda to minimize Congress's foreign policy role in 1858, by exploiting an otherwise obscure dispute with Paraguay. The issue involved redress for the owners of a U.S. weather vessel, the *Water Witch*, which Paraguayan forces had bombed during a survey mission in 1855 (Ynsfran 1958; Peterson 1942). Going well beyond the matter at hand, the president proposed a resolution authorizing him "to adopt such measures and use such force as in his judgment may be necessary and advisable, in the event of a refusal of just satisfaction by the Government of Paraguay." Since the owners of the *Water Witch* were from Rhode Island and no one spoke of annexing Paraguay as a slave state, the crisis seemingly could avoid inflaming sectional tensions, unlike most disputes over inter-American policy since the acquisition of Texas in 1845. As a result, the predated declaration of war sailed through the Democratic-controlled House of Representatives (Moore 1910; *Congressional Record* April 21, 1858; Senate Committee on Foreign Relations 1858).

In the Senate, however, Buchanan's initiative encountered resistance led by Jacob Collamer (Opposition-VT), whose impressive intellect and keen legal instincts earned him the nickname of "Green Mountain Socrates." Collamer wondered how the Senate could consider granting any president the authority to "bombard their cities and towns" and use "the Navy and Army to land upon their shores" to resolve a primarily diplomatic dispute. The Vermont senator's dissent effectively turned Buchanan's tactics against the president by charging that the bill would clothe the executive with "absolute" power to make war. To authorize any "President to commence war at his discretion" was not "proper exercise of the authority of Congress in relation to the subject of war"; therefore, Collamer introduced an amendment to strip the authorization to use force (*Congressional Globe* April 21, 1858; Bogue 1981; Davies 1959). And when the upper chamber voted, the administration suffered a stunning setback: by a margin of 21 to 19, the Collamer Amendment prevailed. The Vermont senator gleefully announced that he did not regard the outcome "as destroying the effect of the resolution, but if so, it should be destroyed" (*Congressional Globe* May 4, 1858, 1929).[2]

---

[2] The *New York Herald* denounced the handiwork of "this disorganized and demoralized Congress" as contrary to "the great ends of international justice." See *New York Herald*, 6 May 1858.

Pro-administration senators regrouped and secured a reconsideration of the vote the following day, after receiving private (and ultimately false) assurances from Buchanan that he would not use force against Paraguay after all. But such parliamentary maneuvers could not conceal the effects of the administration's initial setback. The British minister in Washington, Lord Napier, a friend of Buchanan's from the president's time in London and therefore hardly a hostile observer, perceptively commented on how "the jealous repertory and economical spirit of the present Congress" aggravated Buchanan's international difficulties. Even after subsequently reversing itself, the Senate had sent a message by having initially "refused the liberty of executive action." In the aftermath, the minister doubted that the president could "ask for discretionary powers of action" elsewhere "with any prospect of success" (Lord Napier to William Reed, May 6, 1858; *New York Daily Tribune* August 1, 1860).

Buchanan, however, ignored reality and attempted to replicate his Paraguayan strategy in December 1858, championing a resolution to provide him with authority to use force without congressional consent anywhere in Latin America (the bill was confined to the Western Hemisphere), subject only to his reporting the action to Congress and withdrawing U.S. forces after obtaining a settlement. The United States, Buchanan claimed, could simply not compete with its commercial rivals as long as its constitutional structure prevented the executive from acting rapidly, with force if necessary, to protect U.S. strategic and commercial concerns from the region's "lawless violence." In a worst-case scenario, he conceded, the bill might allow him to initiate hostilities, but, trying to neutralize a resurrection of Collamer's Paraguayan argument, the president's backers contended that "hostilities are not necessarily war." In any case, the administration mouthpiece *Washington Union* claimed, a "vast majority of the American people" preferred to invest the war-making power with the president rather than Congress (quoted in Moore 1910, 259; *Washington Union* 1859; Nichols 1990). Senate debate revolved around the abstract question of how the United States, as a country founded in revolution but now a regional power, should deal with its weaker neighbors (*Congressional Globe* February 18, 1859). But partisan bitterness, the legacy of the Paraguayan resolution, the polarized conception of the U.S. role in Latin America, and the tendency of Republicans of all ideological persuasions to defend the institutional prerogatives of the Senate doomed Buchanan's initiative. While congressional Democrats complained about the actions of a "set of selfish cliques and factious fools," in early March 1860, Secretary of State Lewis Cass privately conceded that the setbacks meant that control of foreign policy now belonged "to the Legislative and not to the Executive Department of the Government" (*Congressional Globe* February 25, 1859, 1334, 1352, 1365; Manning 1939, 285).

Abraham Lincoln, obviously, faced a far different political situation than that confronted by Buchanan: his party overwhelmingly controlled both houses of Congress, and with the legislature out of session when the Civil War began, the president acted unilaterally to defend Union holdouts in the South, suspend habeas corpus, impose martial law in some sections of Maryland, and eventually impose a naval blockade on southern ports, possibly in violation of international law. Yet Lincoln's expansion of executive authority on national security matters was far more cautious than what Buchanan had planned. He obtained retroactive congressional approval for his most aggressive action (suspension of habeas corpus), and as the war progressed, the president faced scrutiny from one of the most aggressive oversight panels in the history of Congress, the Joint Committee on the Conduct of the War. After the conflict's conclusion, meanwhile, a key Supreme Court decision, *Ex parte Milligan* (1866), reined in executive power by overturning Lincoln's use of martial law in states with a functioning civilian court system. The administration's approach, according to the Court, amounted to finding that "republican government is a failure, and there is an end of liberty regulated by law. Martial law established on such a basis destroys every guarantee of the Constitution, and effectually renders the military independent of and superior to the civil power" (*Ex parte Milligan* 1866; Tap 2003).

The generally robust foreign policy role for the 19th-century Congress peaked in the three decades following the Civil War, partly because the era's weak presidents upheld tradition and negotiated substantial agreements with foreign powers as treaties. The failure of the three most ambitious of these treaties – U.S. Grant's scheme to annex the Dominican Republic in 1870, the effort to establish a U.S. protectorate over Nicaragua in 1884, and Benjamin Harrison's gambit to annex Hawaii in 1893 – prompted future secretary of state John Hay to observe that a "treaty entering the Senate is like a bull going into the arena; no one can tell just how or when the blow will fall – but one thing is certain – it will never leave the arena alive" (Leuchtenberg 1952). Meanwhile, the closely divided party structure led to wild oscillations in foreign economic policy, as high-tariff Republicans regularly swapped control of Congress with low-tariff Democrats. In a commentary on where power existed in Gilded Age Washington, President Grover Cleveland turned down media requests to establish a White House press office, suggesting that the real work of governing was occurring on Capitol Hill (Ritchie 1993).

CONGRESS AND AMERICA'S EMERGENCE AS A WORLD POWER

At the turn of the century, a string of presidents – William McKinley, Theodore Roosevelt, William Howard Taft, Woodrow Wilson – terminated the era of congressional dominance on foreign policy questions. After the Spanish-American War, McKinley overcame enormous domestic opposition to obtain Senate approval of the Treaty of Paris, which paved the way for the United States to acquire Puerto Rico and the Philippines. A series of Supreme Court decisions known as the Insular Cases established that the Constitution did not necessarily follow the flag to the new colonies. In *Downes v. Bidwell* (1901), a 5 to 4 majority ruled that since

> those possessions are inhabited by alien races, differing from us in religion, customs, laws, methods of taxation, and modes of thought, the Administration of government and justice, according to Anglo-Saxon principles, may for a time be impossible; and the question at once arises whether large concessions ought not to be made for a time, that ultimately our own theories may be carried out, and the blessings of a free government under the Constitution extended to them. We decline to hold that there is anything in the Constitution to forbid such action. (*Downes v. Bidwell* 1901)

More extreme language accompanied a 1904 decision, *Dorr v. United States*, in which the Court explicitly ruled that the Bill of Rights did not necessarily apply to territories. Otherwise, the Court held, "If the United States, impelled by its duty or advantage, shall acquire territory peopled by savages, and of which it may dispose or not hold for ultimate admission to statehood, ... it must establish there the trial by jury. To state such a proposition demonstrates the impossibility of carrying it into practice" (*Dorr v. United States* 1904).

Though the Insular Cases did not address the appropriate balance of power between Congress and the executive, by placing some elements of foreign policy beyond the Constitution's scope, the rulings reflected a broader reconsideration of constitutional questions in international affairs. And the presidents who followed McKinley did their best to take advantage. When Senate opposition looked as if it might pressure Theodore Roosevelt into constructing a canal in Nicaragua, the president ordered the navy to Panama and (in blatant violation of a 56-year-old treaty with Colombia) assisted a Panamanian "independence" movement (Lael 1987). The new government then negotiated a favorable canal treaty that sailed through the Senate. Two years later, Roosevelt established a customs receivership with the Dominican Republic through an executive agreement rather than a treaty, explaining that he had done so to avoid a robust Senate debate that challenged his vision for Latin American policy. In any such debate, the president scoffed, the Democrats' leading figure on foreign policy issues, Senator Augustus O. Bacon (D-GA), "backed by the average yahoo among the Democratic senators," would block the measure and in the process get "a little cheap reputation among ignorant people" (quoted in Morison 1951, 1144–1145). Roosevelt's successor, William Howard Taft, unilaterally intervened in Nicaraguan domestic affairs; the resulting U.S. military occupation of the country spanned more than two decades.

This newfound pattern of executive unilateralism in foreign affairs accelerated during the presidency of Woodrow Wilson. Ironically a scholar of Congress – Wilson's *Congressional Government*, published in 1887, was the first serious study of Congress from the ranks of U.S. political scientists – Wilson as president repeatedly sent troops abroad without congressional approval. Marine interventions in Haiti (1915) and the Dominican Republic (1916) initiated U.S. military occupations of both Caribbean nations that were only formalized years later through treaties with the new puppet regimes. Wilson twice sent troops to Mexico (1914 and 1916); on the first occasion, Marines already had landed onshore in Veracruz before the Senate considered the resolution to authorize the president's action. Congress overwhelmingly approved the move, but not without some sharp criticism for Wilson; Senator George W. Norris (R-NE) lamented that the Senate needed to "be allowed here to exercise our discretion and our judgment" free from the pressures of passing judgment on an immediate military action (*Congressional Record* 1914, 6999–7000). And Wilson sent U.S. forces to Siberia and Murmansk to intervene in the Russian Civil War, even though Congress never declared war against the Bolshevik regime.

Yet the more powerful presidencies of the Progressive Era did not vitiate an active congressional role in international affairs. The Senate blocked Taft's major international goal – arbitration treaties with Britain and France – primarily from fear that the treaties would provide a backdoor route to minimizing congressional power in the future. Senate opposition likewise delayed and then killed Taft's attempt to establish a customs receivership (in effect a U.S. protectorate) with Nicaragua, although this action did not compel the president to withdraw the Marines sent to prop up the pro-American regime. And even Taft's most significant foreign policy victory – the 1911 reciprocity treaty with Canada – was undone in part due to the effects of the ratification process. The president overcame vehement opposition to the treaty from midwestern senators only by framing the document as a one-sided arrangement from which the United States would disproportionately benefit. Canadian

opponents of the reciprocity seized upon Taft's remarks to fortify nationalist resistance in Canada, which ultimately declined to approve the treaty
(Burton 2004).

Wilson initially avoided his predecessor's difficulties either through bypassing Congress altogether (as in the Haitian and Dominican interventions) or
by translating his academic theories into action and effectively managing the
slim Democratic majorities he enjoyed until early 1919. Wilson's final two
years in office featured a resurgence of congressional power in foreign policy
decisions, most spectacularly through the Senate's rejection of the Treaty of
Versailles. Despite the nullification of the "advise" provision, the prevalence
of treaties heightened the importance of the Senate's role in the conduct of
foreign policy, even though the upper chamber approved 86 percent of the
726 treaties it considered between 1789 and 1926 (Cole 1987, 81; Holt 1933).
Versailles would provide a spectacular exception to this pattern. A combination of diehard ideological opponents (the irreconcilables) and a determined
Senate majority leader (Henry Cabot Lodge [R-MA]) used parliamentary
maneuvers to delay consideration of the treaty for months – allowing stronger
grassroots opposition to the treaty to emerge. Wilson's refusal to consent to
reservations doomed the measure.[3]

The Senate's rejection of Versailles remains the best-known foreign policy battle between Congress and the president to occur during the Wilson
administration. But an equally significant tussle – at least regarding long-term
congressional power – occurred over the intervention in Russia. The more
assertive U.S. foreign policy undertaken by Progressive Era chief executives
required funding; and few contemporary politicians denied that Congress still
possessed the power of the purse. In the 1919 lame-duck session, Senator Hiram
Johnson (R-CA), a (then) progressive Republican who had served as Theodore
Roosevelt's running mate in the 1912 presidential election, introduced a measure to eliminate appropriations for the Russian intervention. Congress had
never cut off funding for an overseas military operation which remained in
the field, and the Johnson Amendment seemed to have little chance of passage. Instead, the same combination of ideologues and partisans that would
doom the Versailles Treaty first showed its potential. The Senate vote ended
even, with Vice President Thomas Marshall forced to cast the tie-breaking

---

[3] The best coverage of the Senate debate over the Treaty of Versailles is Lloyd
Ambrosius, *Woodrow Wilson and the American Diplomatic Tradition* (New York: Cambridge
University Press, 1987); although see also William Widenor, *Henry Cabot Lodge and the
Search for an American Foreign Policy* (Berkeley: University of California Press, 1980); and
Ralph Stone, *The Irreconcilables: The Fight against the League of Nations* (Lexington:
University Press of Kentucky, 1970).

vote to keep appropriations for the operation alive. With Republicans having gained seats in the 1918 election, the new Senate seemed all but certain to cut off funding for the operation unless Wilson acted first. The day after the vote, the acting secretary of state, Frank Polk, understood that the "critical spirit in Congress" left the administration with no choice but to withdraw the troops (quoted in *Papers Relating to the Foreign Relations of the United States, 1918–1919, Russia* 1937, 245–248; Lower 1993).

Johnson as senator never realized his potential and by the 1920s had begun his transformation from a progressive leader into a nationalist, even isolationist, crank. But his tactic of using the appropriations power to influence foreign policy appealed to Senate anti-imperialists, who had scant influence with the executive branch between 1921 and 1933. In 1922, a group of anti-imperialist senators – the peace progressives – teamed with a conservative Democrat eager to reduce federal spending, Utah senator William King, to apply Johnson's tactic to the Haitian intervention. After years of little public notice, Haiti suddenly became a big issue in the 1920 presidential campaign, after the Democrats' vice-presidential nominee, then-assistant secretary of the navy Franklin Delano Roosevelt, boasted about having authored the Haitian constitution when pressed for examples of his government experience. Republican presidential candidate Warren Harding implied that he would bring the occupation to a close, but instead created a commission that recommended minor personnel changes but otherwise maintaining U.S. troops in Haiti indefinitely.

The King Amendment overwhelmingly failed, on a 43 to 9 vote, after most Senate Democrats declined to vote on the measure. (Appearing to support the independence of a majority-black nation was politically impossible for Jim Crow-era southern Democrats, and the 1918 and 1920 election had resulted in the defeat of most Democrats outside the South.) But from 1923 through 1931, an alliance of the peace progressives (mostly Republicans from midwestern states where the GOP was left wing) and Democrats assumed a majority or near-majority in the Senate, resurrecting the type of ideologue-partisan coalition that had blocked the Treaty of Versailles (Johnson 1993).

This coalition exercised a decisive impact on U.S. policy toward the Caribbean Basin in the mid- and late 1920s. Senate resistance neutralized calls for the United States to intervene against the Mexican government during a 1926 dispute over Mexico's land and oil policy. Then, from 1927 through 1929, the peace progressives led a Senate insurrection against the U.S. military occupation of Nicaragua. Since the Taft administration, the United States had stationed troops in the Central American country, hoping to ensure local stability and protect U.S. investments. The breakdown of Nicaraguan politics in

1926, however, led President Calvin Coolidge to dramatically expand the U.S. presence, and by 1928, more than 5,000 Marines patrolled the Nicaraguan countryside in pursuit of guerrilla leader Augusto Sandino. The administration initially beat back a Senate effort to cut off funds by claiming the troops would only provide security for Nicaragua's 1928 presidential election. But when the Marines remained, peace progressive senator Clarence C. Dill (D-WA) introduced an amendment to cut off the funds for the occupation. Dill's efforts encountered fierce resistance (Senator William Bruce [D-MD] claimed that his Washington colleague "would have our nationals scurry out of the country like so many frightened rats"), but the Senate initially approved the measure (*Congressional Record* 1928). The following day, under strong administration pressure, a handful of senators reversed themselves – much as had occurred with the Collamer Amendment more than seven decades before. Nonetheless, the original Dill Amendment spelled the effective end to the occupation, and the incoming secretary of state, Henry Stimson, announced that U.S. troops would withdraw.

The peace progressives failed to survive the Great Depression, either politically or institutionally. The emergence of the New Deal Democratic majority ended the closely balanced Senate upon which their internal power depended. And the economic downturn first led voters to punish senators (such as peace progressive leader John J. Blaine of Wisconsin) they believed had focused excessively on foreign policy and then, more important, triggered a partisan realignment in which the midwestern GOP drifted sharply to the right. By the mid-1940s, the last of the peace progressives (Robert M. La Follette, Jr., of Wisconsin, Burton K. Wheeler of Montana, and Henrik Shipstead of Minnesota) had either retired or had lost bids for renomination. La Follette's defeat had the most national impact – Wisconsin Republican voters cast him aside for a little-known World War II veteran, Joe McCarthy.

Though the peace progressives gradually passed from the scene, one of their number, Senator Gerald P. Nye (R-ND) presided over the highest-profile foreign policy committee of the 1930s, and in the process demonstrated how Congress could use its oversight power to shape national discourse about foreign policy issues. The Nye Committee held hearings exploring the connections between bankers, munitions makers, and the Wilson administration's decision to enter World War I; in the anti-Wall Street atmosphere following the Stock Market crash, the committee's often paranoid conclusions generated surprisingly wide support. In response, a measure co-sponsored by Nye to impose sharp constraints on the president sailed through Congress. The Neutrality Act of 1935, which Secretary of State Cordell Hull considered "an invasion of the constitutional and traditional power of the Executive to conduct the foreign relations of the United States," provided the perfect mechanism (albeit 18 years after the event) for the United States to avoid entry into World War I: it prevented U.S. firms from supplying arms and U.S. banks from making loans to belligerent powers (Cole 1983).

The 1935 law represented a high point of the New Deal-era Congress attempting to restrict FDR's international freedom of action. The Neutrality Act was weakened by amendments in 1936, 1937, and 1939; it effectively was repealed by the 1940 Lend-Lease Act, which allowed the United States to lend military supplies to nations fighting the Axis Powers. That law passed despite congressional recognition that the measure greatly weakened the institution's foreign policy powers; the measure's chief congressional opponent, Senator Robert A. Taft (R-OH), dismissed the president's rationalizing his policy as the equivalent of lending a hose to a neighbor whose house was on fire. The better comparison, the Ohio senator maintained, was to chewing gum; after its use, its original owner would not want it back. The altered international environment also drained support for the kind of tinkering with traditional executive prerogatives that the Neutrality Act had typified. As a result, the efforts of Indiana congressman Louis Ludlow to amend the Constitution to allow for a popular vote on non-defensive war failed to gain majorities in either house of Congress (Bolt 1977).

Even before these debates, significant diminutions to the traditional, formal congressional role in foreign policy already had occurred. Fueled by the backlash against the Hawley-Smoot tariff, the Reciprocal Trade Agreements Act of 1934 stripped from Congress most of its powers over foreign economic policy. Two years later, in *United States v. Curtiss-Wright Export Co.* (1936), a unanimous Supreme Court described a profound distinction between domestic matters, in which the Constitution allocated limited powers to Congress and the president, and international affairs, which implicated questions of sovereignty. The resulting opinion from Justice George Sutherland maintained that not only

> is the federal power over external affairs in origin and essential character different from that over internal affairs, but participation in the exercise of the power is significantly limited. In this vast external realm, with its important, complicated, delicate and manifold problems, the president alone has the power to speak or listen as a representative of the nation. He makes treaties with the advice and consent of the Senate; but he alone negotiates. Into the field of negotiation the Senate cannot intrude, and Congress itself is powerless to invade it. (*United States v. Curtiss-Wright Export Co.* 1936)

Wartime events did little to call into question the prescience of Justice Sutherland's analysis. During World War II, a bipartisan group of senators sponsored a call for the United States to participate in a postwar international police organization, but the Roosevelt administration sidetracked their initiative. Meanwhile, the Manhattan Project established the precedent of "black appropriations," in which Congress would fund national security programs without any oversight on how the money would be spent. This approach would govern intelligence funding after the creation of the Central Intelligence Agency (CIA) and National Security Agency (NSA) in 1947. And congressional oversight was absent regarding the most serious national security–inspired error of the war, the decision to intern Japanese-Americans who lived on the West Coast.

THE COLD WAR CONGRESS

Justice Sutherland's words previewed an era in which Congress's traditional means for influencing foreign policy – the treaty-making power and the power to declare war – went into sharp decline. On the domestic front, a widespread perception existed that the late 1930s had revealed the dangers of an overactive congressional role in foreign policy. Internationally, the Cold War's seemingly all-encompassing nature placed the government on what amounted to a permanent war footing, while the advent of nuclear weapons created the need for instant decision making that was lacking in previous challenges to U.S. national security. This situation gave rise to a new interpretation of constitutional theory that sought to increase the power of the presidency through the commander-in-chief clause.

The Korean War, in which President Harry Truman sent nearly 500,000 U.S. troops into combat absent a declaration of war, symbolized a new era in the war-making power; the administration argued that the concept of limited war necessitated maximum flexibility for the commander in chief. Truman's approach, however, entailed severe political risks, if – as occurred in Korea – the troops became bogged down. Future presidents accordingly devised a different method of side-stepping the war-making power. Harking back to the ideas of James Buchanan, in 1955 Dwight Eisenhower requested from Congress advance authority to use force to resolve a dispute with the People's Republic of China over a handful of islands between China and Taiwan. Eisenhower returned to the tactic in 1957, when he obtained an open-ended authorization to use force to combat communism in the Middle East. John F. Kennedy ushered through a similar resolution in 1962, during the Cuban Missile Crisis; and, most famously, Lyndon Johnson obtained congressional approval to take all necessary measures to respond to North Vietnamese aggression following the Tonkin Gulf incident of August 1964.[4]

Even after the Vietnam War and Watergate weakened public support for expansive presidential authority, Congress struggled to effectively reclaim the war-making power. The War Powers Act of 1973, celebrated as a reassertion of congressional influence, nonetheless allowed the president to unilaterally deploy U.S. troops overseas in hostile situations for up to 90 days, while an amendment to include the CIA under the terms of the bill failed. The measure thus seemed – if unintentionally – to concede the argument that the commander in chief's power gave to the executive a unilateral power to wage war.[5]

Postwar presidents further circumvented Congress by relying on executive or statutory agreements rather than formal treaties. A few statistics underscore the shift. In 1930 (to take a typical pre–World War II year as an example) the United States concluded 25 treaties, as compared to only nine executive agreements. With the important exceptions of NATO, the Southeast Asian Treaty Organization, and the Limited Test-Ban Treaty, however, presidents during the Cold War increasingly turned to executive or statutory agreements rather than treaties when embarking on new foreign policy ventures. By 1968 (again, a fairly typical year for Cold War diplomacy, if not for international events as a whole) the United States entered into just 16 treaties as opposed to 266 executive agreements (Johnson 1984, Moore 1976).

Even though more traditional avenues of congressional influence of foreign policy atrophied in the early stages of the Cold War, members of Congress built on pre-1945 precedents to shape policy. The emergence of what Roger Davidson (1981) has termed "subcommittee government" dramatically expanded the opportunities for foreign policy oversight (Davidson 1981).[6]

---

[4]   For the Formosa Resolution, see Gordon Chang, *Friends and Enemies: The United States, China, and the Soviet Union, 1948–1972* (Stanford: Stanford University Press, 1990); and Robert Accinelli, *Crisis and Containment: United States Policy toward Taiwan, 1950–1955* (Chapel Hill: University of North Carolina Press, 1996). For Congress and the Tonkin Gulf Resolution, see William Conrad Gibbons, *The U.S. Government and the Vietnam War: Executive and Legislative Roles and Relationships*, Vol. 2: 1961–1964 (Princeton: Princeton University Press, 1984); and Edwin Moise, *Tonkin Gulf and the Escalation of the Vietnam War* (Chapel Hill: University of North Carolina Press, 1996), pp. 252–255.

[5]   As one House staffer conceded after Ronald Reagan's refusal to invoke the War Powers Act when sending the Marines to Lebanon in 1983, "War Powers is a law that simply doesn't work in conventional terms. If it works at all, it does so in mysterious ways." See Barry Blechman, *The Politics of National Security* (New York: Oxford University Press, 1992), p. 183.

[6]   Overall, the number of foreign policy subcommittees in the Senate alone grew from seven in 1945–1946 to 31 by 1965–1966, and the number continued to grow into the 1980s.

Procedural gambits allowed legislators to shape international affairs, often outside of the public eye. And, as had been the case in the 1850s and 1910s, the power of the purse provided the ultimate check on executive action.

Perhaps the clearest example of "subcommittee government" affecting the congressional response to foreign policy came in the activities of the heretofore obscure Government Operations Committee, whose charter gave it oversight authority over virtually all federal activities. Between 1953 and 1969, the committee housed three high-profile foreign policy subcommittees, chaired by senators of wildly differing ideological perspectives – the communist witchhunter Senator Joseph R. McCarthy (R-WI), the Cold War liberal Senator Henry "Scoop" Jackson (D-WA), and the anti-imperialist radical Senator Ernest H. Gruening (D-AK).

McCarthy's actions, of course, remain best known. Benefiting from regular FBI leaks as well as access to professional staff and the increased powers granted to subcommittee chairs provided by the Legislative Reorganization Act of 1946, McCarthy convened a series of hearings exploring the alleged infiltration of the national security bureaucracy by communist agents. Ironically, his success in attracting attention (the hearings' television audience peaked in excess of 20 million people) ultimately proved his downfall, since the Army-McCarthy hearings exposed the country to the Wisconsin senator's reckless and bullying tactics (Griffith 1987). But several of his colleagues learned from McCarthy's success at utilizing Congress's newly flexible institutional powers to fulfill his own personal, partisan, and ideological goals. In 1959, Jackson's Subcommittee on National Policy Machinery began hearings and studies critically examined the functioning of Eisenhower's National Security Council (NSC). The subcommittee remained in place throughout the 1960s, and Jackson used its proceedings to criticize both the Kennedy and Johnson administrations for insufficient zeal in waging the Cold War. From the opposite side of the ideological spectrum, in the mid-1960s Senator Gruening's Subcommittee on Foreign Aid Expenditures conducted several highly critical investigations of U.S. foreign and military aid programs (Johnson 1998).

Beyond his policy goals, Senator Gruening squarely addressed the constitutional theories behind his subcommittee's agenda. The Alaska senator conceded that many specific foreign policy functions assigned by the Constitution, such as declaring war, confirming ambassadorial nominations, and approving treaties, had become "perfunctory and routine" in the Cold War period. But, Gruening maintained, senators needed to confront the situation at hand rather than lament the passing of a bygone constitutional framework. Because Congress retained the power of the purse, foreign aid represented a way to influence foreign policy, through tactics such as roll call votes on specific foreign policy questions related to countries that received assistance, generating publicity with hearings, and using the oversight power to pressure executive branch officials (U.S. Senate, Committee on Foreign Relations 1959).

Subcommittee government also allowed the House to increase its traditionally marginal role in foreign policy, as when Representative Otto E. Passman (D-LA) assumed chairmanship of the newly created Foreign Operations Subcommittee, which received jurisdiction over the foreign aid program in 1955 (Haviland 1958, 709). Passman brought a somewhat unusual background to Congress. He had dropped out of school in fourth grade, and then sold appliances before entering politics; capturing the consensus of the Washington establishment, commentators Evans and Novak (1964) ridiculed him as the "shrill-voiced shopkeeper from Shreveport" (*Washington Post* 1964).

Representative Passman, who chaired the subcommittee for more than two decades, was relentless and extraordinarily difficult for executive officials to deal with. As he told one Eisenhower official, "Son, I don't smoke; I don't drink; my only pleasure in life is to kick the shit out of the foreign aid program of the United States" (quoted in Pach and Richardson 1991, 165). Over the course of lengthy annual authorization hearings, Passman returned to two arguments: first, that the United States did not need to provide economic aid, since military aid supplied to dozens of countries freed up money for recipient nations to spend on economic programs; and second, that most foreign countries (he excepted Franco's Spain) did not deserve U.S. assistance, since their socialistic domestic policies were wasteful (U.S. House, Foreign Operations Subcommittee 1957, 162).

Presidents who had the misfortune of crossing Passman's path harbored a uniformly negative opinion of the Louisiana congressman. In 1957, after Passman harangued him at a meeting, Dwight Eisenhower instructed an aide, "Remind me never to invite that fellow down here again" (quoted in Anderson and Pearson 1968, 229).[7] Lyndon Johnson, who privately denounced Passman as "a goddamned Cajun from the hills of Louisiana," told one confidant, "Some day we'll get our way, and if I ever walk up in the cold of night and a rattlesnake's out there and about ready to get him, I ain't going to pull him off."[8]

---

[7] Passman's influence with fellow legislators left Eisenhower "astonished, even astounded, by the apparent ignorance of men of Congress in the general subject of our foreign affairs." See Chester Pach, "Military Assistance and American Foreign Policy: The Role of Congress," in Michael Barnhart, ed., *Congress and United States Foreign Policy* (Albany: SUNY Press, 1986), p. 143.

[8] See President Johnson and Jack Brooks, 10:36 PM 20 Dec. 1963, Tape K6312.13, PNO 6, Recordings of Telephone Conversations – White House Series, Recordings and Transcripts of Conversations and Meetings, Lyndon B. Johnson Library.

By the late 1950s, the London *Times* termed Passman "almost a law to himself on foreign aid" (*The Times* 1960). In 1957, he secured a cut of more than 34 percent from the administration's request. John F. Kennedy went through three foreign aid administrators, partly because no one wanted to deal with Passman. Johnson initially fared no better; in December 1963, Passman outmaneuvered Johnson – no easy task when confronting the man dubbed the "master of the Senate" – and shepherded through the House a 33 percent reduction in the administration's foreign aid request. "Son of a bitch," Johnson hissed the night of the vote.[9]

After the 1964 Democratic landslide, Passman lost control of his subcommittee to a bipartisan pro-foreign aid majority. And he lost his seat entirely in 1976 – ironically following a scandal in which he accepted improper foreign donations (from South Korea's authoritarian regime).

Even after his departure, Representative Passman's subcommittee continued to show how individual House members could shape foreign policy developments, although the figure who next emerged from the subcommittee was about as different as possible in temperament from the dour, Puritanical Passman. Though Charlie Wilson represented a district in the Bible Belt, the Democratic Texas congressman was as well known for his partying ways and his relationships with beautiful women as for his political activities (secretaries in Wilson's House office earned the nickname "Charlie's Angels"). But Wilson was also a serious legislator, first in Austin, when he caucused with the small number of liberals (the "Killer Bees") in the Texas legislature, and then in Washington. Throughout the 1970s, Wilson aggressively championed U.S. assistance first to Israel and then to Nicaragua, two nations he viewed as bastions of Western ideals in an often hostile world. His power increased when he obtained an assignment to the Foreign Operations Subcommittee, which he leveraged in the 1980s to emerge as the leading congressional champion of aid to Afghanistan's mujahedeen. As often was the case with Wilson, a personal connection explained at least some of his interest – at the time, he was dating a Houston socialite who had her own connections to the mujahedeen's chief foreign sponsor, Pakistani president Muhammad Zia-ul-Haq. Aid to Afghanistan eventually achieved considerable popularity, but in the early 1980s, many House Democrats were suspicious of the Reagan administration's zeal for covert operations, making Wilson's support critical to create a bipartisan pro-mujahedeen coalition. And, in the end, U.S. assistance

9   See President Johnson and Larry O'Brien, 4:01 PM, 12 Dec. 1963, Tape K6312.08, PNO 4, Recordings of Telephone Conversations – White House Series, Recordings and Transcripts of Conversations and Meetings, Lyndon B. Johnson Library.

(initially covert, later not-so-covert) helped turn the tide of the war, especially once the United States supplied the rebels with stinger anti-aircraft missiles (Crile 2007).

Subcommittee government of the type seen in the House Foreign Operations Subcommittee and the various subcommittees of the Senate Government Operations Committee was not the only structural change that shaped the ways Congress affected Cold War foreign policy. Government Operations and Appropriations subcommittees vied for influence not only with the Senate Foreign Relations Committee (which had represented what traditionally passed for an official congressional voice on world affairs) but also with the Armed Services Committees of both chambers. The rise of the national security state spread defense spending around the country, forcing members of Congress to consider the Pentagon budget not only through the national interest but from a desire to protect the economic interests of their constituents.

The strongly pro-defense members of both the House and Senate Armed Services committees had no hesitation in aggressively funneling defense projects to their constituents. Representative Mendel L. Rivers (D-SC), who concluded his career as chair of the House Armed Services Committee, was perceived as so zealous in securing projects that many joked that his district's largest city, Charleston, would fall into the sea with the weight of the concrete poured for military bases there. But the congressman denied that patronage explained his action: as Rivers explained in the mid-1950s, the committee viewed itself as "the only voice, official voice, the military has in the House of Representatives." Representative Rivers – and like-minded members of the Senate, such as Senator Richard B. Russell (D-GA) and Senator John C. Stennis (D-MS), who chaired the Armed Services Committee from 1955 until 1981 – rarely challenged executive branch defense proposals, unless they felt the Pentagon was receiving insufficient funding.[10]

Figures like Passman and Wilson exercised disproportionate power not merely because they mastered the rules of subcommittee government, but also because their subcommittees dealt with the power of the purse. After a period of deference to the executive between 1940 and 1960, Congress

---

[10] Rivers quoted in James Lindsay, "Congress and Defense Policy, 1961 to 1986," *Armed Forces & Society*, Vol. 13, No. 4 (Fall 1987), p. 378; see also Barbara Hinckley, *Less Than Meets the Eye: Foreign Policy Making and the Myth of the Assertive Congress* (Chicago: University of Chicago Press, 1994), p. 51; Blechman, *The Politics of National Security*, pp. 23–32; Herbert Stephens, "The Role of the Legislative Committees in the Appropriations Process: A Study Focused on the Armed Services Committees," *Western Political Quarterly*, Vol. 24, No. 2 (Spring 1971), p. 146.

started vigorously reclaiming the appropriations power on foreign policy matters. Initially, this activism was confined to the foreign aid program. What *U.S. News & World Report* dubbed the "foreign aid revolt" of 1963 featured Congress not only slashing the administration's foreign aid request but attaching numerous policy riders to the final bill (*U.S. News & World Report* 1963). These amendments ranged from the trivial (a threat to Peru's foreign aid to protest treatment of U.S. fishing vessels off the Peruvian coast) to the substantial (an amendment to cut off funds to regimes that had come to power through a military coup). By the 1970s, the situation had evolved to such an extent that commentator Robert Pastor could deem the annual foreign aid measure "the nearest thing Congress has to a 'State of the World Message.'"[11]

As the U.S. involvement in Southeast Asia intensified, congressional liberals became more aggressive at using the power of the purse to check executive overseas initiatives. Throughout the early 1970s, Senators George S. McGovern (D-SD) and Mark O. Hatfield (R-OR) annually sponsored an unsuccessful amendment to the Pentagon budget to terminate funding for the Vietnam War. Senator Frank F. Church (D-ID) and Senator John Sherman Cooper (R-KY) achieved a token victory in 1970, when their amendment to block funding for Richard Nixon's invasion of Cambodia was adopted – but only after a protracted debate that gave Nixon the opportunity to withdraw the troops on his own timetable.

Outside of Southeast Asia, however, legislative victories caused one European diplomat to observe that "it isn't just the State Department or the president anymore. It's Congress now" (quoted in Franck and Weisband 1979, 84). A clear sign of the new environment came in 1974, following an aborted attempt to unify Cyprus with Greece. Turkish troops, using weapons supplied by the United States (despite a requirement to employ such arms only in self-defense), occupied the eastern third of Cyprus. The Turks portrayed the move as defensive – to protect ethnic Turks on the island – but it quickly became clear that the Turkish military had no intention of withdrawing.

The Turkish invasion generated intense congressional criticism. Senator Thomas F. Eagleton (D-MO), the Democrats' deposed vice-presidential nominee from two years before, emerged as the key player (Purvis 1984). Linking the invasion to Richard Nixon's failure to follow the law in Watergate ("we have just experienced a period of American history when laws were considered mere 'technicalities' to be rationalized and circumvented to fit the concepts

---

[11] For various policy-related riders, see *Congressional Record*, 88th Congress, 1st Session (14 November 1963), pp. 21840–21842; *Congressional Record*, 90th Congress, 1st Session (17 August 1967), p. 22968.

of policymakers"), Eagleton sponsored an amendment to cut off all military assistance until the Turks withdrew their troops.[12] Overcoming opposition from leaders of both parties, and after a highly-charged ideological debate, the amendment cleared the Senate, 57 to 20. The outcome prompted Arlen Large of the *Wall Street Journal* to conclude that "the Senate is making it plain that its revolt on foreign aid is serious and stubborn" (*Wall Street Journal* October 2, 1974).

In the House, parochial politics played a greater role. The Greek-American lobby, building off the earlier successes of pro-Chinese Nationalist, pro-Dominican, and anti-Castro Cuban American lobbying groups to influence foreign affairs on matters related to their country of interest, mobilized (Tierney 1993; Berger 1975, 224). With no Turkish lobby to counter their efforts, the Greek American activists worked alongside Greek American Representative John Brademas (D-IN), at that time Representative Paul Sarbanes (D-MD), and Representative Peter N. Kyros (D-ME). The House voted 307 to 90 to cut off the aid.[13]

The next year, Congress cut off funds for an existing overseas military operation for the first time since the Nicaraguan affair of the 1920s, a CIA covert operation on behalf of anti-communist forces represented by the National Union for the Total Independence of Angola, known by its Portuguese acronym of UNITA. Shortly after the operation commenced, a freshman senator from Iowa, Dick Clark, chairman of the Subcommittee on African Affairs, traveled to Africa, obtained a sense of the extent of U.S. activities, and returned home convinced that respecting Angolan self-determination would atone for earlier "lack of support for the struggle against colonialism." He then introduced an amendment to the foreign aid bill to cut off all covert assistance to Angola, hoping in the process that adoption would end the "many years of neglect" in congressional oversight of the CIA.[14] Later in 1975, Senator John V. Tunney (D-CA) introduced a companion amendment to the Pentagon budget. Conceding the "tricky" nature of Congress "trying to participate in foreign policy decisions through the use of the purse strings," Tunney detected a "larger meaning" for his amendment: it would restrict executive authority,

---

[12] See Tom Eagleton, "Dear Colleague," 9 September 1974, Box 35, FPD Series, Henry Jackson Papers, University of Washington.

[13] The Greek lobby worked on senators as well; the office of one embargo opponent, Ohio Senator Robert Taft, Jr., struggled to develop a "guide for answering irate Greeks." See Unsigned memo, 2 October 1974, Box 209, Robert Taft, Jr. Papers, Library of Congress; Henry Kissinger, *Years of Renewal* (New York: Simon & Schuster, 1999), p. 233.

[14] See Dick Clark to Pam Kringler, 26 November 1975; Clark to John Haguran, 17 December 1975; both in box 44, Dick Clark Papers, University of Iowa.

either "directly or indirectly," over military policy (*Congressional Record* 1975). Secretary of State Henry Kissinger individually lobbied Senate leaders to no avail; the Tunney Amendment passed, 54 to 22.[15] A few weeks later, the Clark Amendment won approval by a voice vote, thus making permanent the ban on covert assistance.

Unfortunately for Clark and Tunney, conditions in Angola sharply deteriorated shortly after their amendments passed. In early 1976, with strong aid from Cuban paramilitary forces, the communist People's Movement for the Liberation of Angola (MPLA) triumphed in the civil war. Contrary to Clark's predictions, ending U.S. involvement had not ensured the triumph of self-determination in Africa; instead, it had opened the way for the emergence of what critics contended was a Cuban protectorate. Senate Republicans pounced: Senator Dewey F. Bartlett (R-OK) argued that the MPLA's victory "once again gave irrefutable proof that a committee of one hundred is unsuitable for day-to-day foreign policy decisions"; indeed, the "formulation of the issue through a rider on an appropriations bill" illustrated the "careless" process that "greatly reduced" the "odds in favor of correct decisions" (*Congressional Record* 1976, 608–610).

As the 1970s progressed, the idea of an empowered Congress became linked with a liberal, pro–human rights agenda that grew increasingly unpopular. Both Tunney and Clark lost their reelection bids, in both cases amid Republican attacks that their foreign policy activism distracted them from domestic issues of more immediate concern to their constituents (Mink 1981, 65). Two years later, in a symbolic gesture against the decade's institutional activism, the 1980 Republican platform advocated repeal of the Clark Amendment; after Ronald Reagan's election, the incoming secretary of state, Alexander Haig, denounced Clark's offering as "a self-defeating and unnecessary restriction" (*Washington Post* 1981). The next year, the GOP-controlled Senate repealed the amendment, and the House followed suit in 1985.

The Eagleton Amendment, meanwhile, came to be seen by virtually all concerned as an example of congressional overreach. Turkey responded to the amendment's passage not by withdrawing its forces from Cyprus but by closing strategically vital U.S. military bases in the country. The move demonstrated which side had the leverage in the relationship, and it soon became a question of when, not if, Congress would repeal the amendment; even Eagleton's staff conceded that the United States was "at a dead end on the Cyprus issue," with the only remaining question how Congress could "reverse

---

[15] See Bob Wolthuis to Max Friedersdorf, 16 December 1975, box 3, Robert Wolthuis Files, Ford Congressional Relations Office Papers; Dick Clark personal interview.

a moral stand like that."[16] In 1978, the Senate, having grown more conservative since 1974, repealed the amendment; the vote in the House was much closer, but Majority Leader Jim Wright (D-TX) strongly lobbied for repeal and secured a three-vote victory. In the aftermath, the *Washington Post* observed that "many congressmen have come to perceive that vaguely worded riders on foreign economic legislation are a bad way to protect anybody's human rights" (*Washington Post* 1978).

While often effective, therefore, using the power of the purse could expose members of Congress to political attack if their preferred policy option failed to produce the promised results. An alternative existed: using procedural gambits to influence policy. For the most part, given the difficulty both the media and the public had in following arcane procedural disputes, addressing controversial international questions in a backdoor fashion staved off political attacks. But on two key occasions in the Cold War, the approach resulted in members of Congress often becoming associated with untested policy outcomes that lacked sufficient public support. What the *Wall Street Journal* termed "the crippling disease of procedure-itis" occurred when congressional blocs who opposed executive initiatives "for ideological reasons [stuck] to the procedural issues" to hide their failure to build popular support for their agenda (*Wall Street Journal* 1985).

The first example was a set of proposals sponsored as a constitutional amendment by Republican Ohio Senator John W. Bricker, a reactionary conservative who the author John Gunther described in the following way: "Intellectually he is like interstellar space – a vast vacuum occasionally crossed by homeless, wandering clichés" (quoted in Tananbaum 1988, 24). The Bricker Amendment held that any treaty or executive agreement conflicting with the Constitution would have no effect; that all treaties would not apply as domestic law except through valid legislation by Congress or the states; and that all executive agreements would not apply as domestic law except through valid legislation by Congress or the states.

Bricker framed his goal as merely procedural, to guard against "American sovereignty and the American Constitution [being] threatened by treaty law" by giving the House a formal role in the treaty-making process and by ending the constitutional provision making treaties the supreme law of the land (*Congressional Quarterly Weekly Report* 1954). But in fact, the Ohio senator and his allies wanted to reorient Cold War foreign policy away from cooperation with the United Nations, NATO, or European democratic allies and

---

[16] See Ann to Thomas Eagleton, 5 December 1977, Folder 4381, Thomas Eagleton Papers, University of Missouri.

toward an Asia-first foreign policy that would align the United States with far-right anti-communist regimes. Both Truman and Eisenhower recognized the stakes; Eisenhower suggested that "we cannot hope to achieve and maintain peace if we shackle the Federal Government so that it is no longer sovereign in foreign affairs."[17]

In the early 1950s, Bricker's amendment seemed to enjoy wide popular (and Senate) support. But by 1954, he overreached – the backlash against the antics of Bricker's ideological comrade, Senator Joseph McCarthy, had soured the public, the Congress, and the Washington establishment against the far-right agenda that Bricker personified. Eisenhower worked behind the scenes with Senate Democrats, and then-minority leader Lyndon Johnson's (D-TX) parliamentary machinations doomed the Bricker Amendment; by the time his offering came to a vote, Bricker could muster only 42 votes in support. A weaker offering from Senator Walter F. George (D-GA), which sought to invalidate all executive agreements, subsequently fell one vote short of the necessary two-thirds majority. The next time he faced the voters, in 1958, Bricker was upset by a Democrat widely dismissed as a political lightweight, Stephen Young (Caro 2002).

A generation later, another intersection between procedure and policy backfired. In this instance, the key player was Senator Harold E. Hughes (D-IA), a former trucker, governor, and reformed alcoholic (at a time when many did not recognize the disease) who narrowly won election to the Senate in 1968. Hughes spent much of his single term in the upper chamber criticizing the Cold War consensus, and one of his final proposals was a successful amendment prohibiting covert operations unless deemed by the president "important to the national security" and requiring the Foreign Affairs and Foreign Relations Committees, for the first time, to receive briefings on intelligence activities. Hughes admitted the amendment would check "the wide-ranging power of the CIA" only if it were accompanied by a "greater congressional willingness to play its oversight role."[18] But after six years of studying the issue, the Iowa senator knew of no other way to address the problem "other than drawing public attention to it."[19] Like Hughes, House sponsor Representative Leo J. Ryan (D-CA) viewed the amendment as a first step toward bringing

[17] See Dwight Eisenhower to William Knowland, 25 January 1954, Box 6, Dwight Eisenhower Diary, Eisenhower Presidential Library, Abilene.
[18] See Harold Hughes to Robert Hart, 31 October 1974, Box S83, Harold Hughes Papers, University of Iowa.
[19] See Harold Hughes to Hubert Humphrey, 14 February 1974, Box S83, Harold Hughes Papers, University of Iowa.

"the CIA under some kind of jurisdiction by the Foreign Affairs Committee" (*Congressional Record* December 11, 1974).

At the high point of anti-executive sentiment following Watergate and Vietnam, both houses of Congress comfortably approved the Hughes-Ryan Amendment. But by the late 1970s, the altered domestic and international environment produced a backlash against Hughes's agenda. With an election looming in which GOP presidential nominee Ronald Reagan was accusing Democrats of being soft on communism, Congress repealed Hughes-Ryan in 1980. Only 50 members of the House stood in opposition; the Senate did not even have a recorded vote on the decision.[20]

At first blush, the end of the Cold War seemed as if it might prompt a return to the type of executive/legislative relationship more common in the interwar era. After some talk of handling the matter to the United Nations, President George H.W. Bush requested a war authorization from Congress to confront Iraqi forces in Kuwait. House approval was never in doubt, though the administration required hard lobbying in the Senate, where initial vote counts hovered in the 30s. At the last minute, pressure from home-state sources prompted Nevada Democrats Senator Harry Reid and Senator Richard Bryan to vote for the measure, which cleared the Senate with 52 votes (author interview with John Sununu 2011).

In many ways, however, the Gulf War I vote represented a high point for the post–Cold War Congress in foreign affairs. The onset of a hyper-partisan atmosphere, which began with the efforts of Representative Newt Gingrich (R-GA) in the late 1980s, intensified during the Clinton administration's triangulation policy, and sharpened further during the Bush and early Obama years, gradually transformed Congress into a quasi-parliamentary body, with party unity superseding institutional loyalty. Defenders of a powerful congressional role in foreign affairs from the 1990s transformed into aggressive advocates of executive authority when George W. Bush assumed control of the White House in 2001, while 1990s defenders of executive prerogatives generally moved in the other direction. The result was an inconsistent and often indecipherable policy, no more clear than in 1999, when the House defeated, on a 213 to 213, largely party-line tie vote, a measure to approve of Clinton's Kosovo policy – but then consented to continue funding the military operation of which it had formally disapproved (*New York Times* 1999).

---

[20] For the more general altered environment on intelligence oversight issues, see Frank Smist, *Congress Oversees the Intelligence Community* (Knoxville: University of Tennessee Press, 1990), pp. 1–24; and Loch Johnson, *A Season of Inquiry: Congress and Intelligence* (Chicago: Dorsey, 1988).

In recent years, meanwhile, the development of the 24/7 cable news culture has created a wide disparity between the quality of congressional criticisms of the executive (at least when the president belonged to the other party) and the quality of the critique. The current norm – which is, alas, far from the high mark of the congressional role in U.S. foreign policy – brings to mind an event from 1968, after the North Koreans captured a U.S. spy vessel, the *Pueblo*. Worrying about the political consequences of inaction, Senator Stennis sent an urgent message to President Johnson in the Situation Room: "For God's sake, do something." Johnson looked up and told the aide who conferred the report, "Please thank the senator for his helpful advice" (quoted in Blechman 1992, 202).

3

Institutional Challenges Confronting Congress after 9/11:

PARTISAN POLARIZATION AND EFFECTIVE OVERSIGHT

Mark J. Oleszek and Walter J. Oleszek

Numerous internal and external national security challenges confront Congress in the post-9/11 era. Externally, an interdependent world linked by the Internet means that issues or problems that arise in any part of the globe can impact this country, from pandemics to drug trafficking to cybersecurity. What happens in countries little known to most citizens during the pre-9/11 era, such as Afghanistan or Yemen, can affect the United States in consequential ways. Consider that this nation seems engaged in an endless global war (dubbed the "long war" by some analysts) against terrorists and their network of supporters, a marked departure from the pre-9/11 era of conflicts between and among nations. Today's wars appear "limited in scope yet virtually unlimited in duration," where Americans are not asked to sacrifice (except for those in the military and their families) but "to go on with their routines, not change them" (Hampson 2011, 2A).[1] Addressing these challenges and developments can provoke sharp disagreement among our national lawmakers.

On March 10, 2010, for example, the House by a 356 to 65 vote overwhelmingly rejected a non-binding resolution (H. Con. Res. 248), offered by Representative Dennis Kucinich (D-OH), calling for the withdrawal of U.S. troops from Afghanistan within 30 days. Representative Kucinich's basic point was that the cost of the ten-year (and counting) war in financial and other resources, in military casualties, and to nation-building at home is not worth the price. "Our supposed nation-building in Afghanistan has come at the destruction of our own," he argued. The military surge announced by President Barack Obama in December 2009 "cements the path of the United

---

[1] See also Greg Jaffe, "One Percent of Americans Are Touched by This War," *Washington Post*, March 2, 2011, p. A1.

The views and interpretations discussed herein are those of the authors and are in no way attributable to the Congressional Research Service or to Albright College.

States down the road of previous occupiers that earned Afghanistan its nickname as the 'graveyard of empires'" (*Congressional Record* March 10, 2010, H1251). In response, then House Armed Services Chairman Ike Skeleton (D-MO) exclaimed: "Have we forgotten? Have we forgotten what happened to America on 9/11? Have we forgotten who did it? Have we forgotten those who protected and gave [al Qaeda] a safe haven?" (Ibid., H1255) (Skeleton was defeated for reelection in November 2010 when the GOP reclaimed control of the House.)

The disagreement between the two lawmakers underscores a constant challenge for Congress: what issues define "national security" and what policies best promote it? Today, it seems safe to say that national security subsumes far more than the triad of military might, diplomatic sagacity, and intelligence-gathering sophistication. National security now encompasses, among other things, homeland security, climate change, energy independence, scientific research and development, and a strong and expanding economy. Secretary of State Hillary Clinton emphasized that the growing federal deficit ($1.4 trillion in 2010) and debt (over $15 trillion and rising) "undermines our capacity to act in our own interests and it does constrain us where constraint may be undesirable." She added that the inability of our governing institutions to effectively address escalating deficits and debt "sends a message of weakness internationally" (Landler 2010, A6) and makes the United States the largest debtor nation in the world.

Other national security issues include the integrity of our financial system, an up-to-date transportation system, a culture willing to sacrifice for the collective good, and the quality of our schools. "Nearly one-fourth of the students who try to join the U.S. Army fail its entrance exam, painting a grim picture of an education system that produces graduates who can't answer basic math, science and reading questions," according to a think tank report (Armario and Turner 2010, 16). Even obesity is a national security issue. As the former vice chairman of the Joint Chiefs of Staff wrote, Congress cannot afford to put off dealing with the "nation's bulging waistlines" where "one in four young adults is too overweight to serve his or her country" (Giambastiani 2010, 32). In short, national security encompasses a large and expanding array of interconnected issues.

Internally, the institutional challenges for Congress are whether and to what extent it can effectively address this plethora of national security challenges. Critical matters are an internal legislative environment of sharper partisanship as well as insufficient attention to "continuous oversight" – the statutory mandate assigned to every congressional committee by the Legislative Reorganization Act of 1946 – over a huge expansion since 9/11 of the homeland, intelligence, and national security bureaucracy. Acrimonious partisanship and insufficient oversight were certainly evident before 9/11. Post 9/11, the interdependence between the two affects the character of Congress's decision making and the performance of its oversight function. Sharp partisanship infuses virtually all policy making these days, and legislative oversight, a core duty of Congress that requires further strengthening given the massive expansion of the government following 9/11, has also suffered. This chapter considers both developments as they relate to national security policy making in today's political environment.

ACRIMONIOUS PARTISANSHIP

It is useful at the outset to briefly examine partisanship and bipartisanship before outlining the factors that have provoked an acrimonious, or virulent, form of partisanship on Capitol Hill. Partisanship, according to one scholar, "refers to the impact and influence of political parties on the operation of the House [and Senate] and the behavior of its members" (Rohde 1991, 2). Congress has always been a partisan institution, because it is filled with people who generally – though not always, of course – espouse and support the views, ideas, preferences, and procedures of a specific party.

The virtues of partisanship are many, such as providing lawmakers with alternative party agendas; offering minority party corrections or revisions to the majority party's policies; encouraging and energizing voter turnout as constituents evaluate each party's platform and candidates; mobilizing winning coalitions in the House and Senate; or advancing the personal goals of partisan politicians. "I have always said, there is nothing wrong with partisanship," explained Senator Christopher J. Dodd (D-CT). "In fact, the country was not built on anything but partisanship. It was the contest of ideas" (*Congressional Record* April 29, 2010, S2777). Or as a knowledgeable commentator put it, "Partisanship simply reflects the reality of disagreement in a free society" (Dionne 2010, A13).

Bipartisanship has variable meanings depending on how it is defined and the legislative context in which it occurs. Presidents, for example, often emphasize the bipartisan nature of their policies if they attract the support of a handful of opposition party lawmakers, or even only one. Senators, too, share that view. Senator Bob Corker (R-TN) complained that Democratic advocates of the 2010 financial reform bill were reaching out to one or two Republicans to give the legislation a bipartisan veneer. "That is not my idea of a good bipartisan bill," he lamented (*Congressional Record* April 15, 2010, S2334).

Members in the minority party typically suggest that real bipartisanship occurs only when the majority reaches out and genuinely considers the ideas of party and committee leaders on the other side of the aisle. Rahm Emanuel, President Obama's former chief of staff (now mayor of Chicago), declared there is bipartisanship when the majority incorporates ideas from the other party even if no opposition lawmaker votes in the end for the legislative product. In the judgment of then Minority Leader John Boehner (R-OH), "The ultimate measure of whether we have a functioning House is not bipartisanship. Our focus shouldn't be working across the aisle for its own sake," he said. "The true test is whether our ideas, policies, and values are able to stand the test of a fair debate and a fair vote" (quoted in Chaddock 2010, online edition).

Implicit in Leader Boehner's observation is that lawmakers should not seek bipartisanship for its own sake. There are many examples of bipartisan majorities blocking needed legislation or producing watered-downed compromises that allowed issues to fester and worsen for years. Recall the decades-long struggle in Congress and the country to win passage of civil rights legislation. Of course, there are many examples of bipartisanship producing major policy achievements, such as the Marshall Plan and the NATO (North Atlantic Treaty Organization) treaty during the presidency of Democrat Harry Truman, who confronted a GOP-controlled Congress. Or consider President Ronald Reagan's collaboration with Democratic Speaker Thomas "Tip" O'Neill of Massachusetts to end a Social Security funding crisis. Today, party leaders and presidents often make appeals to bipartisanship – an oft-stated wish of voters – but there is a huge chasm between the electorate's wishes and political realities.

Partisan Polarization Trumps Post-Partisanship

President Barack Obama campaigned in 2008 on being a post-partisan chief executive who would change the way Washington works. Neither objective was achieved. The forces of sharp partisanship are simply far stronger than those who advocate the nurturing of cross-party alliances and coalitions. Five forces driving polarization deserve mention.

First, partisan communications networks, along with the alignment of outside interest groups with each party, demonize the opposition and intensify differences between the parties. Second, there are real and fundamental disagreements between the parties on scores of issues (taxes, immigration reform, health care, etc.), which encourage each to craft "wedgislation" (bills that unite one party but divide the other). Third, the parties realize that majority control of the House and Senate is subject to rapid change, creating incentives for minority obstructionism. The days of "one party controlling the House for 40 years, or even 12 years are gone," said noted election analyst Charlie Cook. "Voters have little patience or no patience. If they don't like what's going on in Washington, they'll throw the party out of power and put the other one in. And if they don't like what they're doing, they'll throw them back out" (quoted in Barabak 2010, online edition).

Fourth, changes in the constituency bases of the two parties have made the Democratic Party more liberal and the Republican Party much more conservative. As Senator Orrin Hatch (R-UT) phrased it, "Today, most Democrats are far left; most Republicans are to the right; and there are very few in between" (quoted in Kiely and Koch 1998, 2A). One consequence is that lawmakers rely heavily on their activist bases for money and votes. They recognize that these voters are not reluctant to launch primary challenges against members who "stray from the party's ideological consensus on major issues" (Brownstein 2010, online edition). Fifth, the general electorate, too, appears to be in a more confrontational mood with nearly half of America, according to a Pew Research Center poll, expressing admiration for "political leaders who refuse to compromise" (Garrett 2010, 1). This attitude underscores the difficulty of reaching negotiated settlements on the major issues of the day.

The president did receive public credit for reaching out to the opposition party, but his promises could not be kept for many of the reasons cited above. His problems with Republicans were, in part, his own doing. Democrats had large majorities in both chambers in the 111th Congress (2009–2011), and the president, according to Senate GOP Policy Chairman John Thune of South Dakota, preferred to work with congressional Democrats "to get the things done that they need to get done" (quoted in Pierce 2010, online edition). Private, one-on-one meetings with the GOP leaders of the House and Senate did not occur (Kornblut 2010, A1).[2]

During 2009 and 2010, congressional Republicans were in no mood to cooperate with President Obama in passing his ambitious agenda – such as revamping health care and the financial regulatory system. Both measures expanded the size and reach of the national government, which most Republicans oppose. With 60 votes required to end a talkathon – the new normal for passing legislation in the Senate – Republicans under Senate GOP leader Mitch McConnell of Kentucky were able to use filibuster threats and other parliamentary devices to block or delay action on many bills and

---

[2]   In the 112th Congress, the "meet and greet" situation has changed now that Republicans control the House and more Republicans serve in the Senate, given the "shellacking," Obama's word, Democrats received in the 2010 midterm elections.

nominations. "I wish we had been able to obstruct more," declared Senator McConnell, the architect of the GOP's confrontational "party of no" strategy (quoted in Schneider 2010, 35).

Sharp Partisanship and National Security

Increasingly, the opportunities for bipartisanship on major issues appear fewer and harder to accomplish. As Senator Susan Collins, a moderate Republican from Maine, wrote, "[I]n modern times, I have not seen the degree of bitter divisiveness and excessive partisanship now found in the Senate" (Collins 2010, B4). Witness, for example, that many lawmakers in both chambers do not trust one another; compromise, the essence of governing, often pales in comparison to ideological purity and winner-take-all strategies; Members' motives are questioned and opponents are viewed as political enemies to be "demonized;" and civility and decorum among lawmakers – bedrock elements of the legislative culture – are sometimes replaced by hostile member confrontations and "You lie" outbursts. "The more significant the issue, the more partisan it becomes," observed Senator Olympia Snowe (R-ME) (quoted in Shogren 1995, A18).

From a national security perspective, acrimonious partisanship on Capitol Hill can frustrate national security policy making. On this point, the views of three national security experts are instructive.

*Brent Scowcroft, national security adviser to Presidents Ford and Bush I, stated: "Today, there are simply more lawmakers to the extreme right and left, and the center of both parties has narrowed. That makes it very hard for a president to lead internationally" (quoted in Kitfield 2010b, 18).

*James Steinberg, President Obama's deputy secretary of state. He said: "There is no question that building strong bipartisan support for our foreign policy is critical to the United States' long-term interests.... Nothing is more important for our long-term security as a nation than to find that essential common ground" (quoted in Kitfield 2010c, 21).

*Richard Haas, president, Council on Foreign Relations. "The single greatest threat hovering over world affairs and the future of U.S. leadership is not whether we will soon confront a new global competitor like China, but whether our own domestic politics will rise to the challenges we confront; and on that pivotal question, the jury is still out. I very much hope we can forge bipartisan coalitions willing and able to tackle issues like trade, immigration, energy, and our crushing debt, but it's not obvious to me that as a nation we are up to the challenge right now" (quoted in Kitfield 2010b, 18).

There is little question that Congress's polarized environment suffuses national security policy making despite Barack Obama's 2008 campaign goal of managing a so-called post-partisan presidency. He had little success in his first two years, and the prognosis for the 112th Congress (2011–2013) looks bleak. The ideological divide between the two parties is wide and has gotten wider in the aftermath of the 2010 elections, which witnessed the retirement or defeat of many centrist lawmakers in both chambers and the election of many Tea Party-endorsed or supported candidates. The result is that "the polarization of the parties has become more complete than at any time in the modern era. In both the House and Senate, the most conservative Democrat is more liberal than every Republican and the most liberal Republican is more conservative than every Democrat" (Broder 2010, A19).

Where cross-party alliances and ideological overlaps between the parties were once common, that is no longer the case as party leaders strive to impose internal party discipline and cohesion on major votes. In 1968, only 51 percent of Senate Democrats voted with their party on key issues. Forty-two years later, over 91 percent of Senate Democrats voted with their party (Abrams 2010, 15).[3] The result is that when the parties address their top priorities, Congress functions somewhat like a quasi-parliamentary body: a cohesive majority party – guided by its top leaders – tries to govern but is opposed by an equally united minority party whose aim is to foil the majority's plans and win back control of the chamber in the next election (campaigning against the "do-nothing" Congress.)

Partisanship and Oversight

A key incentive for vigorous oversight, according to scholars, is divided government (one party in control of one or both chambers of Congress and the other the White House). A further motivator would be a polarized political environment like today's. Opposition lawmakers are on the lookout to bash the administration. As a congressional scholar concluded:

> [P]olicy divergence is most likely to occur under divided government, so the majority party in Congress will want to constrain the agencies under the president's control. In addition, members of the majority party may believe that they can benefit from using oversight to emphasize policy differences between their party and the president's party, and if in the case of such hearings and investigations they embarrass a president and his agency, this is not an insignificant [political] side benefit. (Shipan 2005, 437)

---

3 Two well-known Washington journals – *CQ Weekly* and *National Journal* – annually prepare reports on the voting behavior of members and the two parties.

With the 112th House in GOP hands, a major theme articulated by Speaker Boehner is oversight of the Obama administration. The House even adopted a resolution early in the first session directing all committees to conduct aggressive oversight of agencies and departments promulgating rules and regulations viewed as detrimental to businesses and economic growth (*Congressional Record*, Feb. 11, 2011, H686–714). The Environmental Protection Agency (EPA) is a special target of many House committees because of its authority for issuing regulations to curb power plants from emitting greenhouse gases that contribute to global warming. House Energy and Commerce chair Fred S. Upton (R-MI) quipped that he would have EPA administrator Lisa Jackson before his panel so often that he would reserve a Capitol Hill parking space for her. The chief counsel of the Energy panel's Oversight and Investigation Subcommittee highlighted their oversight objectives. "The goal of effective oversight," he said, "is to identify problems, conduct a thorough investigation and see how those problems can be solved – whether that is with legislation, or by eliminating waste, fraud, and abuse, or by rooting out criminal activity, which can then be referred to the Justice Department for criminal prosecution" (quoted in Cohen 2011, 4).

By comparison, under unified government, President George W. Bush did not face the deluge of subpoenas and investigative hearings faced by the Clinton administration.[4] As then-Representative Ray LaHood (R-IL; now Obama's Transportation Secretary) stated: "Our party controls the levers of government. We're not about to go out and look beneath a bunch of rocks to try and cause heartburn. Unless they really screw up, we're not going to go after them" (quoted in Nather 2004, 1190).[5] Another GOP lawmaker observed, "We ended up functioning like a parliament, not a Congress. We confused wanting a joint agenda with not doing oversight".[6] Added an experienced Washington hand, the GOP Congress "viewed itself less as an independent branch of government than as a junior partner to the White House in the American equivalent of a parliamentary system".[7] Why did Congress perform as if it were an adjunct of the White House, allowing party loyalty to trump

---

[4] Susan Page, "Bush Unscathed by Investigations: Here's Why," USA *Today*, August 13, 2003, p. 1A.

[5] David Nather, "Congress as Watchdog: Asleep on the Job?" *CQ Weekly*, May 22, 2004, p. 1190.

[6] Ronald Brownstein, "Treating Oversight as an Afterthought Has Its Costs," *Los Angeles Times*, November 19, 2006, online edition.

[7] Ronald Brownstein, "Who's Watching the President?" *Los Angeles Times*, March 21, 2006, online edition.

institutional responsibility? In the judgment of Representative Barney Frank (D-MA):

> I believe we have seen an overreaching by the President. I believe a seizing of power that should not have been seized by the executive branch. But executive overreaching could not have succeeded as much as it has without congressional dereliction of duty.[8]

Legislative deference to the executive branch changed when Democrats won control of the 110th Congress (2007–2009). A study by the Brookings Institution concluded: "What [was] most striking about the activity throughout the 110th Congress [2007–2009], especially in the House, was the dramatic increase in the amount and scope of oversight of the executive following years of relative inattention and deference under the Republican majority." Moreover, a "good deal of oversight during the 110th Congress, especially in the House, was devoted to Iraq, the dominant public concern, which had been largely neglected in the previous Congress. But oversight ranged across diverse subjects, was mostly serious in its approach, and often had real consequences for policy and Administration" (Binder et al. 2009, online report).[9]

Republicans claimed that with Obama in the White House, the 111th Democratic House did not do an adequate job of overseeing his administration. According to Representative Darrell Issa (R-CA), the chair of the House Oversight and Government Reform Committee in the 112th Congress, the previous Democratic majority on his committee ignored his requests for investigative hearings on "food safety; homeland security; Fannie Mae and Freddie Mac; health-care reform oversight; wasteful stimulus spending; the Minerals Management Service (see BP oil spill); and school choice" (Feldmann 2010, online edition).[10]

"A Failing of Oversight," a lead editorial in the *Washington Post*, highlighted "serious flaws" in Congress's oversight of the Central Intelligence Agency (CIA). The editorial was published in 1984 (*Washington Post* 1984, A26).[11] In a

---

[8] *Congressional Record*, July 13, 2006, p. H5212.

[9] Sarah Binder, Thomas Mann, Norman Ornstein, and Molly Reynolds, "Mending the Broken Branch: Assessing the 110th Congress, Anticipating the 111th," Brookings Institution, January 2009, online report.

[10] Linda Feldmann, "Obama Team Braces for Rep. Darrell Issa, Avid Investigator," *Christian Science Monitor*, November 9, 2010, online edition.

[11] Editorial, *Washington Post*, April 18, 1984, p. A26. The editorial addressed the CIA's involvement in the mining of Nicaraguan harbors, which occurred in the period when the CIA was supporting the "Contras" – a rebel group fighting to overthrow the Sandinista government in Nicaragua.

replay of that theme, the bipartisan National Commission on Terrorist Attacks upon the United States (commonly called the 9/11 Commission) declared that congressional oversight of intelligence and counterterrorism is now "dys-functional" (9/11 *Commission Report*, 420). Commission members urged Congress to strengthen oversight of intelligence by considering the adoption of a number of reforms, specifically, creating a joint committee on intelligence or combining the authorizing and appropriating authorities for intelligence in a single committee in each chamber. As for homeland security, the Commission urged the House and Senate to "create a single, principal point of oversight and review for homeland security" (ibid., 420–421). Each of these recommendations will be discussed in turn.

Creating a Joint Committee on Intelligence

This proposal has been suggested for decades but it has never been adopted by the Congress. The 9/11 Commission recommended that such a joint com-mittee should be modeled along the lines of the Joint Committee on Atomic Energy (JCAE), which was created by public law in 1946 and terminated in 1977. Composed of 18 members (9 representatives and 9 senators), the JCAE exercised nearly total jurisdiction over this new and secretive area, func-tioned in a largely bipartisan manner, and, according to two scholars, might have been "the most powerful congressional committee in the history of the nation" (Green and Rosenthal 1963, 266).

By citing the JCAE as a model for a proposed joint intelligence commit-tee, the 9/11 Commission might have written the idea's obituary. The long-time mood of Congress has been against the formation of joint committees. There are now only four (Library, Printing, Taxation, and Economic), because in 1977 a major Senate committee reorganization initiative pro-posed eliminating all joint committees. A number of reasons account for the demise of the JCAE, and several of them color the formation of a joint intelligence panel. Among the reasons for the demise of the JCAE are the following:

> [C]oncerns inside and outside Congress about the JCAE's close, some thought cozy, relationship with the executive agency it was overseeing; chan-ging executive branch conditions, such as the breakup of the Atomic Energy Commission; new rivals in Congress as the expanding nature of atomic energy and nuclear power extended into the jurisdictions of a number of House and Senate committees; efforts in the Senate [in 1977] to realign and consolidate standing committee jurisdictions and reduce the number of assignments for each Member; and a relatively high number of vacancies on the JCAE (six of 18 seats). (Kaiser 2010, 6–7)

There are other reasons that have discouraged recent Congresses from creating joint committees. (A recent exception is the creation in August 2011 of a joint select deficit reduction panel.) Setting aside "turf politics" – standing committees are not supportive because a joint committee like JCAE, which had "legislative authority" (the authority to receive and report legislation), would erode the jurisdictional authority of existing panels – there are vexing issues of institutional rivalry and many questions to answer: Who should chair the panel: a representative or a senator, and for what length of time? Where would the joint panel meet: on the House or Senate side of the Capitol? What should the funding be for the joint committee? How many lawmakers should serve on the joint panel? Should the composition of the panel be partisan or bipartisan? What are the specifics of its jurisdictional mandate? How should its work be coordinated with the jurisdictionally relevant House and Senate standing committees? Who appoints the staff director, how many staffers are to be hired, and should they be organized on a partisan or a bipartisan basis?

Combining Authorizations and Appropriations in a Single Intelligence Panel

Neither legislative chamber acted on this Commission recommendation, although the House did create a hybrid entity for a limited period of time. During the November 2006 campaign, Speaker-to-be Nancy Pelosi (D-CA) promised to implement all the recommendations of the 9/11 Commission, including the merger of the authorizing and appropriating functions in a single intelligence panel. She fulfilled her commitment, although not exactly as specified in the 9/11 Commission's report. Pelosi no doubt recognized that it would be a messy fight to take jurisdiction away from the Appropriations Committee.

On January 9, 2007, the House adopted a resolution creating a "Select Intelligence Oversight Panel" as part of the Committee on Appropriations. Its membership consisted of 13 lawmakers (8 majority and 5 minority) with 10 selected from the Appropriations Committee and 3 from the Permanent Select Intelligence Committee. The select panel's job was to submit its recommendation for the intelligence community's budget to the Defense Appropriations Subcommittee. That subcommittee then had the responsibility to prepare, as stated in the select panel's authorizing resolution (H. Res. 35), "the classified annex to the bill making appropriations for the Department of Defense."[12]

---

[12] Intelligence funding, estimated to be $80.1 billion, is largely hidden in the classified annex, or section, of the Pentagon's annual budget. See Walter Pincus, "Intelligence Spending at Record $80.1 Billion Overall," *Washington Post*, October 29, 2010b, p. A2.

During floor debate on H. Res. 35, Republicans said the arrangement neither merges the authorizing and appropriating functions in a single committee nor streamlines oversight of intelligence. "As far as I can tell," said one GOP lawmaker, "the only authority this [select panel] has is to write a report to the same people who serve on the [Appropriations Committee]. They could write a report and give it to themselves." In response, Representative David Obey (D-WI), the chair of the Appropriations Committee and a member of the select panel, argued that with the change the intelligence community could not ignore the House's intelligence authorizing committee, because it now had a seat at the table in influencing how much money would be allocated to intelligence. "In this town," replied Obey, "people follow the money."[13]

When Republicans won control of the 112th House, they abolished the select panel. They said it did not track the 9/11 Commission's recommendation, that it was excessive committee bureaucracy, and that the existing standing committees (Armed Services, Select Intelligence, Foreign Affairs, and the Defense Appropriations Subcommittee) were adequate to the task of supervising the intelligence community. Some Democrats suggested that Republicans terminated the select panel because its creation was Nancy Pelosi's idea.

Forming a Standing Committee on Homeland Security

The 9/11 Commission also urged the House and Senate to create a single authorizing panel for homeland security similar to each chamber's Armed Services Committee, which exercises authorizing authority for the Pentagon. The Commission reported that at least 88 congressional committees and subcommittees had some jurisdiction over the Department of Homeland Security (DHS), created in 2002 from the merger of 22 federal entities and employing today over 200,000 personnel. (DHS has since hiked the number of panels claiming jurisdiction from around 85 to over 100; Margetta 2010). The Commission's goals were to minimize jurisdictional conflicts, strengthen oversight, and reduce the number of committees DHS officials had to appear before as witnesses. The House and Senate responded differently to this recommendation.

In the 108th House (2003–2005), the chamber created a temporary Select Committee on Homeland Security with legislative and oversight jurisdiction

---

[13] The Senate Committee on Appropriations and the Senate Select Intelligence Committee reached an agreement allowing selected staff with appropriate security clearances to "attend closed-door markups in both panels" and to have "access to both panels' budgets prior to markups." In the 112th Congress, the House Intelligence chair devised a new arrangement: three appropriators now participate in Intelligence Committee hearings and markups. See Elena Shor, "Rockefeller Releases Deal on Intelligence Budgets," *The Hill*, March 7, 2007, p. 8.

over DHS. One of its missions was to coordinate consideration of homeland security issues lodged under the jurisdiction of numerous standing committees. For example, the Agriculture Committee had authority over animal and plant health; Energy and Commerce over public health; and Transportation over transportation security. The Select Committee's other main purpose was to recommend to the Speaker and the Committee on Rules whether the House should establish a new standing Committee on Homeland Security.

At the start of the 109th Congress (2005–2007), the House replaced its temporary panel with a new standing Committee on Homeland Security. Its jurisdiction included, among other matters, overall authority over homeland security policy and the organization and administration of DHS. However, turf conscious chairs negotiated with their party leaders to maintain some portion of their panel's jurisdiction. The overall outcome in the House was minimal reduction in the "scatteration" of homeland security jurisdiction. When Republicans won control of the 112th House, Representative Peter King (R-NY), the chair of Homeland Security, urged his party's leadership to end the splintered jurisdiction over the DHS and consolidate more authority in his panel. The Speaker and other GOP leaders opposed Chairman King's proposal, in part because they did not want to begin the new Congress with a divisive internal party battle over jurisdictional turf. Moreover, the other chairs opposed relinquishing any of their authority over the DHS. Transportation chair John Mica (R-FL), for instance, argued that the numerous standing committees with shared jurisdiction "should get more homeland security turf, not less" (quoted in Starks 2010, 2901).

A counter to the Commission's argument for consolidated oversight jurisdiction is the benefit associated with inter-committee competition and "creative redundancy." With many panels reviewing similar agencies – which is always the case given bicameralism, the creation of separate authorizing and appropriating panels, and the wide-ranging investigative authority assigned to the government reform panels – lawmakers would have the benefit of more "eyes and ears" monitoring executive agencies and policies. If one panel fails to do its oversight job, several others have the authority to assume the review responsibility.

In the Senate, the chamber's two leaders – Harry Reid (D-NV) and Mitch McConnell (R-KY) – created in August 2004 a 22-person working group that they headed to review the Commission's recommendation for improving oversight of homeland security and intelligence. Two months later the Senate debated the Reid-McConnell plan (S. Res. 445), which renamed the Governmental Affairs Committee the "Homeland Security and Governmental

Affairs Committee" and assigned it some additional jurisdiction for overseeing domestic security and DHS.

When the Senate took up S. Res. 445, turf-conscious chairs of other standing committees won adoption of amendments that reclaimed their authority over DHS that S. Res. 445 assigned to the renamed panel. "We're creating a shell," exclaimed the ranking Democrat, Joe Lieberman of Connecticut, on the renamed committee. "We're calling a committee a homeland security committee. But if you pick up the shell, there's not much homeland security under it" (quoted in Taylor 2004, 1). The panel's chair, GOP Senator Collins, agreed with Lieberman. Dismayed by this turnabout, both voted against S. Res. 445, but the Senate adopted it anyway, on October 9, 2004, by a 79 to 6 vote. The Senate did not act on a proposal in S. Res. 445 to create a separate Appropriations Subcommittee on Intelligence.

The "Swelling" of the Presidency

In 1973, presidential scholar Thomas Cronin testified before a select House committee reform panel and discussed the "swelling" of the presidency and its impact on Congress. From the New Deal to Watergate, he declared, there occurred a "tremendously vast swelling of the Presidency. It is a swollen, overstuffed, compartmentalized growth-institution which I think Congress has not adequately been able to monitor" (Cronin 1973, 429).[14] He identified various reasons for the growth of the presidency (crises, public expectations, and so on) and predicted that the authority of the "presidential branch" would continue to grow in influence in coming decades in both the domestic and international realms. A fundamental task of Congress and the American people, he asserted, is to make "the Presidency safe for democracy" (ibid., 431).

Perhaps the most fundamental challenge confronting Congress since 9/11 is to supervise and hold accountable the dramatic expansion of the homeland security, defense, and intelligence establishment. "Keep us safe" was the assignment Americans gave to the White House, and Congress acted to provide the policies and funds requested by the president to carry out that assignment. If the Founding Fathers returned to observe their handiwork, they would probably be shocked by the role and reach of today's president. Decades

[14] The quotation is taken from Professor Cronin's July 12, 1973, testimony before the Select Committee, p. 429. See *Committee Organization in the House,* Panel Discussions before the House Select Committee on Committees (Washington, DC: U.S. Government Printing Office, 1973).

in the making, the Bush-Cheney administration (2001–2009) accelerated this trend after 9/11, especially in national security affairs.

Assertions of executive authority after 9/11 by President George W. Bush are well known and include such things as domestic wiretapping; blocking White House aides from testifying before congressional committees; the creation of secret prisons abroad; the use of "enhanced interrogation" (torture) on terrorist suspects; "extraordinary rendition" (capturing terrorist suspects and transporting them to undisclosed prisons in other nations for enhanced interrogation); and interpreting certain provisions in laws as he saw fit (so-called signing statements). There was some push-back by Congress against executive claims of authority, such as revising the Foreign Intelligence Surveillance Act (FISA) to provide additional guidelines regarding warrantless surveillance, as well as by decisions of federal courts constraining executive power even in wartime.

The huge expansion of the intelligence community is also noteworthy. In 2009, the *Washington Post* reported, in a three-part major investigative series, that since 9/11, the "government has built a national security and intelligence system so big, so complex and so hard to manage, no one really knows if it's fulfilling its most important purpose: keeping citizens safe" (Priest and Arkin 2010a, A1).[15] There are, for example, 1,271 government organizations, as well as nearly 2,000 private contractors, working on counterterrorism, homeland security, and intelligence in about 10,000 locations across the nation. "Many security and intelligence agencies do the same work, creating redundancy and waste," including the preparation annually of 50,000 intelligence reports, "a volume so large that many are routinely ignored." The authors of the series noted that at least "20 percent of the government organizations that exist to fend off terrorist threats were established or refashioned in the wake of 9/11." They add that the Bush administration and Congress gave intelligence agencies more money – two and a half times what it was pre-9/11 – "than they were capable of responsibly spending" (ibid.).[16]

Significantly, President Obama, while dismantling some of the previous administration's security initiatives, has also kept many. A few examples make the point. The huge intelligence infrastructure remains in place. The president had a "surge" of his own – like Bush in Iraq – sending 30,000 more troops to Afghanistan. Obama retained or expanded 14 intelligence orders of the previous administration, providing the legal basis for the CIA's worldwide activities (Luxenberg 2010, A8). Campaign promises to the contrary, the prison

---

[15]   The other two articles in the series are Dana Priest and William M. Arkin, "National Security, Inc.," July 20, 2010, p. A1, and Dana Priest and William M. Arkin, "The Secrets Next Door," July 21, 2010, p. A1.

[16]   The quoted material in this paragraph is from the July 19 article, pp. A1 and A7.

for terrorist suspects at Guantanamo Bay, Cuba remains open. A former CIA director for the Bush-Cheney White House, Michael Hayden, stated: "You've got state secrets [an assertion by the Justice Department that typically terminates lawsuits involving national security matters], targeted killings, indefinite detention, renditions, the opposition to extending the right of habeas corpus to prisoners," Hayden said. "Although it is slightly different, Obama has been as aggressive as Bush in defending prerogatives about who he has to inform in Congress for executive covert action" (quoted in Rutten 2010, online edition).[17]

Oversight Purposes

Given the reluctance of presidents to relinquish powers once gained, it is worthwhile to identify the array of purposes associated with the implicit constitutional authority of Congress – largely through its committee system – to assert its independent role in holding accountable presidential and bureaucratic power. Briefly, the purposes can be classified as *programmatic* (such as ensuring that agencies and programs are working in an efficient and cost-effective manner); *political* (e.g., generating favorable publicity for lawmakers); and *institutional* (protecting congressional prerogatives, for instance). Two institutional purposes merit further discussion: informing Congress and the public, and protecting congressional prerogatives.

Informing Congress and the Public. Congress's "watchdog" role is crucial, because it shines the spotlight of public attention on scores of significant federal agencies and programs, as well as the White House. The spotlight allows the American people to make informed judgments about executive performance, policy success or failure, and the conduct of officeholders who serve in the nationally elective branches. "The informing function of Congress," wrote Woodrow Wilson in his classic 1885 study of the legislative branch, "should be preferred even to its legislative function." As he emphasized:

> Unless Congress have and use every means of acquainting itself with the acts and dispositions of the administrative agents of the government, the country must be helpless to learn how it is being served; and unless Congress both scrutinize these things and sift them by every form of discussion, the country must remain in embarrassing, crippling ignorance of the very affairs which it is most important it should understand and direct. (Wilson 1885, 303)

[17] Also see Julian E. Zelizer, "Look Who's Back: It's Obama's White House, But It's Still Bush's World," *Washington Post*, August 15, 2010, B1, and Peter Grier, "Obama Orders Guantanamo Tribunals to Resume. Is He Abandoning His Pledge?" *Christian Science Monitor*, March 7, 2011, online edition.

The informing function is particularly important in the intelligence and national security areas where secrecy is often the order of the day. Only an enlightened Congress and citizenry can rein in a runaway executive branch and protect democratic values. Importantly, the CIA has taken many transparency steps both as a result of President Obama's open government initiatives and recognition "that continued public support for the CIA is very much dependent upon public understanding of its mission and activities" (Clark 2011, 20).

Protecting Congressional Prerogatives. Another fundamental goal of oversight is to protect Congress's policy-making role and its place in our constitutional separation of powers system as the "first branch" of government. The massive size and scope of the executive branch has produced a policy-making rival to the Congress. Administrators do more than simply "faithfully execute" our laws according to the intent of Congress (which may be vague). Federal agencies are filled with highly competent and knowledgeable career and non-career experts who, among other things, write rules and regulations that have the force of law; formulate policy initiatives for the White House and Congress; interpret statutes in ways that may expand their discretionary authority or, conversely, undermine legislative intent; and shape policy development by Congress, in part by "selling" their ideas through lawmakers and committee hearings and other means. The large influence of a huge federal establishment post-9/11 highlights the critical role of oversight in checking and correcting unwarranted administrative actions and asserting or reasserting Congress's authority over executive entities.

The checking power of Congress is especially vital when presidents assert that as commander in chief they can do whatever is necessary to keep the nation safe. The practical reality is that during times of crises and wars, there is a tendency for Congress, the courts, and the citizenry to defer to the chief executive, at least initially. And if there is unified government during a polarized era, legislative deference to the president by the majority party often results. But not always. For example, when there was unified government during the George W. Bush presidency, there were some GOP lawmakers who did conduct hard-hitting oversight, such as the review work of the House Oversight and Government Reform Committee. That panel castigated the administration's performance during Hurricane Katrina.

A Few Reform Ideas

The issue of effective oversight has long been a topic of concern on Capitol Hill and remains so post-9/11. A comment made in 1978 by former Speaker

Thomas "Tip" O'Neill (D-MA) (1977–1987) – members "like to create and leg-
islate, but we have shied from both the word and deed of oversight" (*Workshop
on Congressional Oversight and Investigations* 1979, 3) – no doubt still reso-
nates with many lawmakers today. Or as a senator said about the need for
more overseeing rather than overlooking, Congress has "delegated so much
authority to the executive branch of government, and we ought to devote more
time to oversight than we do" (quoted in Earle 2004, 2).

However, since both lawmakers offered their observations, the House and
Senate have adopted various rules changes and passed several laws designed
to prod and encourage more and better oversight of the huge and seemingly
ever-expanding bureaucracy. What also appears evident today is that House
party leaders are requiring committees to conduct oversight of the Obama
administration; moreover, many in the general public appear keen on reducing the size of the national government given trillion dollar fiscal deficits.
Members of both parties are responding to that public sentiment.

House and Senate leaders recognize the importance of oversight, and various lawmakers excel at it and have deservedly earned high praise for their
investigative work. Further, there is no doubt that more oversight activity is
occurring on Capitol Hill than many people realize. Oversight is not easy to
quantify because it is a ubiquitous activity that is subsumed in many hearings, meetings, and informal settings whose purposes may be secondary to
reviewing program and policy administration. Moreover, there is no precise
scholarly consensus on the definition of oversight, and without that it is difficult to determine the extent of congressional oversight activity. Some analysts
refer to it as "after the fact" review of statutory implementation. Others suggest
that whatever Congress does, formally or informally, to affect the executive
branch is oversight. As one scholar stated, how "oversight is defined affects
what oversight one finds" (Ogul 1976, 7). Suffice it to say that undercounting
surely characterizes the amount of oversight carried out by House and Senate
committees (leaving aside the "case work" of individual members) because it
occurs in so many ways and is a byproduct of so many legislative activities.

Still, because it is difficult to get an accurate count of how much oversight
activity takes place in the House and Senate, scholars and journalists often
lament that Congress is doing an inadequate job of oversight. Regularly, legislative reform efforts from the Legislative Reform Act of 1946 to the 112th
Congress (2011–2013) urge more and better oversight. People may disagree on
what constitutes "quality" oversight, but there are several components that
appear to promote its effectiveness. They include (1) a committee chair committed to do oversight on a sustained basis; (2) the willingness of committee
members to devote their time and energy to this enterprise; (3) an experienced

and professional staff; (4) bipartisanship (so the administration cannot play one party against the other); (5) rigorous preparation and documentation in advance of any public hearing; (6) coordination and cooperation with other relevant congressional committees; and (7) follow-through to ensure that recommendations and commitments are acted upon. Three ideas that might strengthen legislative supervision of agency performance and spending are the following:

Outside Oversight Advisory Group. Committees might be encouraged to establish, on a selective basis, an outside advisory group to assist them in their important investigative reviews. The Washington metropolitan area is filled with experts on various topics, such as academics, think tank analysts, or retired lawmakers, who might be willing to assist committees without any remuneration. These ad hoc groups could be created, as needed, by the committee chair in consultation with the ranking committee member. The ad hoc panels would automatically dissolve when their work is over or whenever the chair deems it appropriate.

Oversight and Investigative Staff. For decades, the House Appropriations Committee has had a "survey and investigations" staff. Many of the staff aides are former employees of the Government Accountability Office (GAO), the Federal Bureau of Investigation (FBI), and the Pentagon, or are individuals skilled in investigative work. Much of their work is confidential and in the defense and intelligence fields. Perhaps other committees could be authorized to hire a separate, experienced, full-time professional staff exclusively devoted to the conduct of oversight and investigations. Lawmakers are so busy meeting constituents, attending hearings, traveling to their states or districts, raising money and campaigning, writing bills and amendments, and doing so much other legislative work that they often have scant time for oversight. A separate professional oversight staff could identify duplicative and unnecessary programs under their panel's jurisdiction that might save millions or billions in taxpayer dollars.[18]

The Public as "Watchdog." A rather new oversight trend is the "public as watchdog," or, stated differently, the "democratization" of the review function. The combination of technology and civic-minded individuals and groups has enabled them to monitor federal expenditures and activities. With the federal government posting more of their information and data online, civic-minded bloggers or groups like the Project on Government Oversight (POGO) can visit the sites and assess how their taxpayer dollars are being spent. As the

[18] See Damian Paletta, "Billions in Bloat Uncovered in Beltway," *Wall Street Journal*, March 1, 2011, p. A1. The report was prepared by the Government Accountability Office.

government's chief information officer remarked, the newfound transparency "will elicit a more informed public oversight to help guide federal policies and programs" (Castelli 2010, 13).

Reform ideas have their strengths and weaknesses, and many might not apply to the intelligence and national security communities. Several factors make the conduct of national security oversight challenging for Congress, including these two:

Secrecy. Congress functions in a largely open environment; security activities and operations are necessarily secret. The tension that exists between the legislature's "need to share" information – with colleagues, staff aides, constituents, and others – and the security community's culture of "need to know" influences oversight of the security agencies. The veil of secrecy that usually shrouds intelligence activity means that Congress often finds itself in a "Catch-22" situation. Officials of the CIA, for example, may provide timely notice of planned covert actions to appropriate committee members and party leaders, but lawmakers who possess this information are subject to numerous restrictions that inhibit disclosure of sensitive material to their colleagues, let alone the media or others. It is somewhat paradoxical, though understandable, that the most open of our three national branches of government must conduct most security oversight in secret.

The "closed door" oversight of national security raises numerous dilemmas that are not easy to resolve. Two questions seem especially prominent. First, can Congress function as an effective surrogate for the public in holding the security community accountable for its actions and decisions when these agencies must function in a highly secret environment? Second, in a dangerous world, a challenge for Congress's security committees is balancing their obligation to hold intelligence agencies accountable for their performance without hindering these agencies' ability to carry out their national security responsibilities. In short, how is Congress "to conduct oversight in a policy area deemed of great importance by both the executive and legislative branches but characterized by legitimate needs for secrecy and security that exist in few other policy areas?" (Lowenthal 2003, 63).

Dearth of Outside Assistance. Unless various events or crises precipitate their involvement, relatively few lawmakers focus intensively or extensively on the national security community. Members and staff of the relevant security committees are the principal consumers of information and analysis generated by the many components of the security community. In the judgment of a member of the House Intelligence Committee: "There is no outside organization [like the GAO] that is providing consistent oversight, and whistle-blowing is not a respected tradition in the intelligence community. There is nobody else to help" (quoted in Whitelaw and Kaplan 2004, 36–37). In the post-9/11 world, there is much more debate and information about intelligence and national security affairs, and this development could assuage some of the concerns of the unnamed House Intelligence member. There are many topics or issues that receive scant public notice, however. For example, shrouded in secrecy, the development of "weaponized new software programs is being done outside public view and with little debate about their impact on existing international treaties and on conventional theories of war, like deterrence, that have governed nations for decades" (Clayton 2011, online edition).

SUMMARY OBSERVATIONS

Several conclusions can be drawn from this chapter. First, despite the 9/11 Commission's recommendations, splintered committee jurisdictions over homeland security persist on Capitol Hill. As the Commission report stated, "Few things are more difficult to change in Washington than congressional committee jurisdiction and prerogatives." This reality is not likely to change any time soon. "Turf" reflects power on Capitol Hill. Members and committees do clash over their jurisdictional prerogatives. Committee jurisdictions are a "lawmaker's power base. It is no wonder that committee boundaries are hotly contested" (King 1997, 12). Congressional history suggests that at least three key factors need to be present if shifts of jurisdictional boundaries are to be achieved: significant support from the party leadership on both sides of the aisle; broad bipartisan backing of the chamber's membership; and the willingness, or at least not bitter resistance, of the standing committees that might lose turf to accept a new arrival on the committee stage.

Second, the national security community witnessed a huge surge in federal funding. As one account noted, "After 9/11, U.S. military spending more than doubled" (Barry and Thomas 2010, 30). Defense Secretary Robert Gates announced on January 6, 2011, mindful of the spending cutback ethos abroad in the country and in Congress, $178 billion in spending and program reductions. As Secretary Gates stated: "We must come to realize that not every defense program is necessary, not every defense dollar is well-spent, and that more of nearly everything is simply not sustainable" (quoted in Oliveri 2011a, 1). Secretary Gates's perspective on spending reductions for the military suggests that after a decade of war, the United States might lessen its role as a "global policeman," unless its national safety is directly threatened. As the secretary told the cadets at West Point, "any future defense secretary who advises the president to again send a big American land army into Asia or into the Middle

East or Africa should have his head examined" (quoted in *The Economist* 2011, 40). Some foreign policy specialists call this view "intervention fatigue."

Moreover, there seems little doubt that public alarm at escalating annual deficits and debt will lead to heated debates in Congress about making substantial cuts in the national security budget. For example, the Republican chair of the House Armed Services Committee said "he did not believe it was wise to propose cuts to defense spending in a time of war" (quoted in Oliveri 2011b, 123). Others state that "the defense budget is outrageously bloated" (Wheeler 2011, 22). In the judgment of Commission co-chair Lee Hamilton, "I think we're at the point where I would be skeptical that additional growth is needed in the intelligence community. It looks like we might have more [redundancy] than we need" (quoted in Strohm 2010, 6).

Third, are we safer today than we were pre-9/11 from terrorist attacks? The answer is plainly "yes" in many respects, but not all. For example, there is airport screening of passengers, and security has been upgraded across the country in public buildings and transit facilities. On the other hand, the expectation that intelligence analysts can always "connect the dots" to prevent terrorist attacks is not a reasonable one. Given the superabundance of data that streams every day into the various intelligence agencies, it is a challenge for anyone to recognize a critical piece of information and be able to share it in a timely manner with the relevant agency or person(s). As Tom Ridge, former DHS secretary, observed, "You're never going to eliminate risk. You've got to manage risk" (quoted in Margetta 2010, online edition).

Fourth, the two Commission chairmen, Thomas Kean and Lee Hamilton, wrote, "National security is too important to become a partisan issue" (Hamilton and Kean 2010, 9A). On the other hand, the deep ideological divide between the two congressional parties makes it difficult, if not impossible at times, to address various crises. Most officeholders and attentive citizens recognize that the escalating deficits and debt are national security issues of crisis proportions. Yet it has proven difficult for years to get the two parties together, and with the White House, to deal with entitlement expenditures, such as Medicare. "Compromise," as noted earlier in this chapter, is often a term of derision to many in the public and on Capitol Hill. On many issues, it is a zero-sum environment with many lawmakers unwilling to bargain for a half or even a quarter of a loaf. Instead, as the saying goes, "It's my way or the highway." The point is that partisan polarization can easily degenerate into gridlock on major issues, especially in the Senate because of its rules and procedures.

From President Obama's perspective, if his agenda cannot advance in the 112th Congress (2011–2013), he may concentrate on foreign policy where chief executives typically and constitutionally have greater leeway. The president also has various options in dealing with the 112th Congress. He might use Harry Truman's confrontational approach and blame the GOP-controlled House for not acting on administration priorities; or the president could employ Bill Clinton's triangulation strategy of wooing Republicans to vote for mutually agreed-upon initiatives, mindful of not losing too much support from Democratic lawmakers and outside party activists upset with his actions.

Finally, the Founding Fathers created a complex system of government with an array of checks and balances. Presidents, lawmakers, and the two political parties often disagree strongly about proposed solutions to national issues and problems. This condition is to be expected in a nation as large as ours with so many ethnic, religious, political, economic, and geographical differences. It is the function of representative government to deal with these differences and challenges and reach a consensus on what a majority (sometimes a super-majority) believes to be in the national interest. As James Madison wrote in *Federalist No. 62*: "A good government implies two things: first, fidelity to the object of government, which is the happiness of the people; secondly, a know-ledge of the means by which the object can best be attained." The challenge for President Obama and the Congress in this post-9/11 environment is to attend to Madison's second criterion so they can accomplish Madison's first object.

PART TWO

Oversight Challenges

4

Congress and Defense

Pat Towell

After the 1974 congressional elections swept into office a wave of reform-minded liberals bent on shaking up the House of Representatives, Representative James "Jimmy" Burke (D-MA) – then the third-ranking Democrat on the powerful Ways and Means Committee – blithely dismissed the insurgents' plan to use the rules of the House to carry out what was, in effect, an internal coup against the established power structure. As he walked out of one of the newcomers' planning sessions, Burke scoffed: "You people think this place is on the level."

It is the contrarian thrust of this chapter that, more often – and with greater consequence – than generally is believed, Congress operates more or less on the level in its oversight of the defense establishment. This is to say, acting chiefly through the committees that deal with the Department of Defense (DOD) budget, Congress functions as – among other things – a deliberative body, exercising relatively effective oversight of the U.S. defense establishment. Moreover, some of the committees' efforts to modify the behavior of the defense establishment are sufficiently ambitious to be regarded as policy initiatives.[1]

That thesis challenges a widely held view of Congress's impact on the defense establishment. This prevailing view is that the legislative branch impacts the defense establishment in two ways that fall at opposite ends of the scales of

---

[1] The basic thrust of this chapter reflects the author's observation of the congressional defense committees as the defense reporter for Congressional Quarterly in 1976–2003. Preliminary research for the chapter was conducted in 2003–06 under the auspices of the Center for Strategic and Budgetary Assessments (CSBA) with additional support provided by Boeing, Lockheed Martin, Thales North America and General Dynamics. The views expressed in this chapter are those of the author and are not presented as those of CSBA or the supporting companies, nor are they presented as the views of the Congressional Research Service or the Library of Congress.

budgetary and military significance. On rare occasions, it is acknowledged, Congress is a venue in which armies of lobbyists, partisan strategists, and grassroots activists clash in political battles with billions of dollars, thousands of jobs, and arguably, vital military capabilities hanging in the balance. Such are the battles over the future of a major weapons program (e.g., continued production of the F-22A fighter), far-reaching changes in military personnel policy (e.g., whether retirees should receive DOD medical care for life), or the closure of major defense installations. On the other hand – and far more frequently, the conventional view (accurately) observes – Congress routinely weighs in on matters that are both less important (at the national level) and more important (in the view of constituents) by adding to the annual defense funding legislation hundreds of "member interest" projects, most of them as modest in their impact on national policy (and on the size of the DOD budget) as they are parochial in their scope.[2] Famous examples are provisions of law that require DOD to purchase anthracite coal mined in Pennsylvania to fuel power plants at U.S. bases in coal-rich Germany (Higgs 2006), and report language that directed the Pentagon's Exchange Service to purchase, for sale in PXs, a larger quantity of ripe olives classified as Jumbo, Colossal, and Super Colossal.[3]

These two types of activity appear to account for the lion's share of time, energy, and political capital that most members spend on defense issues. But there is a third class of congressional initiatives – instances in which Congress, acting through its defense committees, participates actively and sometimes constructively in the process of making U.S. defense policy. Consider a few examples of this third type of congressional defense initiative. In 1979–80, prominent members of the two Armed Services committees hammered out legislatively mandated standards for recruits that played a key role in solving the Army's problem of manning the All-Volunteer Force (P.L. 96–342, Section 302).[4] In 1988, largely at the impetus of five women on the House

---

[2] A typical example of this perspective was expressed in a wide-ranging assessment of U.S. national security policy making published in 2004 under the auspices of the Center for Strategic and International Studies: "Congress is engaged in too much of the wrong kind of oversight – too few national debates on major issues, and far too much time and energy being spent on relatively minor and parochial issues," *Beyond Goldwater-Nichols: Defense Reform for a New Strategic Era – Phase I Report*, Washington, DC: Center for Strategic and International Studies, March 2004, pp. 68–69.

[3] See H. Rept. 103–339, the conference report on the FY1994 defense appropriations bill (H.R. 3116), p. 69. The language was sponsored by House Defense Appropriations Subcommittee Democratic member Vic Fazio, whose central California district is home to several ripe olive producers.

[4] See H. Rept. 96–1222, the conference report on H.R.6974, August 18, 1980, pp. 90–91.

Armed Services Committee (HASC) whose politics ran the ideological gamut, Congress responded to the growing number of young, married service members with children by drafting legislation that organized DOD's child day-care system, the largest employer-sponsored child day-care system in the world (P.L. 101–189, Title XV).[5] In 1996, as the defense establishment tried to adapt to a newly chaotic world, the committees ordered a far-reaching Pentagon review of U.S. strategy and force structure – the Quadrennial Defense Review. They also chartered an independent, blue-ribbon commission – the National Defense Panel – to critique the DOD review and offer its own perspective on the path ahead for the U.S. defense program. Together, these two documents helped shape national debate on defense issues in the 2000 presidential campaign (P.L. 104–201, Sections 921–26).[6] And in 2005, the committees concluded that the armed services were circumventing the so-called Nunn-McCurdy law, enacted in 1982 to flag major weapons programs that were experiencing high-cost growth. In response, the committees included in the FY2006 Defense authorization bill provisions that restricted the Pentagon's ability to "rebaseline" programs and required that DOD provide Congress with cost projections if a program reported a "critical" cost increase (P.L. 109–163, Section 802).

In none of these four cases was the congressional initiative the result either of broad-based ideological battles, or of constituency-oriented, retail politics. Rather, each one appears to have been an effort by the committees to solve a problem. Indeed, the last example – the Nunn-McCurdy modification in 2005 – is a striking instance of the defense committees' assertion of an independent role even in circumstances that might have been expected to strongly militate against such an initiative. In the middle of a war, the two committees, led by the president's own party, initiated – over the strong objections of a particularly sharp-elbowed secretary of defense – a significant policy change that had no tangible electoral payoff.

---

[5] See H. Rept 101–331, the conference report on H.R.2461, November 7, 1989, pp. 662–665. See also David F. Burrelli, "Military Child Care Provisions: Background and Legislation," pp. 147–168 in B. Ring (ed.), *The Child Care Disaster in America: Disdain and Disgrace"* (Hauppauge, NY: Nova Science Publishers, 2001).

[6] See H. Rept. 104–724, Conference Report on HR 3230, the National Defense Authorization Act of FY1997, pp. 779–780. The provisions establishing the QDR and NDP are Section 921–26 of the bill, enacted as P.L. 104–201. See *The Report of the Quadrennial Defense Review*, May 1997, available at http://www.fas.org/man/docs/qdr/; *Transforming Defense: National Security in the 21st Century; Report of the National Defense Panel*, December, 1997, available at http://www.dtic.mil/ndp/FullDoc2.pdf; and *The National Defense Panel Assessment of the May 1997 Quadrennial Defense Review*, available at http://www.fas.org/man/docs/ndp_assess.html.

Such stark assertions of the committees' independent role in shaping the defense establishment are by no means an everyday occurrence on Capitol Hill. However, they do occur; and, when they do, they go largely unremarked as do other defense committee initiatives, some of which – while less dramatic from a political standpoint – are potentially significant in their impact on the defense establishment.

HIDDEN IN PLAIN SIGHT

The four examples described support a prima facie case for the following propositions. First, on occasion, the defense committees address significant questions of policy. Second, in at least some cases, these committee initiatives appear to be reasonable efforts to solve problems, and in some cases, they appear to pay off as intended. And third, a more fully rounded assessment of the defense committees' role in the policy-making process is called for, if only to facilitate judgments about, for example, how often and under what circumstances such significant committee initiatives are likely to occur and how their success rate could be improved.

At the outset, it must be emphasized that I do not assume that electorally driven congressional initiatives are necessarily mistaken. For example, although congressional pressure on DOD to buy tens of thousands of Mine-Resistant Ambush-Protected (MRAP) vehicles has been challenged as inconsistent both with the Army's combat doctrine and with its long-range procurement plans, it is arguable that public concern with the mounting rate of IED casualties might have undermined the Bush administration's ability to sustain operations in Iraq had not the politically driven MRAP deployments both reduced casualties and satisfied the public demand that something be done.

Nor, on the other hand, do I assume that all committee initiatives resulting from a relatively deliberative process have been sound. However, while the effectiveness of some defense committee initiatives might be debatable, with few exceptions, their effectiveness has not been debated – indeed, by and large, they have been entirely ignored by students of the defense policy-making process.

This chapter is based principally on a review of policy initiatives contained in the reports filed by the House and Senate Armed Services Committees in connection with the annual National Defense Authorization Acts between calendar years 1975 and 2009 (i.e., the authorization bills for FY1976 through FY 2010). The authorizing committees (that is, the House and Senate Armed Services Committees) were selected for study because, in any given year, they typically intervene on a wider range of issues than do the appropriations com-mittees, perhaps in part because the authorizers have more members and larger professional staffs than their counterpart appropriations panels.

THE AUTHORIZATION PROCESS OVER TIME

Historically, the level of detail at which Congress has tried to control defense policy through its power of the purse has varied over a wide range. In the course of two centuries, the trend has been toward greater specificity of legis-lative control over the use to which appropriated funds could be put. In 1789, for instance, the first appropriations measure enacted under the Constitution funded the entire federal government in 13 lines of text. Separate appropria-tions bills for the War Department and Navy Department appeared in 1794 and 1798, respectively, but initially they were drawn up in relatively general terms. For instance, the Navy bill for 1800 appropriated a total of $2,482,953.99 distributed across 12 categories that were sufficiently broad that Navy Secretary Benjamin Stoddert could purchase the land for six Navy yards at a total cost of $199,000 with no specific legislative mandate (Albion 1980). Over time, the annual defense-related funding bills became increasingly specific, in respects that reflected members' parochial interest in jobs back home. For instance, in 1842, the Navy bill apportioned the service's total appropriation for the year across 32 accounts: one provided $2 million, "for increase, repair, armament and equipment of the Navy, and wear and tear of vessels in commission"; but another provided $2,000, "for building an outhouse and privies at the hospital at Pensacola" (quoted in ibid., 116).

This consistent emphasis by Congress on using the appropriations bills to regulate the recurring administrative minutiae of Army and Navy spending reflected lawmakers' understandable focus on constituent interests anchored in the operation and improvement of facilities. But it also reflected another fact: until the middle decades of the twentieth century when the Army began to mechanize on a large scale and the military services began to invest in large numbers of aircraft, the only major capital investments that afforded Congress leverage on broader issues of defense policy were coastal fortifications and war-ships – items that were budgeted for only episodically. When budget requests for such major investments came along, Congress often weighed in on the substance of broader defense policy; moreover it is arguable that, in at least some cases, when Congress did so, it acted on the basis of policy judgments that were deliberate, if debatable.

For example, Congress consistently was skeptical of schemes by Army engin-eers in the late 18th and 19th centuries to build elaborate forts to protect U.S.

harbors against naval attack. Early in that period, Congress favored earthwork fortifications that were cheaper to build (though more expensive to maintain) and also were more resistant to cannon fire (Kaufmann and Kaufmann 2004). After the Civil War, Congress resisted making major investments to upgrade existing masonry forts on the grounds that rapid improvements in artillery quickly would render the improvements obsolete (ibid.).

Similarly, Congress's decision in 1794 to reconstitute a national navy by building six frigates in response to harassment of U.S. shipping by Algerian corsairs was the upshot of a hard-fought congressional debate over the role of offensive military capability in U.S. foreign policy. So, too, was Congress's decision two years later to fund completion of three of the six ships even though a treaty had been negotiated with Algiers in the meantime and the precipitating crisis had passed (Toll 2006). Congress played an equally decisive – if more controversial – role in shaping U.S. defense policy in 1889 when it mandated that the first three world-class battleships built for the Navy would be "seagoing, coast-line" battleships, deliberately limited in range so they could not conduct the sort of transoceanic, offensive operations against an enemy fleet that were called for by supporters of naval strategist Alfred Thayer Mahan.[7]

But while there are clear examples of efforts by Congress to use its control of the purse to shape the defense establishment in the first century and a half after adoption of the Constitution, it also is the case that well into the 20th century there was no consistency in the level of detail at which Congress controlled appropriations for the War and Navy Departments. As late as 1935, the War Department appropriations bill included both some large, lump-sum appropriations for major elements of the Army – $22.4 million for the Air Corps, for example – and some appropriations that were extraordinarily picayune – $6,232 for the Army Medical Museum, to cite another instance. Executive branch discretion in expending the lump-sum appropriations was quite broad. An amount the Army had justified to Congress as being slated for the purchase of fighter planes might be used instead to buy bombers if the War Department deemed the switch to be in the national interest, although the department typically apprised Congress of significant departures from its budget justification (Huzar 1950).

Through the mid-point of the 20th century, there was even less specificity in the infrequently enacted authorization bills through which Congress set

---

[7]   Congress insisted that the three ships (which served as *Indiana*, *Massachusetts*, and *Oregon*) be designed with only enough coal bunker capacity to steam 5,000 miles. See Harold Sprout and Margaret Sprout, *The Rise of American Naval Power: 1776–1918* (rev. ed.), (Princeton, NJ: Princeton University Press, 1942), pp. 205–213.

the parameters of the defense establishment that it funded through annual appropriations bills. For instance, the authorization legislation governing the Army and Air Force through the decade of the 1950s was the Army and Air Force Authorization and Composition Act of 1950 (64 *Stat* 321) which set only a few limits on broad categories of equipment and people in the service. Those limits were set at levels far above what Congress was requested to fund on an annual basis. For instance, the legislation authorized a ceiling on the quantity of planes the Air Force could operate: not more than either 24,000 planes or 25,000 tons of airframes, "whichever amount the Secretary of the Air Force may determine is more appropriate" (quoted in Kolodziej 1966, 364).

Emergence of the Modern Authorization Bill

The germ of the contemporary annual defense authorization bill was a requirement, enacted in 1951, that the military departments "come into agreement with" the Armed Services committees on most real estate transactions costing more than $25,000. This provision of law got the two committees deeply enmeshed in the deployment during the 1950s of a far-flung network of anti-aircraft missiles and radar systems to defend the country against long-range, nuclear-armed Soviet bombers.

The continental air defense issue put the House and Senate Armed Services Committees in the position of considering the authorization of a large number of new installations, many of which had to be near metropolitan areas because of the relatively short range of the surface-to-air missiles intended to defend the cities. This role afforded the Armed Services panels a prime vantage point from which to observe the debate over a vital military mission as it degenerated into an unusually public inter-service turf war. From 1956 through 1959, the Armed Services Committees watched the Army and Air Force (and the contractors responsible for their respective systems) engage in a public relations battle over the relative merits of the Army's Nike system and two Air Force systems – first, the proposed Talos, and then the Bomarc. Ultimately, the two committees concluded that neither the Defense Department nor the Appropriations committees were compelling the services to collaborate in a coherent air defense program (Dawson 1962). The upshot was Section 412(b) of the Military Construction Authorization Act for Fiscal Year 1960, commonly labeled with the name of Georgia Democrat Richard Russell, the Senate Armed Services chairman who promoted its enactment.[8]

---

[8] Raymond H. Dawson ("Congressional Innovation and Intervention in Defense Policy: Legislative Authorization of Weapons Systems." *American Political Science Review*, Vol. 56,

As originally enacted, the provision required prior legislative authorization for procurement of aircraft, missiles, and naval vessels. However, over the following three decades, Congress incrementally broadened the scope of the requirement until, by the late 1990s the annual defense authorization bill authorized an amount to be appropriated for almost every appropriations account in the DOD budget.[9]

From its inception in the Russell Amendment, the structure of the annual defense authorization bill as we know it today has mirrored those parts of the defense appropriations bill that funded the corresponding sections of the DOD budget. Normally, in both types of legislation, lump sums are authorized (or appropriated) for the same broad categories of activities for which DOD requests funding: aircraft procurement, Air Force; missile procurement, Army; shipbuilding and construction, Navy, for example. But each service "justifies" its lump-sum request for each account by presenting a detailed explanation of how the funds would be spent – how much money is slated to buy how many units of each type of weapon funded by that account. The use of broad funding categories in the text of the legislation gives the executive branch some flexibility in accommodating unforeseen developments since, within fairly broad limits, the services can shift money from one program to another by obtaining the consent of the authorization and appropriations committees through a so-called reprogramming process that does not entail enactment of new legislation.

In the reports the committees write to explain each of the annual bills they draft, the panels elaborate their expectations of how DOD and the services will allocate the various lump-sum appropriations, based on so-called justification books submitted to Congress with the annual budget request and any

No. 1 [March 1962], pp. 42–57) contends that congressional dissatisfaction with DOD's handling of the air defense issue gained strength during 1958 as Congress debated President Dwight D. Eisenhower's post-Sputnik proposal for reorganization of DOD (pp. 50–53). A sense that the authorizing committees needed to play a more directive role in setting defense policy came out of that experience, Dawson says. See also Joshua E. Klimas, *Balance Consensus, Consent, and Competence: Richard Russell, the Senate Armed Services Committee and Oversight of America's Defense, 1955–1968*, Ph.D. diss. (Ohio State University), pp. 395–415.

9   To this day, annual authorization is not required by law for the military personnel accounts that provide pay and benefits for uniformed members of the armed forces. However, the Armed Services Committees routinely include in the authorization bill an overall total authorization for military personnel. Even if the bill did not set a specific authorization amount for military personnel appropriations, it would largely determine the amount of that appropriation since it also authorizes the principal components of the military personnel appropriation: the number of active-duty personnel and of those reservists who qualify for compensation and any changes in military pay.

changes to those plans the committees may direct. Prior to 2009, military construction projects were the only items for which specific authorization amounts routinely were included in defense authorization bills. All other authorization amounts below the appropriations account level were listed in funding tables included in the committee reports which, while not legally binding, were generally accepted as a serious assertion of the committees' intent as to how the funds in each account would be allocated. Beginning with the authorization act for FY2010 (P.L. 111-84), the funding tables were incorporated into the authorization bill. However, the amounts in those tables remain subject to change by reprogramming.

Clout: What Kind? And to What End?

Often it is asserted that the annual defense authorization bills derive their significance from their supposedly binding effect on subsequent defense appropriations legislation, a relationship that the Russell Amendment clearly was intended to establish. This view is summed up in the claim that the authorization bill sets a ceiling on the amount that can be appropriated for a given appropriations account. A usually silent corollary of that proposition is the assumption that the authorization measure's control of the amounts appropriated – limited though it is – is the basis of the House and Senate Armed Services Committees' clout.[10] But if the committees' influence on defense policy depended on their supposed (indirect) control of annual appropriations, they would be in trouble, because the widely held belief that they control through authorization ceilings has little evidence to back it up.

In terms of congressional practice, direct clashes between the Armed Services and Appropriations committees over major programs are rare, and the record is ambiguous.[11] One explicit test of whether the "ceiling" interpretation is generally accepted came in 1985, when the Senate Appropriations

---

[10] The Armed Services panels have, in effect, long since acquiesced in the fact that the appropriators need not await action on the authorization bill before marking up the companion appropriations measure. The frequent occurrence of a situation in which the defense appropriations bills are passed prior to action on the authorization bills that supposedly regulate them routinely instigates news stories predicting "the demise of the defense authorization process" and relegation of the Armed Services Committees to the more limited influence typical of most other legislative committees in the House and Senate.

[11] In a simple turf battle within the House and Senate, one might expect the Appropriations committees to easily overpower the Armed Services Committees or any of the other legislative panels (with the possible exception of the tax-writing committees). While the good will of the Armed Services Committees is useful to many members and vital to some, the good will of the appropriators is extremely important to nearly all members.

Committee fought Senate Armed Services to a draw on the appropriators' inclusion in the 1986 continuing resolution of $7 billion worth of defense programs not included in the already enacted defense authorization bill (Towell 1985).[12]

If the relationship between defense authorization and appropriations legislation is ambiguous in terms of practice, the situation is all too clear – to the disadvantage of the Armed Services panels – from a purely legal perspective: the Government Accountability Office (GAO), which Congress accepts as the controlling legal authority on appropriations law, gives short shrift to claims that the Russell Amendment constrains the Appropriations committees:

> An authorization act is basically a directive to Congress itself, which Congress is free to follow or alter (up or down) in the subsequent appropriation act. A statutory requirement for prior authorization is also essentially a congressional mandate to itself. Thus, for example, if Congress appropriates money to the Defense Department in violation of 10 U.S.C. § 114 [i.e., the Russell Amendment], there are no practical consequences. The appropriation is just as valid, and just as available for obligation, as if section 114 had been satisfied or did not exist.[13]

But the facts on the ground strongly suggest that this cannot be the last word on the power of the Armed Services committees and of the annual authorization bills that account for the bulk of the committees' work. Talented members of the House and Senate – including some whose constituencies are not home to any major military base or contractor – seek seats on those committees and invest considerable time and effort in their work. DOD routinely accommodates the authorizing committees' demands for briefings and hearings involving the department's senior civilian and military leaders and complies with directions in the authorization bills (and accompanying committee reports) that relate to authorized programs. House and Senate leaders almost always find time to schedule several days of floor debate on the authorization bills. Another consideration is that the Appropriations committees frequently cite prior action by their counterpart Armed Services panel as the

---

[12] A procedural deadlock on the FY1986 continuing resolution was broken when Defense Appropriations Subcommittee Chairman Ted Stevens (R-AK) agreed to seek the Armed Services panel's informal approval of the unauthorized programs. See Pat Towell, "Defense Add-Ons Revive Senate Turf Fight," *Congressional Quarterly Weekly Report*, December 14, 1985, pp. 2617–2618.

[13] Office of the General Counsel, General Accounting Office [*sic*], *Principles of Federal Appropriations Law* (3rd ed.), (GAO-04026iSP), volume 1, pp. 2–41, 2–42. Reflecting its original publication date, this source (generally referred to as "The Red Book) identifies GAO by its original name.

reason for appropriating less than the administration requested for a particular program. So the political reality on Capitol Hill appears to be more complex than a simple question of whether or not the Appropriations committees are required to accede (at some level of detail) to spending caps set by the authorization process.

To sum up, there seems to be a disconnect between the way the legislative process actually works and a widely held belief about why it works that way. On the one hand, the Armed Services committees frequently exercise substantial influence over significant aspects of U.S. defense policy, though they do so episodically and reactively – as one would expect from a legislative body. The annual authorization process seems to be, somehow, an integral element of the Armed Services committees' policy-making role; yet there is no obvious reason for why that process should operate, at all. What's going on?

One or more of the following dynamics may be at work. In many cases, the House and Senate Armed Services Committees – like other congressional committees – exercise power in ways that have little to do with enacting legislation, simply by publicizing executive branch errors or malfeasances through hearings, staff investigations, roving congressional delegations, and the like. To this extent, the authorization process simply provides a specific mandate under which the committee pursues routine oversight activities. Even if it is clear that the authorizers cannot constrain the amounts appropriated for a particular program, it is not at all clear to what extent the authorizing committees can set conditions on the expenditure of the appropriated amounts, particularly in authorization legislation that is enacted subsequent to the appropriation.[14] There may be enough constituent interests engaged in the voluminous non-funding-related provisions routinely included in the authorization bill – particularly provisions that touch on military compensation and benefits – to give party leaders an incentive to fit the bill into the floor schedule. This may be particularly true if it is clear that the final version of the bill will include no "poison pill" provisions that would ensure a veto. In many cases, the Appropriations committees may simply follow the lead of their counterpart authorization panel, which can muster three times the number of committee members and four times the number of professional staff to probe the massive DOD budget.[15] The authorization bills may simply

---

[14] This argument depends on the fundamental procedural rule that later-enacted legislation controls previously enacted legislation. Ironically, this mechanism could work only if the authorization bill is enacted after the appropriations bill, rather than prior to it as the Russell Amendment clearly contemplates.

[15] In view of the simplistic assumptions about members' motivation that pervade the relevant academic literature, it is worth emphasizing that there is no assumption here that the

"keep on keeping on," out of sheer political momentum driven by the perceived importance of defense issues, combined with the seniority, persistence, and political savvy of Armed Services committee leaders.

The political dynamic that gives the Armed Services committees' leverage through the annual authorization process may be, at once, more subtle and more powerful than a simple matter of legal requirements. The key impact of the Russell Amendment may be the simple fact that it provides an incentive and rationale for the House and Senate Armed Services Committees to scrutinize annually every part of the DOD budget and to employ a professional staff large enough and sufficiently diverse in its expertise to assist the committee in such an annual review. At the very least, this "expands the base of knowledge in Congress for the critical analysis of defense issues" (Dawson 1962, 57)

COMMITTEE ASSETS

A grasp of what the Armed Services committees can and cannot do by way of taking policy initiatives – and of how they do the things they can – requires an appreciation of the many sources of leverage the panels bring to their oversight task. Underpinning the committees' legislative armory is the fact the Constitution assigns Congress a degree of authority over the organization and equipage of the armed services that has no parallel in terms of the relationship of the legislative branch with other executive branch agencies.

While Congress can probe and fine-tune the operations of any federal agency using the "power of the purse," the Constitution explicitly grants Congress uniquely far-reaching authority concerning the military establishment, specifically the powers "To raise and support Armies. To provide and maintain a Navy," [and] "To make Rules for the Government and Regulation of the land and naval Forces." These mandates frequently are cited by the congressional defense committees as the basis of their authority to review any administration's defense program at a much finer level of granularity than is typical of congressional oversight of other major executive branch agencies.

committees' program funding decisions are politically immaculate conceptions born out of utterly disinterested analysis. Nor is there any assumption that there is no institutional rivalry between authorizing and appropriations committees. Rather, the assumption is that, in addition to trying to secure their own reelection, a critical mass of Appropriations Committee members (and staff) attempt to review the administration's program on its merits and that, in making those assessments, they may take cognizance of the authorization committees' work.

Access to the Military

Congressional defense committees exercise a degree of direct access to career DOD personnel – particularly senior military officers – that has no parallel in other committees' relationships with the agencies they oversee. With the advent of the Cold War, the congressional defense committees routinely insisted on obtaining the personal and professional judgments of top military leaders on pending issues. Moreover, the National Security Act of 1949 (P.L. 81–216) specifically authorized any member of the Joint Chiefs of Staff to present to Congress any recommendation, on the officer's own initiative, after first informing the secretary of defense

The Senate Armed Services Committee draws particularly strong leverage from the fact that promotions for military officers – unlike those for civil servants – require Senate confirmation. Nominations for promotion to flag and general officer grades are individually scrutinized by the Senate Armed Services Committee staff and nominees to the two highest grades – general and lieutenant general and the corresponding Navy ranks of admiral and vice admiral – sometimes are required to appear before the committee at a hearing and to promise that, if confirmed, they will provide Congress with their candid professional opinions, when asked, even if these conflict with administration policy. Generally, nominees also are required to promise that they will inflict no reprisals on subordinates who divulge, in response to congressional inquiries, information that either the nominee or his political superiors do not wish to disclose.[16]

At the other end of the military hierarchy, members of Congress concern themselves with the well-being, morale, and preparedness of junior enlisted personnel, routinely demonstrating a responsiveness to that group they do not extend to rank-and-file civilian federal employees. Service members, wherever they may be stationed, are the relatively young sons and daughters of constituents all across the country, whose parental concern for the troops' well-being generates interest among many more members than those whose constituencies host military bases. But the defense committees have additional incentives, in that DOD relies on a complex system of compensation and a massive network of supporting social service infrastructure. By one estimate, these personnel and personnel-related costs may account for nearly half

---

[16] The Senate's rein on officers in the two senior grades is reinforced by the fact that officers are confirmed at those grades for a particular assignment. If a three-star or four-star officer is assigned to another position at the same grade – as was the case with General David Petraeus – he or she must be nominated by the president and confirmed by the Senate to hold the new position at the same grade.

of the $518 billion the Bush administration requested for DOD's base budget in FY2009 (Kosiak 2008, 16). Finally, DOD's ability to carry out its missions arguably depends on the talent and morale of service members – particularly relatively junior officers and enlisted personnel – in a way that civilian federal agencies do not depend on the morale of the civil service.

The upshot of all this is that the defense committees routinely involve themselves more deeply in the organizational fabric of the armed services than other committees do in the career ranks of the agencies they oversee. As a by-product of this, the defense committees may have a much richer picture of the agency within their purview, which presumably informs their oversight and choice of policy initiatives.

Advocacy Oversight

In addition to being unusually intrusive (compared with other legislative committees), the Armed Services Committees take as their point of departure a basic sympathy with DOD. Most Armed Services committee members and staff see themselves as advocates and supporters of the defense establishment, in a way that goes beyond whatever parochial interests the members might have in the way of bases or contractors back in their constituencies. Critics lament that this makes DOD's congressional overseers lapdogs rather than watchdogs. But that complaint both exaggerates the practical effect of the committees' policy slant and ignores the ways in which it facilitates their oversight activity.

At least since the end of the Vietnam War, there has been a broad consensus in Congress on most of the (relatively few) aspects of defense policy that have been salient in the national political arena. The significant exceptions to that rule – aside from debates over presidential decisions to commit U.S. forces to combat – have been the occasional debates over the overall size of the annual defense budget, the debates over strategic arms policy in the 1980s, and the continuing debate over the size and thrust of the U.S. antimissile defense program. But it was inevitable that those national issues were going to be resolved in the Senate and House as a whole (or in the electoral arena) rather than within the circumscribed arena of the Armed Services Committees.

In sum, on the relatively few defense-related issues that gain traction in the broader political arena, the views of the defense committees are not necessarily dispositive in any case. It is on relatively technical questions regarding the manning, organization, and equipment of U.S. forces – issues that typically do not have a partisan aspect – that the defense committees have their greatest impact as policy initiators. Put another way, since the committees are relatively free of internal debates over fundamental issues such as the overall size of the defense budget – issues that, in any event, would be resolved in a broader political arena than a committee – they are free to focus time and energy on narrower problems to which they can apply their expertise and independent perspectives with some expectation of coming up with a solution that their parent chamber will accept. In this respect they stand in sharp contrast to some other congressional committees that routinely are riven by fundamental disagreements over the cardinal premises of major programs within their purview – indeed, sometimes by existential debates over the legitimacy of federal action in an entire sphere of policy.

Independent Perspective

The committees function as a market within which executive branch policies can be constructively challenged and probed. Since the committees are "pro-defense" rather than "pro–Defense Department" they have provided the services with a court of appeal against (or, as critics would have it, an avenue for end-runs around) decisions of the DOD political leadership. A mundane but potentially significant example of this is the routinization since 1995 of the "unfunded priorities lists" – each service's prioritized list of how it would allocate additional funding, should it become available in the course of congressional action on the president's budget request.

The committees sometimes have tried to incentivize OSD or the services to reconcile internal contradictions in their programs – or simply to come to terms with unpleasant realities – sometimes simply by highlighting the anomalies. For example, in an effort to compel DOD to resolve the long-festering problem of reconciling long-term Navy shipbuilding plans with realistic budgets, the 2000 Defense bill required DOD to submit its plan for acquiring ships for the following 30 years, (P.L. 106-65, Section 1013). Three years later, they included in the 2003 Defense bill a requirement that such a 30-year shipbuilding plan be submitted to Congress with each budget (P.L. 107-314, Section 1022).

The committees also have championed bureaucratic orphans – important capabilities that either fall between bureaucratic stools or routinely lose out in the competition for funds (and promotions) to prestigious combat forces that represent the services' marquee capabilities. The committees' efforts to make the services increase funding for strategic lift investments – most dramatically through the Congressionally Mandated Mobility Study (CMMS) mandated by the 1981 Defense bill is one example of the committees' ability to boost a key capability that was not prioritized by the services (P.L. 96-342, Section 203b).

On occasion, the committees have reached further down into the services, to challenge the entrenched views of a specialized – and prestigious – fraternity. For example, House Armed Services Chairman Les Aspin in the late 1980s and HASC Subcommittee Chairman Duncan Hunter in the mid-1990s used various investigative and legislative tactics to pressure the Navy's nuclear submarine community to consider incorporating various novel technologies into the U.S. submarine program which, in the view of some critics, had grown hidebound and imprudently dismissive of developments being explored by potential adversaries (Polmar and Moore 2001, 314–315).

Expertise

Yet another important resource at the disposal of the Armed Services committees is the members' expertise – of a particular sort. Typically, at any given time, there are a few members of each Armed Services Committee who have clearly relevant military experience or technical expertise. Others acquire "expertise-by-osmosis" from interested parties in their constituencies. But substantive expertise is not a prerequisite either for election to Congress or for selection to a particular committee.

The greatest value added by the committees to the policy process is their potential to combine technical know-how with political acumen: to mediate the relationship between the defense establishment and the body politic it serves, persuasively conveying the special requirements of the armed services to their legislative colleagues and, conversely, ensuring that the military's programs are tolerable to the broader society, both financially and socially.

> Expertise, in the congressional context, is really a system in which generalists learn enough about a given subject matter to help other generalists – their colleagues.... Congressional information is not the type of expertise that comes from undertaking a detailed study or being on an operational firing line. Rather, its major characteristic is a blend of the substantive and the political, the academic and the pressure group information, the bureaucracy and the constituency. Members and staffers are exposed to an impressive variety of information – studies, Administration arguments, leaks, interest group pressures, complaints from the districts, concerns of constituents – and the combination of these various communications is different from the perspectives of others in the [policy-making] system. (Kingdon 2002, 38)

Any effective congressional committee will have a significant number of members with those eminently political skills. What sets the Armed Services Committees apart is that, alone among the legislative committees, they have in the annual authorization bill an instrument that gives them an incentive to regularly apply that political expertise to oversight of the entire scope of activity of the agency within their jurisdiction.

Staff and Specialization

For the two Armed Services panels, committee reforms in the early 1970s encouraged a process of specialization within the broad scope of committee jurisdiction that has continued. Subcommittees with fixed jurisdiction had been created in both Armed Services Committees by the mid-1970s. The number of professional staff – subject matter experts and analysts as distinct from clerical and administrative personnel – ballooned. In recent years, both committees have divided their staffs between a larger group responsible to the committee's partisan majority and a smaller group responsible to the minority, so one must allow for the likelihood that there is considerable overlap between the work of the two partisan staffs. On the other hand, both committees' highly touted tradition of bipartisanship may mean there is less duplication on the Armed Services panels than on many other committees that allocate their staff on a partisan basis. In any case, the increase in staff resources available to committee members is striking, as is the background and tenure of staff members. Most have a substantial professional background relevant to their duties on the staff, and many of them stay through enough budget cycles to gain considerable experience with parts of the budget relevant to their responsibilities. In 2008, for instance, six of the 38 professional staff on Senate Armed Services had served with the panel for at least 10 years. The 47-member House committee staff included five 10-year veterans.

Members, too, typically stay with the Armed Services Committees for the long haul. In 2008, the House committee's 62 members included 20 who had been on the panel for 10 years or more. That same year, the Senate panel numbered among its 25 members seven who had been on the panel for at least 10 years, and two more who, in 1998, were serving on House Armed Services Committee and joined the Senate panel as soon as they were elected to the Senate.

Think Tanks

In addition to their organic staff, any congressional committee can call on three congressional support agencies: the Governmental Accountability Office

(GAO), the Congressional Research Service (CRS), and the Congressional Budget Office. All three agencies are charged with providing objective, non-partisan analysis to Congress. The defense committees also draw on other sources of independent expertise: private, non-partisan think tanks; certain policy analysis organizations with a clearly partisan orientation; federally funded research and development corporations; university-based experts; and a number of small but high-powered centers within the executive branch. These various non-DOD sources of information and analysis contribute to policy debates independent of the legislative process, but the two Armed Services Committees also tap them formally in their annual hearings.

In hearings during 2008 that were not focused on specific nominations, Senate Armed Services heard a total of 154 presentations by witnesses.[17] Of that total, 25 presentations were by "outside" experts (i.e., persons not representing the Bush administration, DOD, or one of the armed services). Four of those outside witness-appearances were by staff of the congressional support agencies. Also in 2008, House Armed Services hosted 310 appearances by witnesses, of which 92 were by outside experts, including 21 by congressional support agency staff.

COMMITTEE TACTICS

To cope with the complexity of defense issues and the sheer bureaucratic inertia of an agency as large as DOD, the defense committees have developed a repertory of tactics that allow them to exercise on DOD and the services various degrees of leverage that range from bureaucratic nudges to sweeping assertions of legislative authority over agency operation.

In a handful of cases – the tightening of Army enlistment standards in the early 1980s, the Goldwater-Nichols DOD reorganization of 1986, and the establishment of the Special Operations Command in 1987, to name three conspicuous examples – the committees have enacted laws imposing significant change on DOD and the services. Far more often, however, the committees use actions short of legislation to incentivize DOD leaders to address emerging problems themselves. In those cases in which the committees have had recourse to legislation to mandate some action by DOD, they typically

---

[17] These data refer to the number of witness-appearances before the two committees, not the number of witnesses. Several witnesses from the Department of Defense and some from outside sources testified more than once to each committee and are counted separately for each appearance. The data are drawn from the House and Senate Armed Services Committees' websites cataloging hearings held during the 110th Congress (2007–2009).

have taken that step only after less coercive tactics have failed to nudge the agency into addressing a situation that the committees saw as problematical.

Hearings: At the low end of the spectrum of legislative "coerciveness" is the ability of the committees to shape the political climate on an issue by public hearings. In some cases, a narrowly circumscribed controversy can be defined – and even resolved, in political terms – by a hearing that is generally perceived as offering the protagonists a fair chance to state their respective cases and join the issue. This function may be particularly effective in an era when blogs offer any dedicated advocate a way to pitch his case directly to the public, bypassing the gatekeeper function traditionally performed by the press. In June of 2007, for example, a House Armed Services hearing with Army officials and outside experts substantially damped down controversy over a novel type of body armor (called Dragon Skin) which the Army had rejected – unfairly, according to an energetic publicity campaign waged by the manufacturer.

Legislative Reports: The committees sometimes include in the voluminous reports accompanying their bills language expressing concern over a problem but without directing DOD to take any particular steps to deal with it. On occasion, such an expression of committee concern turns out to be the first step in a multi-year process leading to more decisive legislative action, such as in 1977, when Congress decried a decline in the quality of Army recruits, and in 1984 when lawmakers warned that the services were allowing U.S. special operations capabilities to atrophy even as the Soviet Union was expanding its special ops capability.

The statement of managers on the conference report on a defense authorization bill may also direct DOD or one of its components to take (or refrain from) some particular action. For instance, the joint explanatory statement accompanying the final version of the 2009 defense bill complained that the Missile Defense Agency (MDA) was not conducting operational tests of the national anti-ballistic missile system at a sufficiently rapid rate, and objected to MDA's having canceled one very important test without the approval of other interested Pentagon agencies (including the director of Operational Test and Evaluation [DOT&E]). The conferees directed MDA – in the explanatory statement, not in a provision of the bill – to consult with DOT&E and other appropriate DOD officials before canceling any more scheduled major tests.[18] While MDA could ignore this language on grounds that it is not legally

---

[18]   House Armed Services Committee Print No. 10, 2008, p. 570. For procedural reasons, there was no official conference report on the enacted version of the FY2009 defense authorization act. This document is the functional equivalent of the conference report.

binding, such action would have risked provoking the Armed Services committees to incorporate more draconian mandates in future legislation. The committees may include in the text of the bill non-binding language expressing the "sense of Congress" that a particular course of action should be pursued. In 2008, for instance, Congress included such a provision in the defense bill calling for DOT&E to have a five-year tenure (P.L. 110–181, Section 909).

Investigative Reports: Occasionally, a committee, one of its components, or a group of committee members, sponsor investigative reports which, while not embedded in the authorization legislation, have significantly shaped debate within the defense policy community on a particular issue. While these reports may become the basis for specific legislative proposals, they also may have a broader impact within the defense policy community, forcing issues toward the top of the agenda and forging what had been disparate elements of information into an actionable critique of then-current policy. In April 1989, for example, a House Armed Services panel chaired by Representative Ike Skelton (D-MO) concluded a wide-ranging investigation of DOD's network of "war colleges" with a report that instigated numerous efforts to make the professional military education program more intellectually rigorous.[19]

Congress's penchant for ordering reports from various sources on issues great and small, either in provisions of law on in report language, is a staple element of the widely held view that the legislative branch plays no consequential role in formulating U.S. defense policy. At best, the assertion often is made, most of the studies required by the defense authorization bills are pointless exercises; at worst, they are counterproductive impositions on DOD personnel.[20] However, even a report that is arguably trivial in its substance can perform a useful function, for instance, by truncating what otherwise could be a prolonged and contentious floor debate on some issue. But the Armed Services Committees also request reports of substance on important issues, often with the aim of forcing some issue higher on the agenda of senior DOD officials.

---

[19] *Report on the Panel on Military Education of the Committee on Armed Services of the House of* Representatives, Committee Print, April 21, 1989.

[20] Former Defense Secretary Donald H. Rumsfeld, a frequent critic of congressional reporting requirements, lamented their cumulative effect in a speech to students at the National Defense University in Washington, DC early in 2002: "We file over 950 reports every year to the Congress. I don't think anyone reads them. We're just killing trees all over the world.... [N]o one report is wrong or bad, but it's the cumulative effect of all this." Department of Defense, Office of the Assistant Secretary of Defense for Public Affairs, "Remarks of Defense Secretary Donald Rumsfeld, National Defense University, Washington, DC, January 31, 2002. Accessed August 15, 2011, http://www.defense.gov/speeches/speech.aspx?speechid=183.

In some cases, the committees simply ask an agency to analyze a potential solution to an acknowledged problem or to reconcile apparent contradictions within its program. For instance, the House Armed Services Committee, in its report on its version of the 2006 Defense authorization bill, directed the services to report on the utility of paying for junior officers to obtain graduate degrees from civilian universities as an incentive to remain in the service.[21] In other cases, the committees ask DOD – or one of its components – to reconcile policy inconsistencies. For example, the 2009 defense authorization bill required the secretary of defense to provide an annual plan for buying, maintaining, and scrapping the entire array of aircraft required by the Navy and Air Force over the following 30 years, the latest in a litany of (thus far unsuccessful) efforts by Congress to make OSD force the services to come up with affordable, long-term aircraft modernization plans (P.L. 110–417, Section 141).

Outside Analysis: Another option, sometimes used when the committees are grappling with technically complex issues, is for the panels to request an analysis by a competent public or quasi-public agency other than the one directly in charge of the activity under study: one of the auditing and review offices within DOD, one of the congressional support agencies, or some other established group with relevant credentials. The FY2009 authorization bill, for example, required DOD to commission an assessment by the National Academy of Sciences of the technical feasibility of so-called boost-phase anti-missile defenses (P.L. 110–417, Section 232).

Ad Hoc Commissions: On occasion, when the issue at hand is complex and any resolution seems likely to be politically challenging, the committees have mandated creation of an ad hoc, bipartisan commission comprising individuals with both substantive expertise and political clout and who, as a group, reflect a broad span of the political spectrum. This group, then, is charged with proposing one or more potential solutions for later consideration. Such commissions have had a significant impact on the public debate concerning the issue within their purview both because of the apparent competence of their analysis and the consensus reached among members who approached the issue from different political perspectives. The debate over whether to deploy a nationwide anti-missile defense system was significantly affected by the report of such a congressionally mandated commission, established by the FY1997 authorization bill, which was chaired by then-former (and future) Defense Secretary Donald H. Rumsfeld (P.L. 104–201, Sections 1321–29).

---

[21]   H Rept. 109–89, pp. 314–315.

In some cases, the committees have required a report from DOD with the proviso that it be reviewed and critiqued by an independent group – either an established organization like GAO, or an ad hoc blue-ribbon commission. This approach may be particularly useful if the desired analysis requires an extensive knowledge of DOD and the services at such a fine level of granularity that not even the most knowledgeable and prestigious of outside experts could do the job from scratch, whereas they could usefully critique an in-house analysis. A prime example of this approach is the National Defense Panel chartered by the FY1997 authorization bill to critique DOD's in-house Quadrennial Defense Review (QDR) and to offer its own views on emerging U.S. defense needs (P.L. 104–201, Sections 921–26).

Periodic DOD Reports: To facilitate oversight of chronically problematic programs, the committees may require DOD to provide certain quantitative indicators on a regular basis, either at set intervals or when certain parameters – cost increases or delays, for example – exceed some threshold that raises questions about a program's well-being. In addition to informing the committees, these requirements probably ensure that the information in question will receive closer attention from senior DOD leaders than would be the case if the data were not going to Capitol Hill. An early example of this was a provision of the FY1976 authorization bill requiring DOD to regularly give the defense committees its Selected Acquisition Reports (SARs), which DOD had created as an internal management system in 1967 to track changes in the projected cost and schedule of major weapons programs (P.L. 94–106, Section 811).

Legislation: From time to time, usually after several more subtle efforts to elicit action from DOD, the committees will simply take on the department and/or the services and mandate a course of action in the plain letter of the authorization law. These initiatives can be as sweeping as the provisions of the free-standing 1987 Goldwater-Nichols DOD organization bill. Far more often, however, they are less ambitious in scope. On rare occasions, faced with what they deem refractory opposition within the executive branch, the committees have micromanaged the execution of already enacted law. After Congress established the position of assistant secretary of defense for special operations and low-intensity conflict (ASD/SOLIC) in 1988, over DOD's strong opposition, the Reagan administration delayed nominating a candidate to fill the job. Eventually, it nominated in succession two officials who had been prominent opponents of the legislation. Senate Armed Services then added to the 1989 defense authorization bill a provision stipulating that, pending Senate confirmation of a nomination for the SOLIC job, the duties of that position would be carried out by the secretary of the army who was former House member

John Marsh (D-VA), a man the committees trusted to see to it that the duties of the new job were carried out in good faith (P.L. 100–180, Section 1211).[22]

THE ARMED SERVICES COMMITTEES' AGENDA: INTERNAL
AND EXTERNAL POLITICS

Facts on the ground may have more impact on the Armed Services committees' oversight agenda than anything else. At any given time, the security environment the country confronts may draw the Armed Services Committees' attention to some facets of the defense establishment more than others. For instance, the panels may be more likely focus on the duration of deployments and on the ratio of time spent deployed to time spent at home when high-tempo combat operations have lasted several years. But besides reflecting the immediate security situation facing the country, the committees' agendas at any given time also are influenced by six factors that affect both their overall level of activity and the likelihood that they will engage particular issues.

Long-Term Political Dynamics

From time to time, the rules of the legislative game change in a fundamental way that persists over decades. One example is the huge expansion in analytical staff to support members of Congress, which dates from the mid-1970s. That increase in staff resources – in members' offices, on committees, and in the three congressional support agencies – was partly a response to what many saw as the high-handed treatment of Congress by the Johnson and Nixon administrations, particularly in their conduct of the Vietnam War. It was an essential enabler of the whole array of policy initiatives that have become routine parts of the defense authorization process over the past three decades.

Another such long-term dynamic – one that limited the Armed Services committees' autonomy – is the evolution between the late 1960s and the early 1980s of sharper partisan divisions in Congress than had been apparent for at least two decades after World War II. Even when the lines are as sharply drawn as they are now, there are only a handful of defense policy questions on which broader partisan battles preempt the defense committees. However, a high level of ambient partisanship can constrain the Armed Services Committees in a number of ways.

Some issues are so fundamental to the differences between the two major parties that the committees would be preempted by debate across Congress. For

---

[22] H Rept 100–446, pp. 680–684.

example, as long as the two parties divide in general terms over federal spending, there will be an irreducible, and probably significant, guns versus butter aspect to the debate over the gross level of Pentagon spending. Other defense issues, while not so clearly rooted in fundamental partisan disagreements, have become partisan shibboleths by adoption. For example, the urgency of deploying missile defenses has evolved over the past quarter century as one of the few concrete defense issues over which Democrats and Republicans reliably divide. Non-defense, but highly contentious issues – such as abortion – can have a powerful impact on the timing (or even the likelihood) of action on the defense authorization bill because the issues loom large in the broader arena and the authorization bill is one of many venues in which those larger fights are waged (Burrelli 2002). And finally, an authorization bill can simply become hostage to procedural roadblocks arising from battles on other bills, battles that may be more likely to arise in a highly partisan environment. In 2010, for example, the overall budget debate was so contentious that the FY2011 defense authorization act did not become law until January 7, 2011.

Short-Term Political Dynamics

Other aspects of the political environment, which can change more rapidly, also affect the scope of the Armed Services Committees' initiatives, as well as their overall level of activity. For example, it is a cardinal premise of recent critiques of the national security policy-making process that Congress has been much less assertive on these issues in the past several years than it had been in the preceding decades (Murdock et al. 2004). However, the most important factor at work may have been the country's tendency to rally around the president in wartime, a historic pattern that may have been reinforced by the shocking and unprecedented character of the terrorist attacks of September 11, 2001, and by the unconventional adversaries confronting U.S. forces in Iraq and Afghanistan.

Another significant, but transient, political factor in the level of committee activity is the partisan relationship between the majority in each chamber of Congress and the president. From 2001 through 2006, the Republican majorities in the House and Senate evidently were less inclined to challenge the Republican administration than were the Democratic majorities elected in 2006 and 2008. This could have been due to loyalty or simply to the likelihood that Republicans' views were more congruent with President Bush's policies than were Democrats'.

Finally, the range of issues that the Armed Services Committees can deal with from a relatively non-partisan, problem-solving perspective probably depends on whether the defense budget is expected to expand or contract. If the budget is contracting in real terms, members may be under stronger pressure to assess any proposed initiative – however analytically neutral it may be – in terms of its implications for the members' favored services, programs, installations, and so forth.

Committee Organization and Procedure

Any organization is optimized, by its organization and standard operating procedures, to focus on some aspects of its operational environment more than on others. On any committee, a handful of members likely will make that panel a principal focus of their work. But most members have to spread their attention across many activities, and have little "down" time in which to pursue matters not vital to their constituencies (and their reelection prospects). Accordingly, they may be particularly likely to accept the selection and definition of issues that emerge from the committee's standard operating procedures. In turn, the committees are likely to focus on issues that fall within the purview of their established subcommittees and panels. For example, during two periods when the committees devoted considerable effort to reforming DOD's acquisition process, one or the other of the panels had an organizational component that focused specifically on that process – not as one aspect of a set of acquisition programs, but as an issue in its own right and the focus of the unit's work.[23]

Issue Type

The record suggests that some types of issues are inherently more difficult than others for congressional committees to decisively influence. In a crisis, both public sentiment and the exigencies of the situation typically tip the balance strongly in favor of presidential initiative. Since the end of World War II, this has been true even for decisions involving the commitment of U.S. forces to combat, notwithstanding Congress's effort to assert itself through the War Powers Resolution. The president also has an inherent advantage over Congress in many decisions about national strategy that hinge on declaratory policy, to the extent that a presidential declaration of a strategy is

---

[23] In 1980–81, House Armed Services chartered a task force on acquisition, chaired by Dave McCurdy. For its part, Senate Armed Services had a full subcommittee dedicated to the acquisition process from 1985 to 1996. See Jeff Bingaman, "The 12th Annual Gilbert A. Cuneo Lecture: The Origin and Development of the Federal Acquisition Streamlining Act," *Military Law Review*, Summer 1994, pp. 149–165.

self-executing. For example, if the president announces that it shall be U.S. policy to guarantee the territorial integrity of a particular country, or that the United States renounces the first use of nuclear weapons, such a declaration creates the policy. The obvious exceptions to that generalization are cases in which a declaratory policy is embodied in a treaty requiring the consent of a two-thirds majority of the Senate.

On the other hand, Congress has considerable leverage over strategies that require for their execution that Congress appropriate funds, say, for the acquisition of a certain weapons system. For instance, in 1967, in the context of rising political discontent over U.S. interventions in Vietnam and in the Congo, Congress rejected a proposal to fund a fleet of Fast Deployment Logistics Ships intended to facilitate the rapid dispatch of U.S. ground forces to distant trouble spots. As a rule, decisions about how large a force to maintain and how it should be equipped require the appropriation of funds; sometimes they require significant changes in the organization of DOD. Both actions require congressional assent, and neither – as a rule – affords the president much scope for cashing in, politically, on his role as commander in chief. In general, it is easier for Congress to block a presidential initiative than to force some course of action on a reluctant executive, simply because it is easier to mobilize a blocking coalition, comprising members who oppose an initiative for different reasons.

Institutional Prerogatives

The committees also have difficulty with initiatives that are seen by any of the services (or by cohesive components within one of the services) as an infringement on their ethos by unqualified outsiders. The problem, in these cases, is rooted in the interaction of two factors: the strength of the target institution's commitment to its established priorities and procedures and the degree to which successful implementation of the proposed change depends on the enthusiastic assent of the target institution.

In the words of Representative Les Aspin (D-WI), spoken a few years before he became chairman of the House Armed Services Committee:

> If it looks like a close call, we ought to go with the services. For just bureaucratic reasons and having the system work correctly, we ought to go with the system that the services want. Otherwise, it can be a disaster. We can list a whole bunch of things that, when we have crammed them down the throats of the services, turned out to be a disaster, for all kinds of bureaucratic reasons. (*Congressional Record*, July 21, 1982, H 17341–44)

Coherence of the Debate

The range of issues over which the Armed Services committees can effectively assert their claim to unique expertise (i.e., can assert a claim in which their parent legislative chambers and DOD acquiesce, if only grudgingly) depends partly on the extent to which the national political elites share a common definition of the national security situation facing the country at that time. Some such broad frame of reference is the fundamental characteristic of a well-defined policy arena: one within which many cardinal premises are generally accepted, DOD is trying to solve complex problems within those premises, and a handful of big issues are open to debate within circumscribed limits.

For at least the decade and a half between the fall of South Vietnam and the collapse of the Soviet Union, the U.S. political system navigated the issues of national security policy within such a relatively consensual frame of reference. There was general agreement on the identity of the enemy – the Soviet Union – and on the threats that adversary posed to vital U.S. interests, namely, that U.S. allies in Europe could be intimidated in politically significant ways by massive Soviet conventional military forces if they acquired an apparent superiority over the outnumbered NATO conventional forces against which they were poised; and that an apparent Soviet superiority in strategic nuclear forces might undermine the U.S. government's ability to offset the intimidating effect of Soviet conventional numbers by pledging nuclear retaliation against Moscow for any move against major U.S. allies.

Within those broad premises, only a handful of issues were seriously debated in the political arena. Those debates – most of which turned on questions of what would constitute unacceptable Soviet superiority in either the nuclear or conventional realms – were intense and were fraught with some significant implications for U.S. defense policy and budgets. But with few exceptions, the political battles were conducted within a complex intellectual framework largely shaped by the defense establishment and consisting of an elaborate and closely coupled set of assumptions about the nature of the military balance in question (nuclear or conventional) and highly technical calculations about the operational characteristics of the myriad types of equipment proper to each sphere. The political system dealt with most aspects of nuclear weapons policy, and with practically all facets of conventional arms policy, within those complex frameworks of assumptions and technical calculations. Mastery of those established intellectual constructs marked one as an "expert" to whom most non-experts deferred on relevant issues. That was the political context within which, in 1977, Senate Armed Services members Nunn and Bartlett wrote a 15-page critique of NATO strategy that hit the Alliance like a jujitsu maneuver. Citing several recent improvements in Soviet conventional forces, the two senators argued – convincingly to many – that when those new developments were taken into account, NATO's contemporary defensive plans failed on their own terms.[24]

Today, by comparison the national security policy arena is far less organized around a consensual definition of the situation. In contrast to the widely shared assumptions that structured policy debates of the late Cold War period, there is no comparable frame of reference of any real specificity that commands a broad a consensus within the U.S. defense policy community. Thus, there is no analytical fulcrum over which the defense committees can exert leverage on DOD policy by identifying ways in which it was falling short, taken on its own terms.

The documents that ostensibly map the country's security environment and its response – the National Security Strategy, the National Defense Strategy, and the National Military Strategy – are cast in general terms that set few priorities. None of those documents offer guidance that would shape a defense investment plan likely to survive the tight federal budgets in the offing, which will allow little room for hedging by buying a wide enough array of capabilities to cover any of several possible future security environments. The various authoritative statements produced by the individual armed services are characterized by their robust assertions that the parent service's marquee systems are just the ticket for the future security environment – whatever it might be.

The relatively undefined character of the current national security policy debate need not hamstring the Armed Services committees. Indeed, the current practice of drafting detailed, annual authorization bills was instigated by the Armed Services committees' frustration with an inchoate debate over continental air defense in the mid-1950s. The far greater uncertainty surrounding today's defense debates may offer the committees a wider opportunity: rather than critiquing DOD's performance within an established strategic framework, the committees' challenge today is to try to shape a process that could create such a framework, a task surely as daunting as the creation of the Cold War consensus in the two decades after the end of World War II.

CONCLUSION

There are some fundamental and highly contentious questions about the defense posture of the United States – the overall size of the Pentagon budget,

---

[24] *NATO and the New Soviet Threat, Report of Sen. Sam Nunn and Sen. Dewey F. Bartlett to the Committee on Armed Services, United States Senate,* Committee Print, 1977.

for example – concerning which the defense committees seem unlikely to have a decisive impact: the stakes simply are too high for too many players to imagine that the contemporary U.S. political system could cede authority over them to a relative handful of legislators claiming specialized knowledge.

This chapter argues, however, that there are many other issues – highly consequential for the U.S. national security posture, but engaging relatively few political interests outside the defense community – concerning which the defense committees have asserted themselves. Moreover, on the face of it, these committee initiatives have been sufficiently significant in their intended impact that they deserve more attention than they have received from students of the defense policy-making process. The circumstances that broaden or narrow (and otherwise shape) the committees' agenda are one aspect of the committees' oversight activity that warrants more systematic analysis.

5

Congress and Homeland Security

Timothy Balunis and William Hemphill

Fragmentation is not an uncommon trend in government. Among congressional committees, executive agencies, and organized interests, the tendency toward dispersal and decentralization is prevalent. Considered in terms of separation of powers, fragmentation can be as much a blessing as a challenge. The splintering of legislative and executive authority ensures a diversity of perspectives, a wide range of access points, and layered accountability. In this regard, the nature of the congressional challenges facing the Department of Homeland Security (DHS) is not unfamiliar.

How much is enough? Beyond some optimum point, fragmentation becomes hyper-fragmentation. The scope of the fragmentation challenge, and its implications for DHS's missions, is anomalous. Although other fledgling departments have been beset by fragmentation – some degree of this is the norm – the expanse of missions and agencies, not to mention myriad committees with tangential interests, have amplified this trend to a degree unmatched currently, and perhaps historically. Moreover, the sprawling oversight of DHS among congressional committees continues to have daunting implications not only for the department's senior leadership but also for the execution of DHS operations on the national front lines.

This chapter will begin by tracing the substantive and institutional evolution of homeland security. Particular emphasis will be given to the overall homeland security policy subsystem and how the emergence of homeland security as a "new" issue had significant reverberations, not only for executive governance but for congressional structure and politics as well. An analysis of the resulting fragmentation among committees will include a discussion

The views expressed herein are those of the authors and do not reflect the position of the United States Coast Guard Academy, Department of Homeland Security, United States Military Academy, the Department of the Army, or the Department of Defense.

and application of committee and subsystem theory. Subsequently, this chapter will compare the congressional experience of DHS to three other executive departments – Defense, Energy, and Transportation – in both the 110th Congress (2007–2009) and in their own respective infancies. Having made this contrast, this chapter will seek to explain these differences and – perhaps more important – consider the implications of congressional fragmentation for DHS.

The question that permeates this discussion, the question that must endure, is how the structural phenomenon of fragmentation among congressional committees impacts homeland security at the policy, strategic, operational, and tactical levels. In the trenches – waterborne security zones, airport security checkpoints, border crossings, and marine terminals nationwide – fragmentation ceases to be an abstract conflict among policy makers and becomes a critical stressor on the viability of homeland security nationwide.

CONSOLIDATION AND FRAGMENTATION: THE INSTITUTION EVOLUTION OF HOMELAND SECURITY

The nation reeled, seemingly under attack from some amorphous foreign threat. Frustration in the Middle East with American intervention and military presence in that region boiled over, triggering a dramatic and unexpected response – widely seen as a brazen attack – against the United States. In addition to the significant human costs, the economic effects were jarring: the stock market crashed, consumer confidence and demand plummeted, and the United States stumbled into a recession. Viewing this most recent challenge to U.S. hegemony, some allies continued to stand with Washington; others openly questioned their commitments, as well as U.S. motives in the Middle East. Beyond the staggering effects at home, the crisis reinvigorated calls at home for energy independence and American disentanglement from Middle Eastern affairs.

The macropolitical responses in Washington were dramatic. Deeply concerned with preventing another attack, the president proposed the creation of a new department – a major reorganization of executive agencies – which eventually stood up after years of wrangling with Congress. In the House and Senate, the response was organizationally inverse, but similarly significant. Jurisdiction over a "new" policy area was not clearly awarded by House Rule X or Senate Standing Rule XXV, prompting congressional committees to battle fiercely for the right to oversee the fledgling department. Whereas one chamber of Congress did eventually create a new committee to oversee the department, the other awarded jurisdiction to a long-standing, powerful committee.

Nonetheless, the resulting fragmentation in the House and Senate had substantial implications for policy making and presented numerous hurdles for the new department.

The institutional effects of the 1973 Arab oil embargo still linger today. A striking parallel to the September 11 attacks, the embargo was initiated by the Organization of Petroleum Exporting Countries (OPEC) in response to U.S. support for Israel during the 1973 war with Egypt. Beyond its immediate economic effects, the embargo brought new urgency and new definitions to debates over energy policy in the United States. Between Congress and the executive branch, the institutional reactions were polar opposites: while bureaucratic control over energy issues was consolidated in the Department of Energy, Congress responded with decentralization and fragmentation. (Jones and Strahan 1985, 153). In the 1970s, as many as 83 committees and subcommittees exercised jurisdiction over energy policy, prompting the Select Committee on Committees – named the "Bolling Committee" for its chair, Representative Richard W. Bolling (D-MO) – to recommend creation of a new energy committee in 1974 (Ornstein 2003, 35). Amid competition for "property rights" over energy policy, the House Interstate and Foreign Commerce Committee absorbed primary jurisdiction in 1974, eventually becoming the Energy and Commerce Committee. (Johnson 2003, 10–11) The Senate created the standing Committee on Energy and Natural Resources in 1977, which was granted primary authority over energy policy amid a contentious field (Schneider et al. 2003, 16–23).

The sudden trauma of September 11 was characteristically different from the oil crises of the 1970s. However, as homeland security consumed the national consciousness, it was beset by similar, conflicting responses: aggregation in the executive branch and disaggregation in the legislative branch.

Theoretical Foundations

At its core, jurisdictional fragmentation is about subsystem politics and committee competition. The evolution of homeland security in the United States is best understood in terms of its policy subsystems, relatively closed networks of committees, executive agencies, organized interests, academics, and/or opinion leaders that tend to dominate a certain policy area (Baumgartner and Jones 1993, 7–8). As public debates calm, as definitions stabilize, as interests congeal, as supporting institutions are created, subsystems enjoy a high degree of autonomy amid low attention. The result is partial political equilibrium characterized by limited external access, negative feedback, and incremental change (Baumgartner and Jones 1993, 21).

Subsystem governance is often the norm in American politics, as an array of institutions process myriad policy issues in parallel. Yet dramatic change does occur. Examining the phenomenon of stasis punctuated by significant change, Baumgartner and Jones (1993) discuss how partial equilibrium can give way to rapid reform. As new issues reach the public agenda, or well-known issues are repackaged or redefined, widely held policy images change. Disenfranchised interests mobilize, and political conflict expands. Entrenched subsystems or institutions, long hegemonic in their respective policy area, must compete with new players. As macropolitical attention refocuses on the contested policy area, feedback changes from negative to positive, precipitating institutional responses. Long-standing policy monopolies are shattered and substantive reform often follows (Baumgartner and Jones 1993, 19–22).

The energy subsystem provides a compelling illustration. Long viewed in economic terms, energy policy simmered quietly off the public agenda. But as energy came to be seen increasingly as a national security issue following the oil shocks of the 1970s, its policy image morphed. The institutional reactions were severe. Presidential proposals for new executive agencies, such as the Federal Energy Administration and the Energy Research and Development Administration, came to fruition. Committees in Congress clashed furiously over a policy area whose jurisdiction had never been clearly assigned in the past. The result was a destabilized subgovernment and degree of fragmentation that further complicated, rather than rationalized, energy policy making through the end of the 1970s (Jones and Strahan 1985, 175–176).

Within the dynamics of subsystem politics, congressional committees are a key political unit. Baumgartner and Jones (1993) note that congressional reorganization often reflects or reinforces external change, particularly as policy issues are redefined and conflict expands. Committee jurisdictions are particularly supple with regard to issue dynamics (Baumgartner and Jones, 195–198). Theories on the structure and dynamics of the committee system – its purpose, its fierce competition, its continual evolution – abound. Most prominent among them are the *distributive benefits*, *party-cartel*, and *informational efficiency theories* (Groseclose and King 2001). Each theory has tremendous explanatory power for addressing the fragmentation that surrounds homeland security. *Distributive benefits*, which conceives of the congressional committee system as a highly evolved product and protector of ingrained interests (Groseclose and King 2001, 48–49), may explain much of the competition over DHS and the emergent homeland security policy subsystem after the September 11 attacks. Though most every interest in the Congress is itself a minority, *distributive benefits* suggests that the committee system serves as a mechanism for the rapid creation and dissolution of coalitions to advance those interests as issues arise (Groseclose and King 2001, 46–47). The ambiguity of so many aspects of homeland security, the range of special interests, and the lucrative stakes involved combine to enable and encourage the dispersion of jurisdiction among so many eager committees.

In the past, the control of party and committee leaders inhibited efforts to create new committees and, correspondingly, pare off the jurisdiction of existing committees. According to the *party-cartel* theory, the committee system is a mechanism for rewarding faithful partisans with committee assignments, advancing the party agenda, enhancing its image on highly publicized counterterrorism efforts, and assuring reciprocal loyalty between party and committee leadership (Groseclose and King 2001, 50–51). The fragmenting homeland security subsystem over DHS has provided numerous outlets and opportunities to pursue these ends. The failure of numerous past reform attempts in both chambers attests to the enduring strength of these features of a coordinated party cartel.

Last, *informational efficiency* posits that the committee system is, foremost, a mechanism to develop decentralized expertise and process numerous issues and bills in parallel. The exponential growth in congressional business in the young United States necessitated a means of policy specialization and workload management. By the 13th Congress (1811–1813), an early system of ad hoc committees had given way to one of standing committees. These developments underpin the informational basis for the congressional committee system. Diverse committees, whose membership *does* generally reflect that of the median voter in each house, enable members to develop and leverage selective expertise (Krehbiel 1991, 20–21).

The Executive Consolidates

On October 8, 2001, President George W. Bush issued Executive Order 13228, establishing the Office of Homeland Security (OHS) within the Executive Office of the President, and the Homeland Security Council (HSC), modeled after the National Security Council (NSC). The OHS, under the direction of former Pennsylvania Governor Tom Ridge, would develop, oversee, and coordinate a comprehensive national strategy for homeland security. The HSC, consisting of Cabinet members with homeland security responsibilities, would advise and assist the president on homeland security issues and serve as an additional mechanism for coordination (Bush 2001).

However, many in Congress sought a more substantial, enduring organizational change in the executive. Faced with the challenges of managing disparate agencies and functions, stifling terrorism, and satisfying the public imperative to better secure the homeland, policy makers grappled with the most effective organizational model: coordination or consolidation? Proposals favoring coordination included a continuation of the Office of Homeland Security (OHS) in the White House, with increased budgetary and statutory authority for its director, then-Governor Tom Ridge. The assignment of a lead federal agency, such as the Department of Justice (DOJ), for terrorism or disaster response, comprised a moderate option. Further toward consolidation along the spectrum of alternatives, others proposed either a new, independent agency dedicated to homeland security or a department level reorganization (Conley 2002, 4–6).

Along the coordination-consolidation spectrum, the eventual outcome – a Cabinet-level Department of Homeland Security – was far toward the consolidation end. The scale of the new department, which opened its doors on March 1, 2003, was far beyond that of DOE. Embodying consolidation over coordination, the Homeland Security Act of 2002 (H.R. 5005) mandated the integration of 22 diverse agencies and over 200,000 employees into DHS, including the Animal and Plant Health Inspection Service, Coast Guard, Federal Emergency Management Agency, Immigration and Naturalization Service, and Secret Service. The result was a department that was heterogeneous in terms of its mission, culture, structure, and administration. Additionally, DHS was initially budget-neutral, adding the considerable new mandates of "homeland security" to the legacy missions of component agencies. In many cases, the traditional missions of component agencies had connections to homeland security that were tangential at best (Cohen et al. 2006, 685–686).[1] "There is no place else in the literature – or in the history of U.S. political institutions," notes Donald Kettl (2003, 268) "where reformers merged such a wide range of large and important agencies into a new department, charged them with a broad and expansive mission, and at the same time directed them to continue unabated with their existing responsibilities." While bureaucratic reorganization has been a traditional response to coordination problems, such as those leading up to the September 11 attacks, certain parameters have generally applied. Along with budget neutrality, governmental reorganizations in

[1]   Cohen, Cuellar, and Weingast assert that the imposition of new responsibilities on top of legacy agency mandates, combined with the requirement for budget neutrality, was actually an intentional strategy by the White House to erode legacy missions and achieve ulterior policy goals (i.e., deregulation, devolution). Moreover, Cohen et al. cite the similar use of bureaucratic reorganization as a means to attain substantive policy goals, such as President Roosevelt's Federal Security Agency and President Carter's Department of Energy. See Dara K. Cohen, Mariano-Florentino Cuellar, and Barry R. Weingast, "Crisis Bureaucracy: Homeland Security and the Political Design of Legal Mandates," *Stanford Law Review*, Vol. 59 (2006), pp. 746–749.

U.S. history have typically been zero-sum in terms of agency responsibilities. Where organizational mandates have increased, resources have commensurately increased (Kettl 2003, 268–269). In this sense, the institutional design of DHS was anomalous and underlies continuing concerns over the operational effectiveness of the department.

The Congress Fragments

Congress did not respond in parallel. As with the energy crises of the 1970s, the institutional response in Congress was a stark contrast to the consolidation in the executive branch. Committees, eager to build jurisdiction over a "new" policy area that was not clearly assigned in either chamber's rules, commenced combat. Echoing similar struggles over health care in the 1950s and energy in the 1970s, over 80 committees in the House and Senate called hearings, requested briefings, and demanded the testimony of numerous DHS personnel. In 2004, only a year into the life of the new department, DHS personnel testified at 165 committee hearings, delivered 1,747 briefings, and responded to 3,632 questions for the record. By 2006, these numbers would increase to 206, 2,242, and 3,745, respectively (Chertoff 2007, 2–3). Heading into the 110th and 111th Congresses (2007–2009 and 2009–2011), these numbers – a strong indication of fragmentation – would only increase.

The congressional tendency toward fragmentation was neither unprecedented nor unforeseen. The Advisory Panel to Assess Domestic Response Capabilities for Terrorism Involving Weapons of Mass Destruction – known as the "Gilmore Commission" for its chair, then-Virginia Governor James Gilmore – called for jurisdictional consolidation as early as December 2000. Among its recommendations was a single authorizing committee in each house with jurisdiction over counterterrorism and homeland security (Gilmore 2000, 18). In early 2001, the Hart-Rudman Commission on National Security in the 21st Century sagely recommended a DHS-type reorganization to prevent terrorist attacks and enhance domestic security (Hart-Rudman 2001, 7). In parallel, Hart-Rudman advised, "Congress should rationalize its current committee structure so that it best serves U.S. national security objectives; specifically, it should merge the current authorizing committees with the relevant appropriations subcommittees" (Hart-Rudman 2001, 112). In its report, the 9/11 Commission expressed concern over the dozens of congressional panels overseeing DHS. Arguing that committee reorganization was critical to achieving crucial unity of effort, the commission recommended "one authorizing committee and one appropriating subcommittee in each house," echoing the Gilmore Commission (Kean and Hamilton 2003, 421).

The Homeland Security Act validated these recommendations, albeit more vaguely, by expressing the "sense of Congress that each House of Congress should review its committee structure in light of the reorganization of responsibilities within the executive branch by the establishment of DHS" (H.R. 5005 2002). Throughout, the common motivating principle was simple: if executive reorganization is not paralleled by congressional reorganization, gains in bureaucratic efficiency and coordination will be muted (Cohen et al. 2006, 706–707).

These proposals were partially fulfilled at best. In January 2003, the House Appropriations Committee realigned the jurisdictions of its subcommittees to create a 13th Subcommittee on Homeland Security. At the same time, five other committees in the House internally reorganized to create subcommittees oriented toward homeland security or terrorism; among them were the Judiciary Subcommittee on Crime, Terrorism, and Homeland Security and the Intelligence Subcommittee on Terrorism and Homeland Security (Koempel 2005, 5–7). The House did establish a Select Committee on Homeland Security in the 107th Congress (2001–2003), which continued into the 108th (2003–2005). The temporary committee's charge included the development of recommendations related to the Homeland Security Act, oversight of the creation of DHS, and the continuing review of "laws, programs, and Government activities relating to homeland security" (H. Res. 5, 2003). The Select Committee's jurisdiction did not immediately change that of other committees holding authority over aspects of homeland security. However, the Select Committee's work did culminate in the establishment of the standing Committee on Homeland Security on January 4, 2005. A rare creation – no standing committee had been created in the House since the Committee on the Budget in 1974 (Koempel 2007, 51) – the new committee was granted jurisdiction over "homeland security policy," "the organization and administration of the Department of Homeland Security," and "functions of the Department of Homeland Security" (House Rule X 2009, cl. 1[i]). In terms of jurisdiction, this change carved off little from other House committees, thereby limiting the reach of the new committee.

In early 2003, the Senate Appropriations Committee responded similarly, creating the Subcommittee on Homeland Security and adjusting the jurisdiction of its previously existing subcommittees. On the authorization side, the Senate did not use a select committee, instead relying on private negotiations and deliberations before the full chamber. Scant proposals to create a new, independent Committee on Homeland Security were stifled almost immediately (Laskow 2009). In October 2004, the Senate passed Senate Resolution 445, renaming the Governmental Affairs Committee as the Homeland

Security and Governmental Affairs Committee (HSGAC). While the change was not purely cosmetic, the confined homeland security jurisdiction of HSGAC was detailed in Senate Resolution 445, and took effect in the 109th Congress (2005–2007; Koempel 2005, 4)

On the surface, the changes in the House and Senate were significant. However, they occurred with minimal substantive changes to the jurisdiction of other committees. Whereas the two authorizing committees gained authority over DHS itself, explicit jurisdiction over functional aspects of homeland security (i.e., immigration, natural disaster management) and specific DHS agencies remained with legacy committees. In other cases, particularly the Senate, chamber rules were more specific regarding what the homeland security committees would *not* have jurisdiction over. This continuing lack of clarity over jurisdiction enabled continued fragmentation between committees over homeland security legislation, functions, and agencies. In the 110th Congress (2007–2009) alone, DHS officials would testify at 374 hearings, before 95 different committees and subcommittees.

As opposed to a short-lived response, the legislative tendency toward disaggregation has not only continued in response to the emergence of homeland security; it appears to have accelerated. However, one cannot consider the experience of DHS in isolation. The congressional landscape of homeland security may appear daunting, but it also demands comparison to other policy areas. The macropolitical evolution of energy policy and institutions in the 1970s is but one cautionary tale. Through a comparative analysis with other executive departments, the relative plight of DHS and homeland security can be more completely understood.

A COMPARATIVE ANALYSIS OF FRAGMENTATION

Fragmentation in the 110th Congress

Congressional fragmentation over the Department of Homeland Security, and homeland security in general, has been lamented since the department's inception (Laskow 2009). However, this phenomenon must be examined in comparative context. DHS has not been the first executive department to lament its frequent visits to Capitol Hill; homeland security is not the first substantive policy area to inspire competition among congressional committees. How has congressional jurisdiction over other executive departments evolved since their inception? With this question in mind, we will look cross-sectionally at the 110th Congress (2007–2009) and compare the congressional experiences of three other, relatively new departments: Defense, Energy, and

Transportation. They are diverse in terms of size, personnel, budget, and mission, and each was created under different circumstances through the amalgamation of different agencies. But the key commonality – the process and degree of jurisdictional consolidation since departmental inception – represents a dynamic that all have experienced. Compared to older departments, they share a newness that permits a more salient analysis of their own experiences with fragmentation.

Before proceeding, a critical distinction must be made. Committee jurisdictions as awarded by House Rule X and Senate Standing Rule XXV are both quite clear and quite ambiguous. As in the U.S. Constitution, this balance between clarity and ambiguity establishes legal authority while inviting competition, thereby ensuring that power does not accumulate excessively in one institution. However, the notion of "committees of primary jurisdiction" is a basic but necessary generalization. For a particular department or policy area, which authorizing committee in the House and the Senate possesses primary responsibility for legislating and overseeing their agencies and functions? As committees typically evolve in tandem with the creation of a new executive department, a focus on one committee of primary jurisdiction enables one to most effectively examine that relationship. How should "primary jurisdiction" be determined? In some cases, authority over a department or agency is clearly comprehensively granted to certain committees. For example, the House and Senate rules specifically award jurisdiction over the Department of Defense to their respective Armed Services Committees (Rule X, cl.1(c)(4); Rule XXV, cl.1(c)(1)3.); jurisdiction over the Coast Guard is explicitly given to the transportation committees in each house (Rule X, cl.1(r)(1); Rule XXV, cl.1(f)(1)1.). Where formal jurisdictions are less clear, others have suggested alternate bases of primary committee authority: preponderance of hearings concerning a department or agency (Adler 2002, 95); bill referrals (King 1997, 126–134); explicit jurisdiction over component agencies, functions, or policy areas (Adler 2008, 85–86); or budget dollars controlled for component programs and policy areas (Adler 2002, 95).

For purposes of this study, committees of primary jurisdiction, as noted in Table 5.1, were determined based on explicit jurisdictions over departments in the House and Senate rules wherever possible. In the few cases where this was unclear, clear grants of authority over component functions or policy areas also factored in the determination of "primary" status. An examination of jurisdictions in House Rule X and Senate Standing Rule XXV resulted in the designation of the committees of primary jurisdiction shown in Table 5.1.

This cross-sectional analysis included data from all committee and subcommittee hearings in the 110th Congress (2007–2009) at which DHS, DOD,

TABLE 5.1. *Committees of primary jurisdiction*

Department	House	Senate
Defense	Armed Services	Armed Services
Energy	Energy and Commerce	Energy and Natural Resources
Homeland Security	Homeland Security	Homeland Security and Governmental Affairs
Transportation	Transportation and Infrastructure	Commerce, Science, and Transportation

Department	Number of Committees, Subcommittees before which Department Testified	Number of Hearings– 110th Congress	Number of Hearings– Committees of Primary Jurisdiction	Percentage of Hearings– Committees of Primary Jurisdiction
DOD	43	261	126	48.28%
DOE	36	104	53	50.96%
DHS	95	376	187	49.73%
DOT	32	125	87	69.60%

FIGURE 5.1. Departmental hearing data (110th Congress) – Committees of primary jurisdiction.

DOE, and DOT officials testified. The data were drawn from the legislative/governmental affairs websites of each department, and included the chamber in which the hearing was held; the committee/subcommittee holding the hearing; the executive department and subagency testifying at each hearing; the position and affiliation of departmental officials testifying at the hearing; and subject matter of the hearing. As illustrated in Figure 5.1, across all four departments, these data provided a comparison of each department's legislative activity.

Overall, these data demonstrate that DHS is challenged in several ways. Whereas the other three departments answer to an average of 36 different committees and subcommittees, DHS testified before 160 percent more (95). The 374 hearings before the House and Senate involving DHS were clearly more numerous than those of the other departments, although the newest department is disproportionately smaller in terms of personnel (DOD has more) and funding (DOD and DOE have bigger budgets). Committees of primary jurisdiction conducted the majority of hearings for DOE (50.94 percent), and a considerable 69.9 percent of hearings for DOT. In contrast, less than

50 percent of hearings involving DHS – as well as DOD – were before their respective committees. More recently, Deputy DHS Secretary Janet Holl Lute asserted that the number of committees overseeing DHS had climbed to 108 in the 111th Congress (2009–1011; NPR 2010).

This emphasis on committees of jurisdiction provides a general sense of the autonomy of those committees and the scope of congressional demands upon parallel departments. However, the picture is incomplete. By this measure, DOD seems to have a more fragmented experience under the Armed Services Committees than DHS under its primary committee. When the focus is solely on primary committees, jurisdictional clarity surrounding the corresponding department may not be readily apparent; the committee of primary jurisdiction may have a single competitor or numerous committees attempting to build jurisdiction through hearings and non-legislative activity. To provide a more holistic appraisal of fragmentation, several other measures of jurisdictional clarity have been developed. For example, Baumgartner and Jones (2000) applied a model of congressional jurisdictional entropy that incorporated the number of committees overseeing a given policy area, the number of distinct subtopics on which hearings were held, the size of professional committee staff, the number of hearings conducted, and the presence or absence of recent structural reform (Baumgartner and Jones 2000, 340)

A more modest but pertinent methodology has been the use of Herfindahl analysis – commonly used by economists to analyze market concentration – to measure jurisdictional clarity. Applying the approach of Hardin (1998), Baumgartner and Jones (2000) examined "overlap" over certain policy areas by cross-referencing the number of committees active on that issue. By comparing the proportion of activity by all committees in a policy area, a measure of jurisdictional concentration – the Herfindahl index – is determined. On a scale of 0 to 100 (index is multiplied by 100 to ease comparison) a value of 100 represents complete jurisdictional clarity, a situation in which one committee conducted all hearings on a topic. A score of 0 would mean total fragmentation or overlap, showing that a maximum of committees exercised jurisdiction over a policy area. The strength of this measure is that it integrates the activity of all committees exercising jurisdiction over a policy area.

As opposed to policy areas, Table 5.2 presents Herfindahl indices – a measure of overlap or jurisdictional clarity – for each of the four departments discussed earlier.

While reaffirming some of the relative trends between departments, these indicators of jurisdictional clarity provide additional detail in distinguishing between the House and Senate. In more absolute terms, a Herfindahl index of 50 would indicate equal hearing activity between two committees over

TABLE 5.2. *Jurisdictional clarity (Herfindahl index)*
in 110th Congress, by department

Department	House	Senate
Homeland Security	26.66	40.09
Defense	39.63	27.74
Energy	17.90	61.91
Transportation	49.85	50.89

a contested department (or policy area); among four committees, the index would be 25.

The jurisdictional clarity surrounding DHS is therefore low in relative and absolute terms. This indicates a high degree of fragmentation, particularly in the House. The picture appears less bleak in the Senate. What is remarkable is that the Herfindahl index for DHS is not the lowest among the four departments. At first glance, it appears that House oversight over DOE is even more fragmented, while DOD experienced greater fragmentation in the Senate. However, this is deceiving.

An examination of the modality of departmental oversight is illuminating. The low jurisdictional clarity surrounding DOE in the House is due to a particularly active rival to the Energy and Commerce Committee (E&C), the Science and Technology Committee (S&T). Oversight of DOE was effectively bi-modal; while E&C held 34.3 percent of hearings where DOE testified, S&T hosted 22.9 percent. No other House committee held more than 8.5 percent of DOE hearings. DOD, which appears subject to greater jurisdictional ambiguity than DHS in the Senate, faced the same scenario. While the Senate Armed Services Committee hosted 48.5 percent of hearings where DOD testified, the Homeland Security and Governmental Affairs Committee (HSGAC) held 22.1 percent; the next closest competitor – Veterans Affairs – hosted 13.2 percent. Whereas a primary competitor poses a challenge, it monopolizes the competition in ways that mitigate jurisdictional competition. In other words, having a strong rival can effectively monopolize the competition, minimizing strong jurisdictional claims from other aspiring committees.

The fragmentation of DHS oversight was not bi-modal in either chamber. In the House and Senate, there was no strong rival to the committees of primary jurisdiction. Instead, there were dozens of them. Among those committees providing the strongest challenges to the House Committee on Homeland Security (CHS) and Senate HSGAC – the judiciary and transportation committees – their enhanced engagement of DHS was due to their *clear* jurisdiction over component agencies (i.e., Coast Guard) or functions (i.e., natural disaster management, immigration) of DHS. The range of other competing committees emerged from wide jurisdictional seams in the House and Senate rules. With such tremendous jurisdictional ambiguity regarding homeland security, combined with intense macropolitical attention on the issue, fragmentation is the likely result.

Fragmentation in the "Infant Congress"

A cross-sectional analysis of these four departments in the 110th Congress (2007–2009) is revealing. However, each department is a different age. As the jurisdictional regime in Congress evolves in tandem with a corresponding department or policy area, it is equally important to consider these committee-department or committee-policy relationships in political time. King (1994, 49–50) notes that committees, in their quest to build jurisdiction over contested policy areas, often do so gradually and incrementally. As a result, jurisdictional control and the relationships between committees, agencies, and policy areas are ever changing. To accurately compare the severity of fragmentation over the fledgling DHS, one must consider DOD, DOE, and DOT at similar points in their own bureaucratic "lives." More grandly stated, committee dynamics must be examined longitudinally, as well as cross-sectionally (Baumgartner and Jones 1993, 657–658). Although the oversight picture for DHS may be daunting, it may be that extreme fragmentation is a common growing pain for a young department.

To analyze the experience of each department in parallel political time, the notion of an "infant congress" is necessary. In the political life of an executive department, an "infant congress" refers to the first complete, two-year congress following the inception of that department. In almost every case, new departments do not open their doors the same time a new congress is sworn in. Therefore, to ensure consistency in departmental comparisons, data on the experience of DHS, DOD, DOE, and DOT were drawn from the first full congress following the creation of each department. As a measure of jurisdictional clarity for the congressional activity surrounding that department, Herfindahl indices were again calculated using hearing data. Table 5.3 captures jurisdictional clarity for each department in its "infant congress," further broken down by House and Senate.

In comparison to the other three departments, DHS experienced a higher degree of fragmentation during its first full, two-year congress. In particular, the score of 10.64 indicates extremely high fragmentation over homeland security oversight in the 109th House (2005–2007). Although the same measure in the 109th Senate (2005–2007) was higher – 19.92 – jurisdiction over homeland

TABLE 5.3 *Jurisdictional clarity (Herfindahl index) in "Infant Congresses,"*
by department

Dept.	House			Senate		
	Committee of primary jurisdiction	Congress (years)	Jurisdictional clarity	Committee of primary jurisdiction	Congress (years)	Jurisdictional clarity
DHS	CHS	109th (2005–2007)	10.64	HSGAC	109th (2005–2007)	19.62
DOD	HASC	81st (1949–51)	52.90	SASC	81st (1949–51)	49.62
DOE	E&C	96th (1979–81)	15.55	E&NR	96th (1979–81)	28.17
DOT	T&I	91st (1969–71)	22.67	CS&T	91st (1969–71)	38.33

security was far more ambiguous than for the other departments. What the fledgling DHS is experiencing seems to be worse than the jurisdictional competition affecting the other departments in each chamber of Congress. The exception is energy in the 96th House (1979–1981), the first full congress following the establishment of DOE. Recalling the earlier discussion of the energy crises of the 1970s and the resulting warfare between congressional committees over energy jurisdiction, this indicates a low level of jurisdictional clarity in the House. Nonetheless, fragmentation over homeland security is relatively high, even when compared to other departments in their youth.

IMPLICATIONS FOR POLICY

[C]reating the Department of Energy was child's play compared to creating this new department [DHS].... If the 88 committees of some jurisdiction in the Congress are dealing with the Department of Homeland Security, they cannot successfully achieve that common mission of protecting the homeland. Thus, it will wind up that some committees, some committee members, some staffs will say to that Department of Homeland Security, unless you do X, unless you give us this response, we are going to take it out on the department. And you will have fragmentation that will be pulling the department apart. It will be responding to the fragmentation that would continue to exist on Capitol Hill.
James Schlesinger, former Department of Energy
Secretary (2003, 24)

Homeland security is a case study in extreme congressional fragmentation. On an abstract level, this is a problem of jurisdictional ambiguity, an example of how the distributive and electoral pressures of Congress heighten existing rivalries as new, undefined issues emerge. Committees compete. Across the range of motivations for committee activity – informational, distributive, partisan – the incentives to accumulate jurisdiction and influence over a policy area like homeland security, or a young department like DHS, are considerable. As with energy policy in the 1970s or health care policy in the 1990s, the result is a complex web of oversight and a dizzying network of relationships between executive agencies and congressional panels. Approaching the operational and tactical levels, the governance implications of fragmentation on homeland security are far from abstract. The question posed at the beginning of this chapter – how a structural phenomenon like fragmentation or "hyperfragmentation" impacts policy making and implementation – reverberates at the level of senior leadership and across the tactical frontlines of homeland security.

Policy Coherence in Homeland Security

There is the general concern of policy coherence – the degree to which consensus exists on goals, public problems and policy areas are commonly understood, and policies are clearly targeted to key constituencies such as executive agencies or organized interests. Regardless of whether policy is "good" or "bad," May et al. (2006) note that the degree of coherence will determine the clarity of guidance to "policy targets" (i.e., executive agencies) and the viability of implementation. Where there is dominant involvement by congressional committees and executive agencies, policy tends to be clearer and more cohesive. Fragmentation has the opposite effect.

A lack of policy coherence tends to be self-reinforcing. Bellavita (2008) discusses the elusive nature of "homeland security" and how the lack of a common definition has heightened fragmentation, undermined unity of effort, and inhibited the commonality of culture within DHS. Is homeland security purely about terrorism? Should it include natural disaster preparedness, response, and recover? Should the definition of "disaster" or "hazard" be more broad, to include "all hazards," other natural or man-made incidents, or even social trends that threaten the stability of American society? Or is homeland security whatever DHS does, to include the legacy missions of agencies such as the Coast Guard, Animal and Plant Health Inspection Service (APHIS), or the Secret Service? Ambiguity obscures common definitions and purpose, thereby fostering fragmentation; as competition continues between congressional committees, efforts to develop common terms of reference and fashion coherent policies are further inhibited.

May et al. (2009) demonstrate how the misalignment between a fragmented committee system and an amalgamated DHS has undermined the
cohesiveness of homeland security policy and the department. Applying a
broad definition of homeland security, including eight policy subsystems –
border security, domestic security, food safety, information security, natural
disaster preparedness, public health emergencies, technological hazards, and
transportation safety – they analyze the correlation between agency and committee control. As regards border protection and natural disaster preparedness, coordination and cohesion have improved since the inception of DHS.
Indeed, these two policy subsystems represent cases where more powerful
congressional committees *did* cooperate to effect important institutional
innovations: the integration of legacy immigration agencies into Immigration
and Customs Enforcement (ICE), Citizenship and Immigration Services
(CIS), and Customs and Border Protection, and the Post-Katrina Emergency
Management Reform Act (PKEMRA) of 2006. In other areas studied, however, the integrative impacts of executive consolidation and congressional
fragmentation have been modest or negative, attributable to these divergent
institutional responses since September 11 (May et al. 2009).

Implications for Departmental Leadership and Agencies

More practically, fragmentation poses considerable challenges for the leadership, direction, and vision of DHS. By any standard, the sheer workload
created by hundreds of hearings and thousands of briefings and reports
in a two-year congress seems daunting. In a memorandum to the House
Committee on Homeland Security in 2007, Secretary Chertoff estimated
that the average time to prepare and rehearse testimony for a routine hearing was 60 work hours, with some hearings requiring over 200 work hours
(Chertoff 2007, 9). Multiplied by the 370+ hearings and 5,000+ involving DHS in the 110th Congress (2007–2009; NPR 2010), the demands on
the time and energy of departmental leadership is striking. In a hearing
before the House Select Committee on Homeland Security in 2003, former
House Speaker Thomas S. "Tom" Foley (D-WA) argued, "[T]here is not
only a need to bring some focus and scope to the oversight function, but
there is a critical need to avoid the [distraction] of members of this new
Department from having to respond day by day to dozens and dozens of
different requests for testimony, and that is predictable" (Foley 2003, 7). One
must wonder what the opportunity costs have been for the DHS Secretariat
or the heads of the department's operational components. "It does get to the
point that it is distracting to other objectives that you're trying to achieve,"

noted Asa Hutchinson, former Administrator of the Transportation Security Administration (Laskow 2009).

"[Testimony] consumes an awful lot of time. But truthfully … most people miss the biggest problem. And that is that the direction you get from the committees tends to be inconsistent" (NPR 2010). DHS is equally accountable to committees with legislative jurisdiction and, to a degree, oversight jurisdiction. However, as the range of congressional panels overseeing DHS expands, the same committees and subcommittees are not accountable to each other; nor must their direction to executive agencies be uniform. This creates tremendous potential for inconsistent, competing, or contradictory guidance.

As the Coast Guard balances its legacy missions with the mandates of homeland security, the agency has had to navigate the conflicting emphases of different committees. In the 110th Congress (2007–2009), the House Transportation and Infrastructure (T&I) Committee responded to the concerns of maritime industry by closely scrutinizing the Coast Guard's performance of its marine safety missions – merchant mariner licensing, inspection of deep draft and small passenger vessels, marine casualty investigation. Then Transportation and Infrastructure Chairman James L. Oberstar (D-MN) challenged ADM Thad Allen, then the commandant of the Coast Guard, to explain the connection between marine safety and homeland security missions. While Allen articulated the relationship between maritime safety and security, as well as a pointed defense of the service's search and rescue mission, the exchange reflected the jurisdictional cross-pressures on the Coast Guard (Allen 2007). Against concurrent demands in the 110th Congress (2007–2009) to increase armed patrols and screening of maritime cargo – including the requirement in H.R. 1 to scan or inspect 100 percent of all foreign containers entering U.S. ports (H.R. 1, 2007) – the Coast Guard continues an operational balancing act shared by other DHS agencies. Similarly, FEMA's emphasis on legacy functions, beyond pure terrorism response and recovery, continue amid T&I's proposals that it should be removed from DHS, rebalance its mission priorities, and be restored to independent Cabinet-level status (*Congressional Record* 2009, E412). Both examples evoke the wide range of definitions for homeland security, and the tension between the new mandates of homeland security and legacy missions of DHS agencies.

In both cases, Transportation and Infrastructure's oversight has represented a desire to reaffirm its authority over agencies within its legislative jurisdiction and leverage its informational expertise over DHS policy making and implementation. This is one of many challenges to the autonomy of the House Committee on Homeland Security, an embodiment of dispersed authority and jurisdictional competition.

To a degree, diverse guidance is a function – and perhaps a benefit – of the informational aspects of committees. Widespread specialization and expertise are primary functions of a diverse committee system. Much of the initial resistance to new homeland security committees came from established committee chairs. In defense of fragmentation on informational grounds, John D. Dingell, Jr. (D-MI; 2004), former chairman of the House Energy and Commerce Committee, remarked:

> I went through the energy crisis, in the 1970s, and I have gone through a number of other problems of similar character, and I never found that there was anything other than benefit to be achieved by having a large number of committees viewing these questions from the standpoint of their own experience and expertise. And I would say that this happened very much during the time of the 1970s when the Energy Administrator or the chairmen of the regulatory bodies or later the head of the Department of Energy would come up to report to different committees about how they were conducting their business. (Dingell 2004, 49)

However, for all its advantages, decentralized expertise also creates the potential for redundant oversight. For example:

- In the 109th Congress (2005–2007), DHS testified before five different committees and subcommittees on *worksite enforcement* between June and July 2006.
- Between July and November 2006, department officials testified seven times, before five different committees and subcommittees, on *border security*.
- In the 110th Congress (2007–2009), between February and April 2007, DHS officials testified five times on the issue of *post-Hurricane Katrina housing* before four different congressional panels (Chertoff 2007, 4–6).

Redundancy, and the distraction it can pose for senior departmental leadership, illustrates that informational efficiency can be double-edged. Given the activity of 108 committees and subcommittees in the 111th Congress (2009–2011), congressional fragmentation over homeland security may represent more of an imbalance between information and efficiency.

Another effect of fragmented jurisdiction is delay. With its array of veto points, the legislative process in the House and Senate is inherently complex. The competition and dispersal of authority among committees – and the potential for joint or multiple referrals – further complicates the path that homeland security legislation must follow. Whereas appropriations may be delayed, but will eventually pass, the enactment of authorization bills has not been a given. In 2008, Congress did not pass the annual DHS Authorization Bill, owing largely to the number of committees involved with negotiation (Strohm 2008). In the 109th Congress (2005–2007), chemical security legislation was delayed for months due to jurisdictional posturing between the House Homeland Security and Energy and Commerce Committees. Evidencing the importance of issue framing, bill draftsmanship, and jurisdictional clarity, both committees fought overall referral of the bill, with the Energy and Commerce Committee attempting to redirect the legislation by striking the word "terrorism" from its text. In 2006, the Senate Committees on Finance, Homeland Security and Governmental Affairs, and Commerce, Science, and Transportation wrestled over a port security bill for months. Ken Nahigian, a counsel for the Commerce, Science, and Transportation Committee, observed, "We had almost identical bills for port security coming out of each committee. For 30 straight days we were locked up in a room from 7:00 A.M. to 1:00 A.M. arguing about jurisdiction" (quoted in Laskow 2009). After four years without a Coast Guard authorization bill – owing largely to disagreements between committees in sequential referral – Congress passed H.R. 3619 on September 28, 2010. Enacted were a number of provisions for Coast Guard modernization and acquisition reform that had been delayed for years (H.R. 3619, 2010). In each case, distributive and informational pressures exacerbated the conflict between committees, extending the normal timeline for homeland security authorizations.

The effect of committee fragmentation at the operational and tactical levels of homeland security is an open question. As an overarching concern, it pertains to any functionally responsible executive agency that is accountable to multiple congressional panels. The connection between everyday DHS operations and the coherence of the homeland security subsystem may be indirect. However, the clarity and consistency of policy, and the focus of senior DHS leaders, connects very closely to "the field." In an early plea for jurisdictional consolidation, Richard S. Conley noted, "With responsibility for components of this DHS spread out across thirteen committees, Congress must rationalize the authorization and appropriations process or the department's operations may be hindered" (2003, 8). For leaders and operators in homeland security, that possibility may be sobering.

CONCLUSION

After September 11, the emergence of homeland security as a new policy area placed a tremendous stress on the political system. The institutional reactions in Congress and the executive branch were opposite but equally momentous:

fragmentation versus consolidation. Whereas the creation of the Office (OHS) and Department of Homeland Security (DHS) – in which Congress was a key partner – were attempts to resolve widespread coordination problems, the House and Senate did not act in parallel. Jurisdictional competition, the central collective action problem characterizing Congress, drove dozens of committees toward the issue of homeland security and attempts to define it in terms favorable to their explicit jurisdiction. This is the essence of subsystem and committee politics. Drawing a parallel to the energy crises of the 1970s, this chapter has explored the evolution of legislative-executive relationships and has attempted to understand how the distributive, information, and partisan cross-pressures on committees drive the phenomenon of fragmentation in an emergent policy area.

Institutional reform is a perennially popular and quixotic cause in American government. During the House's hearings to assess the need for a new homeland security committee, Thomas Mann observed, "Congressional history is littered with the failure of jurisdictional reform" (Mann 2003, 28). Nonetheless, Congress has periodically reformed itself, and committee jurisdictions are continually changing. On occasion, the House and Senate have passed bold statutory reforms to committee jurisdictions and internal procedures, such as the Legislative Reorganization Act in 1946, which abolished 47 standing committees and streamlined others. In other cases, procedural measures such as sequential referrals can be used to control the path of legislation or limit the scope of committee activity. Most typically – and perhaps meaningfully – the process of committee reform is ongoing and incremental, a process of "common law" change as jurisdictional conquests become rooted in precedents and bill referrals (King 1997, 126–134). As the committees of primary homeland security jurisdiction evolve in tandem with DHS, the more subtle common law approach will likely be their most viable strategy in the short term.

The congressional fragmentation of homeland security oversight has been unmatched by the experiences of other executive departments, even in their respective youths. The dispersal, the ambiguity of jurisdiction in Congress, has diminished the overall clarity and coherence of homeland security policy and has presented the DHS leadership with a significant opportunity cost that may exceed the informational benefits of the committee system. In this regard, the parallel to the energy crises of the 1970s is sobering. In the years since energy policy emerged as a new jurisdictional battleground, its policy-making environment – legislative and executive – has stabilized a great deal. This invites optimism. However, as the relationship between DHS and Congress evolves, the implications of fragmentation for those on the front lines – tactical coxswains, airport screeners, Border Patrol agents, marine inspectors – remains the most salient inquiry.

6

Congress and Intelligence

Loch K. Johnson

Sixteen federal intelligence agencies comprise America's Intelligence Community – a vital first line of defense to protect the nation against terrorists and other threats (Johnson 2011a). Yet, in the manner of other government organizations, they can fall prey to Lord Acton's well-known prophecy that "power tends to corrupts and absolute power corrupts absolutely."[1] History reveals that time and again a nation's secret services have turned their disquieting capabilities for the surveillance and manipulation of enemies against the very citizens they were meant to shield. Efforts by lawmakers in Congress to maintain accountability over intelligence agencies ("oversight," in the awkward expression of American political scientists) has proven difficult and has often failed.

The thesis that secret government organizations can be a danger to open societies should hardly astound. After all, intelligence agencies are made up of human beings, flawed by nature; consequently, one can anticipate intelligence failures and abuses. No mere mortal is omniscient, nor can any human lay claim to Kantian purity in government affairs. Yet societies seem regularly taken aback by the occurrence of intelligence failures and scandals. They express amazement and dismay that espionage services have been unable to provide a clairvoyant warning of impending danger; or that they have spied or plotted against citizens at home, not just adversaries abroad. In contrast to this naivety, the American founder James Madison understood that nations were led not by angels but by mere mortals; failure and scandal were inevitable.

With admirable Midwest common sense, President Harry S. Truman echoed Madison's cautionary words found in *Federalist Paper 51* about the

---

[1] In a speech presented in July 8, 1975, Senator Frank Church (for whom the author served as a speech-writer at the time) suggested that Lord Action's famous admonition should be rephrased: "All secrecy corrupts. Absolute secrecy corrupts absolutely."

importance of constitutional safeguards against government abuse. "You see," Truman said, "the way a government works, there's got to be a housecleaning every now and then" (quoted in Miller 1973, 420). Citizens in the democracies can throw up their hands in despair over the fact that intelligence errors and misdeeds are inescapable; or they can acknowledge the limits and the foibles of human beings and adopt measures to lessen their effects.

THE EVOLUTION OF SAFEGUARDS AGAINST INTELLIGENCE ABUSE IN THE UNITED STATES

Efforts to fashion methods of accountability to supervise America's secret agencies have gone through several phases since the Republic's early days. The first phase lasted from the signing of the Constitution in 1787 until a major domestic espionage scandal came to light during the Watergate era almost 200 years later.

The Era of Trust (1787–1974)

Throughout the Era of Trust, intelligence was set apart from the rest of the government. The dominant attitude among members of Congress was that the honorable men and women in the intelligence agencies would have to be trusted to protect the United States against dangerous and unscrupulous forces at home and abroad. "No, no, my boy, don't tell me," a leading Senate over-seer, John Stennis (D-MS), told Director of Central Intelligence (DCI) James R. Schlesinger in 1973 when the spy chief attempted to provide a full account-ing of operations abroad conducted by the Central Intelligence Agency (CIA; Johnson 1994a). "Just go ahead and do it, but I don't want to know."

While most of the nation's intelligence officers have indeed been honorable individuals, the writers of the Constitution could have predicted that eventu-ally power – perhaps especially secret power – would be misused. Resonating this bedrock principle of government accountability, Supreme Court Justice Louis Brandeis reminded Americans two centuries later that the founders had strived "not to promote efficiency but to preclude the exercise of arbitrary power. The purpose was not to avoid friction, but, by means of the inevit-able friction incident to the distribution of the governmental powers among three departments, to save the people from autocracy" (*Myers v. United States*, 1926).

Yet this sound constitutional doctrine gave way to the exigencies of fighting against enemies of the state, whether the Barbary pirates of yore or commu-nists of the Cold War. The United States, the world's first democracy, would follow the practice of regimes around the world and throughout earlier history, setting its secret agencies outside the framework of checks and balances and accountability that are the trademarks of democratic societies. A hostile world demanded no less; efficiency would have to take pride of place over civil liberties.

This is not to say that the U.S. intelligence agencies were devoid of all vestiges of accountability. During the Cold War, most of their activities were approved by officials in the White House and the National Security Council. Further, from time to time, the CIA would report, or at least try to report, to lawmakers, only to find deaf ears on Capitol Hill. Now and then, as in the aftermath of the Bay of Pigs fiasco, the embarrassing U-2 shoot-down over the Soviet Union in 1960, and the controversy surrounding CIA subsidies for the National Student Association in 1968, a few lawmakers would call for inquiries and intelligence reform; but there were never enough reformers in Congress to bring about significant change. While Barrett (2005) argues that the devotion of lawmakers to intelligence oversight has been underrated in the scholarly and popular literature, congressional approval of intelligence programs seems nonetheless to have been highly discretionary during the Era of Trust. For the most part, presidents and lawmakers provided DCIs and other intelligence managers with broad authority to conduct secret operations at home and abroad as they saw fit.[2] In the autumn of 1974, all this would change.

The Era of Uneasy Partnership (1974–1986)

Belief in intelligence exceptionalism underwent radical revision in the United States when the *New York Times* reported in 1974 that the CIA had been engaged in domestic espionage against our own citizens.[3] The Bay of Pigs, U-2 shoot-downs, and CIA student subsidies were one thing, but spying on

---

[2]   For research that has found little meaningful accountability in these early days, see Ransom (1970) and Walden (1975). For more current accounts that continue to find Congress weak in the exercise of intelligence oversight, see Kathleen Clark, "'A New Era of Openness?' Disclosing Intelligence to Congress under Obama," *Constitutional* Commentary, Vol. 26 (2010), pp. 1–20; Jennifer Kibbe, "Congressional Oversight of Intelligence: Is the Solution Part of the Problem?" *Intelligence and National Security*, February 2010, pp. 24–49; Anne Joseph O'Connell, "The Architecture of Smart Intelligence: Structuring and Overseeing Agencies in the Post-9/11 World," *California Law Review*, Vol. 94 (December 2006), pp. 1655–1744; Amy B. Zegart, "Domestic Politics of Irrational Intelligence Oversight," *Political Science Quarterly*, forthcoming; and Amy Zegart and Julie Quinn, "Congressional Intelligence Oversight: The Electoral Disconnection," *Intelligence and National Security*, 25 (December 2010), pp. 744–766.
[3]   See the reporting of Seymour Hersh in the *New York Times* throughout the autumn and winter months of 1974, especially from December 22 to 31.

American voters quite another. In the context of this stunning revelation, con-current *Times* reporting on the agency's covert actions against the Allende regime in Chile – a democratically elected government – took on added weight and drew further criticism of America's secret operations. Reacting with rare alacrity, Congress set up panels of inquiry in January of 1975: first the Church Committee in the Senate (led by Democratic Senator Frank F. Church of Idaho) and what eventually became the Pike Committee in the House (led by Democratic Representative Otis G. Pike of New York). Not to be left behind, the Ford administration established a presidential investigative commission, led by (and named after) Vice President Nelson Rockefeller.

The Church Committee, on which the author served as assistant to the chairman, dug deeper than the other panels, spending 16 months on its inves-tigation and issuing a set of public reports that stood over six feet high, as well as other reports that remain classified (U.S. Senate 1976).[4] The Church Committee confirmed that the *Times* was correct about CIA surveillance within the United States, as well as covert action against the democratic government of Chile; but the panel found that the newspaper accounts had only scratched the surface of wrongdoing by America's intelligence organiza-tions. The investigative findings demonstrated, for example, that the CIA had opened the mail to and from selected American citizens, which generated 1.5 million names stored in the agency's computer bank (Operation CHAOS). Moreover, Army intelligence units had compiled dossiers on 100,000 U.S. citizens during the Vietnam war era; and the vast computer facilities of the National Security Agency (NSA) had monitored every cable sent overseas, or received from overseas, by Americans between 1947 and 1975 (Operation SHAMROCK), and had engaged as well in questionable wiretapping within the United States (Operation MINARET).

Among the most chilling of the Church Committee findings emerged from the vaults of the Federal Bureau of Investigation (FBI): Operation COINTELPRO. The bureau had created files on over one million Americans and carried out more than 500,000 investigations of "subversives" from 1960 to 1974 – without a single court conviction. As then-Senator Walter F. Mondale (D-MN), a member of the Church Committee, recalled (Johnson 2000): "No meeting was too small, no group too insignificant" to escape the

---

[4] The Church Committee also issued two special reports: U.S. Senate (1975a) and U.S. Senate (1975b). The leading works about the Church Committee are Loch K. Johnson, *A Season of Inquiry* (Lexington: University Press of Kentucky, 1985); and Frederick A. O. Schwarz, Jr., and Aziz Z. Huq, *Unchecked and Unbalanced: Presidential Power in a Time of Terror* (New York: New Press, 2007).

FBI's attention.[5] From 1956 to 1971, the bureau carried out secret smear campaigns against thousands of groups and individuals, simply because they had expressed opposition to the war in Vietnam or criticized the slow pace of the civil rights movement. The Klu Klux Klan made the bureau hit list as well – seemingly any group that failed to fit into J. Edgar Hoover's Norman Rockwell image of a loyal American. Target Number One for Hoover, though, was the civil rights leader Martin Luther King, Jr., the victim of many a campaign of lies and innuendo perpetrated by the bureau, including a blackmail attempt in 1964 that sought to push Dr. King into suicide on the eve of his acceptance speech for a Nobel Peace Prize.

Historian Henry Steele Commager correctly observed (1976, 32) that "perhaps the most threatening of all the evidence that [stemmed] from the findings of the Church Committee" was "the indifference of the intelligence agencies to constitutional restraint." As a result of the *Times* reporting and the congressional and the Rockefeller inquiries, lawmakers vowed to change this indifference through the institution of laws, regulations, and, above all, a new philosophy of meaningful and consistent legislative review of intelligence activities. It was time to say farewell to the earlier era of benign neglect.

The *Times* reporting and the investigations of 1975 led to a sea change in attitudes within the United States, and soon after inside other democracies around the world as well, about the need for better supervision of the secret services. On December 31, 1974, Congress passed the Hughes-Ryan Act, a law that was revolutionary in concept. It required the president to explicitly approve ("find" – therefore, the approval is called a "finding") all important covert actions. By requiring a statement of purpose about the covert action, endorsed by the commander in chief, this first step effectively ended the doctrine of plausible deniability, whereby presidents had sought to evade responsibility for covert actions and supposedly protect the reputation of the United States as a result. Next, the finding had to be reported to Congress in a "timely manner." Since 1976 and 1977, the reports are presented orally (in executive session) to SSCI and HPSCI.

The Hughes-Ryan law did not go so far as to require congressional *approval* of covert actions, but it did set up an opportunity for lawmakers to influence these operations. After a covert action briefing, nothing would stop members of the Senate Select Committee on Intelligence (SSCI) and the House Permanent Select Committee on Intelligence (HPSCI), meeting separately for the briefings, from expressing their opposition – or even having a vote

[5] See also Walter F. Mondale, with David Hage, *The Good Fight: A Life in Liberal Politics* (New York: Scribner, 2010).

on the merits of the covert action. Neither the opinions nor the vote would be legally binding, but a committee that was riled up over what members considered an ill-advised operation could only be ignored at political risk by the DCI.[6]

The nature of the opposition on Capitol Hill would matter. If it were only a junior member or two, the president might choose to ignore the criticism. If the opponents included powerful members of SSCI and HPSCI – say, the chairs – that would be a different story and a president would probably want to reconsider going forward with the covert action. Backing away might be prudent, as well, for a president facing majority opposition in both commit-tees. So while Hughes-Ryan provided no formal legal authority for Congress to stop a covert action in its tracks by committee votes, it did require reporting on these operations to legislative overseers and that sets the stage for political opposition to form against moving forward with the proposal.

Further, if SSCI and HPSCI opposed a covert action, but a president ignored this "suggestion," members of the two committees could convene a secret session of Congress and vote up-or-down to shut off money for the operation – an extreme contingency, but exactly what Congress did with the Boland Amendments to stop covert action in Nicaragua during the 1980s.[7] Constitutionally, an irate set of lawmakers could (but never have so far) bring impeachment proceedings against a president considered out of control in his or her conduct of a particularly questionable covert action.

Short of these more extreme responses, members of Congress could vote against replenishment of the CIA's Reserve for Contingency Fund, through which lawmakers annual provide seed money for covert actions so the White House can move swiftly if necessary in ordering the use of the "third option" in emergency situations. Just as one should think twice about pulling on the tail of a tiger, so does a president and a director of National Intelligence (DNI) think twice about entering a fight with a congressional committee. This sense of executive branch prudence gives to the Hughes-Ryan Act an added unwrit-ten dimension, even if the law is devoid of explicit authority for lawmakers to approve or disapprove these decisions.

Other statutes designed to define the boundaries of probity for the secret agencies would soon be passed in the wake of Hughes-Ryan, such as the

---

[6] As of 2004, the DNI office has been split into a separate director for the CIA, known as the Director of the Central Intelligence Agency or D/CIA, and a National Intelligence Director or DNI.

[7] On the seven Boland Amendments, each more restrictive, see *Congressional Quarterly,* "Boland Amendments: A Review," *Weekly Online* (May 23, 1987), 1043; and Henry K. Kissinger, "A Matter of Balance," *Los Angeles Times,* July 26, 1987, VI.

important Foreign Intelligence Surveillance Act (FISA) in 1978, which banned warrantless national security wiretaps. Two years later, Congress enacted a far-reaching law to further tighten supervision over America's secret agencies. Although only two pages in length, this Intelligence Oversight Act of 1980 has sharp teeth, requiring *prior*, not just timely, notice to SSCI and HPSCI, and on *all* important intelligence operations – collection and counterintelligence, too, not just covert action.

Beginning with the Hughes-Ryan Act and carrying on until the Iran-*contra* scandal of 1987, lawmakers, presidents, and DCIs attempted during this experimental Era of Uneasy Partnership to fashion a workable relationship between democratic openness, on the one hand, and effective espionage, on the other hand – that is, between liberty and security. The result was a dramatic increase in attention on Capitol Hill to intelligence activities. The difference between pre-1974 and post-1974 is as stark as night is to day. The Iran-*contra* affair would demonstrate, however, that this New Oversight was far from foolproof.

The Era of Distrust (1986–1991)

Efforts by the NSC staff and a few CIA officers during the Reagan years to bypass Congress and conduct covert actions against the Sandinista regime in Nicaragua – even though prohibited by the Boland Amendments – displayed a disquieting failure of the New Oversight that had been established in 1974–1980. Even when SSCI and HPSCI leaders directly questioned NSC staffers, including national security advisers Robert C. McFarlane and Vice Admiral John M. Poindexter, about the rumored super-secret organization, "The Enterprise," created by the NSC staff to carry out the covert actions, the lawmakers were deceived. The NSC simply lied to the lawmakers about their illicit operations.

Following their investigation into the scandal, lawmakers enacted new legislation to further tighten executive and legislative supervision over the secret agencies. The Inspector General Act of 1989 established a meaningful inspector general (IG) office at the CIA, confirmed by the Senate and with a mandate to keep the members of Congress regularly and fully informed of any improper activities at Langley. In addition, the Intelligence Oversight Act of 1991 clarified the meaning and the limits of covert action and required formal written approval by the president in a finding, not just a slippery verbal assent. With these measures, the government would launch another attempt at making the experiment in intelligence accountability work.

The Era of Partisan Advocacy (1991–2001)

A product chiefly of redistricting decisions across the country that produced an abundance of safe congressional districts, along with a harsh take-no-prisoners form of campaign rhetoric inflamed by a new Republican Speaker, Newt Gingrich of Georgia, the post-Iran-*contra* atmosphere in Washington proved poisonous to constructive bipartisan support for intelligence within SSCI and HPSCI. This sudden partisan divide on the oversight panels was a startling departure from the past (Barrett 2005, 459). Except for some acrimony and split votes generated by disagreements over whether to allow CIA covert actions in Nicaragua during the Reagan years, the committees had almost always registered unanimous votes as they decided on intelligence policies, with members from both parties driven by a sense that intelligence was an especially sensitive policy domain and ought to be placed above the normal partisan fray in Washington.

Yet in the period after the Republican takeover of the Hill in the 1990s, notes Aberbach (2002, 20), a new mood arose, one that was "hostile not only to the intent and behavior of political appointees, but to the missions of many federal programs and agencies." Both HPSCI and SSCI proved vulnerable to this rising partisan storm. Knott (2002, 57) attributes the growing polarization, in part, to a Republican wariness toward President Bill Clinton's foreign policy, as well as to a "simple partisan payback for years of perceived Democratic hectoring of Republican presidents." Acrimonious partisan politics swirled around the nomination of Robert M. Gates for DCI in 1991 – his second try, this time successful by the narrowest vote margin of any DCI nominee before or since. By 1997, intelligence – once considered above politics – had become as vituperative as any other policy domain. The candidacy of Anthony Lake, the incumbent Democratic national security adviser for DCI in 1996, led to a deeply bitter struggle between Democrats and Republicans in Congress, with Lake finally withdrawing his name from consideration. The hearings, described by an observer as "vitriolic" were punctuated by the most heated public exchanges across the aisle in SSIC's history (Ott 2003, 87).

The Era of Ambivalence (2001–Present)

Partisan squabbling over intelligence continued to roil SSCI and HPSCI after al Qaeda's attacks against the United States in 2001. Indeed, according to a keen observer of Congress, the bickering grew even more heated. "One could only marvel at the degree to which partisanship had come to infect the work of the two committee," writes L. Britt Snider (2005, 245), former SSCI counsel and a former CIA inspector general. "Once held up as models of how congressional committees should work, they now seemed no different from the rest" (ibid.).[8] Added to this internal political stress on the intelligence committees was a new ambivalence among their members toward the nation's secret agencies, displayed when the lawmakers merged temporarily into a Joint Committee to probe the tragic 9/11 intelligence failure. Some members of the Joint Committee scolded the intelligence agencies for their errors leading up to terrorist attacks against the United States. Even SSCI's chair, Senator Pat Roberts (R-KS), once an arch-defender of the CIA, bemoaned in 2004 that not a single official in the intelligence community had been "disciplined, let alone fired" for the mistakes related to 9/11, or for the faulty prognosis about weapons of mass destruction (WMD) in Iraq. In dismay, he concluded that the "community is in denial over the full extent of the shortcomings of its work" (Drogin, A1).

While Roberts and a few other once reliable champions of the intelligence agencies occasionally displayed flashes of ambivalence and rebellion, for the most part SSCI and HPSCI members fell into an oversight stupor. They forgot the warnings of Madison and the wisdom of the Constitution. Oversight came to mean rallying behind the president and the intelligence community to support the fighting that ensued in Iraq, Afghanistan, and against global terrorism. This was an amplification of a trend visible even before 9/11. Prior to the terrorist attacks on the American homeland that day, SSCI had held only a couple of hearings on the subject of Al Qaeda. On the House side, the oversight record was just as dismal. According to the Kean Commission, led by former governor Thomas H. Kean (R-NJ), members of HPSCI held only two hearings on terrorism from 1998 to 2001 – the fewest of any conducted by a security or foreign affairs panel on Capitol Hill in the period leading up to the 9/11 attacks (Kean Commission). In another measure of their relative inactivity, from 1976 to 1990 the two intelligence committees averaged fewer than two public hearings a year (Johnson, 96). Zegart (2011) found a low number of intelligence hearings in later sessions of Congress, as well.

"We really don't have, still don't have, meaningful congressional oversight [of the intelligence agencies,]" observed a GOP leader, Senator John McCain (R-AZ), in 2004 (McCain 2004). That same year the Kean Commission (2004, 420) concluded that "congressional oversight for intelligence – and counterterrorism – is now dysfunctional." A former staff member

---

[8]   See also L. Britt Snider, *The Agency and the Hill: CIA's Relationship with Congress, 1946–2004* (Washington, DC: Center for the Study of Intelligence, Central Intelligence Agency, 2008).

of the Church Committee observed further in 2009 that "unfortunately, the process of congressional oversight of intelligence, including covert action, so carefully crafted in the 1970s, is now regarded as something of a joke in Washington" (Treverton 2009, 232). When news broke in December of 2005 about warrantless wiretaps secretly carried out by the second Bush administration, some SSCI and HPSCI members complained publicly about the violations of the Foreign Intelligence Surveillance Act, but they never did much about it. According to a seasoned reporter with an intelligence beat (Gertz 2002, 113), the relationship between the oversight committee and the intelligence community had "degenerated into a mutual admiration society for secret agencies." Lawmakers seemed to have concluded that it was time to rally behind the secret agencies, even if some (like Roberts) felt occasional twinges of ambivalence toward the secret agencies because of the disturbing intelligence failures that had occurred from 2001 to 2003.

A SHOCK THEORY OF INTELLIGENCE ACCOUNTABILITY

The oversight performance of SSCI and HPSCI has fluctuated widely during the Cold War and since. Several observers have commented on these ups-and-downs. Writing about oversight in the years before the Church Committee investigation, for example, Ransom (1975, 38) noted that intelligence accountability had been "sporadic, spotty, and essentially uncritical." Even after the introduction of the New Oversight in 1975, students of the subject discerned little serious attention to this responsibility in recent years.[9] The chief cause of the inattentiveness derives from the nature of Congress: lawmakers seek reelection as their primary objective and they usually conclude that passing bills and raising campaign funds is a better use of their time than the often tedious review of executive branch programs. This is especially true for intelligence review. The examination of secret operations must take place in closed committee sanctuaries, outside of public view. Absent public awareness, the chances for credit-claiming, which is vital to a lawmaker's reelection prospects, becomes difficult (Mayhew 1974).

---

[9]   See, for example, Joel D. Aberbach, *Keeping a Watchful Eye: The Politics of Congressional Oversight* (Washington, DC: Brookings Institution, 1990); Christopher J. Deering, "Alarms and Patrols: Legislative Oversight in Foreign and Defense Policy," in Colton C. Campbell, Nicol C. Rae, and John F. Stack, Jr., eds., *Congress and the Politics of Foreign Policy* (Upper Saddle River, NJ: Prentice-Hall, 2003); and Loch K. Johnson, "Presidents, Lawmakers, and Spies: Intelligence Accountability in the United States," *Presidential Studies Quarterly*, Vol. 34 (December 2004), 828–837.

An examination of intelligence accountability in the United States since the Year of Intelligence in 1975 indicates a cyclical pattern of stimulus and response. A major intelligence scandal or failure – a shock – transforms the perfunctory performance of oversight into a burst of intense program scrutiny. This burst is followed by a period of reasonably attentive oversight activities that yields remedial legislation or other reforms designed to curb inappropriate intelligence operations in the future. Then comes the third phase of the shock cycle: a return to a middling practice of oversight. McCubbins and Schwartz (1984) offer the useful metaphor of "police patrolling" and "firefighting" to highlight these differences in commitment by lawmakers to oversight responsibilities. Patrolling consists of steadily checking up on the executive bureaucracy: the shining of a flashlight into darkened windows, a jiggling the lock on the door, walking the streets with a keen eye. In contrast, firefighting requires an emergency reaction to a calamity after it occurs. Lawmakers like firefighters jump on the fire truck when the alarm sounds and try to put out the conflagration. A prominent member of Congress has recently used the policing analogy. "There has been no cop on the beat," said Representative Henry A. Waxman (D-CA), then-chair of the House Oversight and Government Reform Committee, who accused Republicans of abandoning their oversight responsibilities. "And when there is no cop on the beat, criminals are more willing to engage in crimes" (quoted in Shenon 2007, A18).

Sometimes the high-intensity police patrolling that follows firefighting can last for months and, if the original shock was strong enough to produce extended media attention, even years. Once the firestorm (an intelligence failure or scandal) has subsided and reforms are in place, however, lawmakers return to a state of relative inattentiveness to intelligence activities – low-intensity, or perhaps even non-existent, police patrolling. This pattern is depicted in Figure 6.1.

To reach the level of a shock (or fire alarm), an allegation of intelligence failure or impropriety has to have sustained media coverage, with at least a few front-page stories. In 1974, for example, the *New York Times* had an unusually high run of stories on the CIA from June through December: some 200 articles. In December alone, nine stories on the agency made the front page – unprecedented at the time. Here was a steady drumbeat of chiefly negative reports, setting the stage for a strong public – and, therefore, congressional and presidential – reaction to the most explosive of these news items: Operation CHAOS, the CIA domestic spy scandal. On the eve of the next major intelligence scandal, the Iran-*contra* scandal, the *Times* carried 11 front-page stories in both October and November of 1986 about possible intelligence abuses

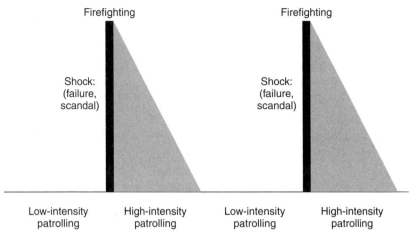

FIGURE 6.1. The cycle of intelligence shock and reaction by congressional overseers, 1974–2010.

related to a covert war in Nicaragua. The number jumped to 18 front-page stories in December, setting the stage for the Joint Committee investigation into the scandal in 1987.

Congress has greater authority than the media to investigate intelligence operations – from the power of the purse to the power of the subpoena and, ultimately, impeachment. The media, though, seems to have more will power to conduct oversight, driven in part by a profit motive to sell newspapers by exposing government scandals and failures. Intense media coverage may not be enough in itself to bring out the firefighters on Capitol Hill. The warrantless wiretaps of the second Bush administration, for instance, garnered considerable media attention but no major congressional inquiry. Such considerations as the personalities of congressional overseers – especially the attitudes of the SSCI and HPSCI chairs – and the existence of divided government can play a role, too (Johnson, Kuzenski, and Gellner 1992).

The Intelligence Shocks

Thirty-six years have passed since Congress began to take intelligence oversight seriously, near the end of 1974. During this time, lawmakers have devoted about six years of their time to intensive investigating (firefighting), stimulated by five major intelligence controversies or shocks (alarms). During the other 30 years (83 percent of the total) their time was spent in police patrolling – sometimes vigorously in the immediate aftermath of shocks, but for the most part in a perfunctory manner.

Major Alarm No. 1: The Domestic Spy Scandal (1974). The government of the United States responded to news allegations of CIA domestic spying with the Church, Pike, and Rockefeller inquiries. The findings of these panels led to the creation of SSCI and HPSCI, the FISA warrant requirements of 1978, and the Intelligence Oversight Act of 1980 with its dramatic requirement of prior notice to Congress for all important intelligence operations (Schwarz and Huq 2007; Johnson 1985).

Major Alarm No. 2: The Iran-Contra Scandal (1986). The Inouye-Hamilton Committee, chaired by Senator Daniel K. Inouye (D-HI) and Representative Lee H. Hamilton (D-IN), examined the Iran-*contra* allegations and disclosed unlawful intelligence operations by the NSC staff and a few CIA officials (U.S. Congress 1987). Its findings led to enactment of the CIA Inspector General Act of 1989, creating an inspector general (IG) with responsibilities to keep Congress informed of agency improprieties; and the Intelligence Oversight Act of 1991, which clarified covert action definitions and tightened its approval procedures.

Major Alarm No. 3: The Ames Counterintelligence Failure (1994). In response to the discovery of Aldrich Ames's treachery, the Congress created a presidential-congressional panel of inquiry, known as the Aspin-Brown Commission and led by Les Aspin and Harold Brown, both former secretaries of defense. The commission published a report calling for reforms across the board of intelligence activities, but with special emphasis on the need for a stronger DCI and for revealing to the public the annual aggregate intelligence budget figure (Aspin-Brown Commission 1996).[10]

Major Alarm No. 4: The 9/11 Attacks (2001). The failure of the intelligence agencies to warn the nation about the catastrophic terrorist attacks against the American homeland in 2001 led Congress to form a Joint Committee of inquiry (U.S. Congress Joint Committee 2002), known as the Graham-Goss Committee, after its leaders, Senator Bob Graham (D-FL) and Representative Porter J. Goss (R-FL). Subsequently, Congress urged the creation of a presidential investigative panel (Kean Commission) to probe further into the disaster. Moreover, HPSCI released to the public a critical evaluation of the CIA's human intelligence activities around the world, stressing the lack of good assets in key locations (U.S. House 2004).

Major Alarm No. 5: The Absence of WMDs in Iraq (2003). In light of an incorrect intelligence judgment about the likely presence of WMDs in Iraq, expressed in a National Intelligence Estimate of October 2002, Congress supported the creation of a presidential commission on intelligence to

---

[10] For an account of the commission's work, see Loch K. Johnson, *The Threat on the Horizon: America's Search for Security after the Cold War* (New York: Oxford University Press, 2011).

investigate this analytic failure. This panel was known as the Silberman-Robb Commission (2005), after its chairs: Judge Laurence H. Silberman and former senator Charles S. Robb (D-VA). Moreover, SSCI under Senator Roberts undertook a parallel but separate probe into the faulty WMD estimate, focusing on the CIA's errors, but elected not to examine questions about the poor use of warning intelligence by the Clinton and second Bush White Houses (U.S. Senate 2003).

As shown in Table 6.1, Congress embraced 13 key initiatives related to intelligence during the time span from 1974 to 2010. Only two occurred outside the context of a response to a major fire alarm. The first, the Intelligence Identities Act of 1982, was the result of a conclusion reached by members of Congress that a law was needed to provide stiff penalties against anyone who revealed, without proper authorization, the name of a U.S. intelligence officer or asset.[11] The second, the Whistleblowers Protection Act of 1998, evolved within SSCI and HPSCI over a long period of time, moved forward by a sense that an intelligence officer with a serious complaint against his or her agency should be provided protection by the Congress against retaliation by the agency for contacting lawmakers (if initially rebuffed by the agency's own oversight staff).[12] The other initiatives were the result of specific shocks and the sounding of major alarms, followed by inquiries and a finite period of aggressive patrolling.

A KEY ISSUE OF INTELLIGENCE ACCOUNTABILITY: WHO SHOULD BE INFORMED?

Several prominent issues have dominated the ongoing debate over how legislative oversight should be conducted with respect to the intelligence agencies. Among the most important is who should be kept informed on Capitol Hill. Before 1974, the answer was just a few lawmakers on the small intelligence subcommittees of the Armed Services and Appropriations Committees – if indeed the DCI deigned to tell them anything, or if the lawmakers were (unlike Senator Stennis) willing to listen. Today the "witting circle" on the Hill has widened to include members of SSCI and HPSCI, as well as (on some topics) selected members who serve on the appropriations, armed services, foreign affairs, and judiciary committees – with the top four leaders of Congress (two from each party) also informed on some emergency occasions. Intelligence officials, though, are not beyond playing games with these reporting rules,

---

[11] See Title VI, Sec. 601, 50 U.S.C. 421; Public law 97–200.
[12] Title VII, Intelligence Authorization Act for FY 1999; see Snider, *The Agency and the Hill*, pp. 71–72.

TABLE 6.1. *Intelligence shocks and oversight responses by U.S. lawmakers, 1974–2010*

Year	Stimulus	Oversight response	Purpose of response
1974	FA (#1)	Hughes-Ryan Act	Controls over covert action
1976–77	FA (#1)	Oversight committees established; critical reports	More robust oversight
1978	FA (#1)	FISA	Warrant process for wiretaps
1980	FA (#1)	Intelligence Oversight Act	More stringent oversight rules
1982	P	Intelligent Identities Act	Protect intelligence officers and agents
1987	FA (#2)	Critical report	Improve intelligence oversight
1989	FA (#2)	Inspector General Act	Improve internal CIA oversight
1991	FA (#2)	Intelligence Oversight Act	Further tighten oversight rules
1996	FA (#3)	Aspin-Brown critical reports; DCI assistants established	IC management improvements; strengthening of counterintelligence
1998	P	Whistleblowers Act	Protect intelligence whistleblowers
2001	FA (#4)	Patriot Act; authorization of attacks against Al Qaeda and Taliban regime; increase in counterterrorism funding	Increased surveillance of suspected terrorists; paramilitary counterattacks against Al Qaeda and Taliban
2004	FA (#4)	Critical reports	improvements in humint and analysis
2004	FA (#4, #5)	Intelligence Reform and Terrorism Prevention Act (IRTPA)	Strengthening CI, IC coordination

Abbreviations:

FA = fire alarm

#1 = domestic spying   P = patrolling
#2 = Iran-contra   humint = human intelligence
#3 = Ames   IC = intelligence community
#4 = 9/11 attacks   FISA = Foreign Intelligence
     Surveillance Act

#5 = Iraqi WMDs errors

sometimes attempting to whisper only in the ear of a committee chair – DCI Turner's ploy with Representative Edward P. Boland (D-MA) in their early relationship, until Boland began to wonder how much he could really peer into the activities of the intelligence agencies while locked in a bear hug by the DCI.

On other occasions, intelligence managers may seek to limit their briefings on a finding or some other key intelligence decision to a "Gang of Eight" (the top four congressional leaders and the top four SSCI and HPSCI leaders from both parties); or even a "Gang of Four," by limiting the witting circle to only the leaders of the two intelligence committees, or sometimes the phrase is used to refer to the four top congressional leaders (Cumming 2010). The Gang of Four concept is strictly an invention of the executive branch, used from time to time by presidents of both parties since 1980; nowhere is this provision allowed by statute. The Gang of Eight is a group, it should be emphasized, that was supposed to be used only in times of emergency and only with respect to covert actions, not for other intelligence activities. Yet in 2002 the second Bush administration briefed – all too briefly, according to recipients – only the Gang of Eight for its questionable use of warrantless wiretaps, an operation revealed by the *New York Times* in 2005.

In another bit of trickery, intelligence managers often do their best to make sure that no staff is present for briefings on covert action to the Gang of Eight or the Gang of Four. It is a clever strategy, relying on the fact that members of Congress usually don't have enough time or expertise to question an operation deeply, while experienced staff aides might raise serious objections for the members of Congress to consider. As Clark notes (2010, 14), the executive branch will deign to inform the Gang of Eight sans staff support, then claim that it had the support of Congress for an operation – as if eight lawmakers represented the Senate and the House. Sometimes the staff on SSCI and HPSCI are partisan, inexperienced in the procedures of oversight, or have limited knowledge about intelligence. Good staff is vital, because the members are often too busy to address the details of intelligence initiatives advanced by the CIA and the other secret agencies. "The staff has to take the lead," concludes a former CIA officer who has observed Agency-Hill relations for 35 years (Johnson 2010). "You ultimately must choose the right people and pay them well to stay" (ibid.).

Clark has concluded (2010, 13) that "the Obama Administration has continued the Bush Administration practice of resisting robust intelligence disclosure to Congress." The Obama administration, for example, has refused to report to Congress on covert actions beyond the Gang of Eight. It bears repeating that the intent of Congress in the 1980 and the 1991 Intelligence Oversight Acts was to allow a Gang of Eight just in emergencies, after which ("in a few days" – interpreted to mean 48 hours) the Eight were expected to ensure that the full complement of SSCI and HPSCI members would be properly briefed. Here is the standard to which the Congress should return, insisting at the same time that if there is a genuine need for a Gang of Eight briefing, then a few senior and knowledgeable staffers will be included in the briefing and the entire SSCI and HPSCI membership will be informed that the Gang of Eight provision has been temporarily evoked.

Sometimes the favorite number of lawmakers to brief on Capitol Hill has been zero – a "Gang of None" – as was clearly the case with Operation CHAOS, CONTELPRO, SHAMROCK, MINARET, and the CIA assassination plots. The longest-serving DCI, Allen Dulles (1953–1961), once said that he felt obliged to tell the truth to only one person: the president – if he asked (Ransom 1976, 4). On another occasion Dulles widened the circle by one. "I'll fudge the truth to the oversight committee," he said, "but I'll tell the chairman the truth – that is, if he wants to know" (quoted in Braden 1975, 14)

In sharp contrast, the intent of the 1980 and 1991 Intelligence Oversight Acts was to have *all* the members of SSCI and HPSCI briefed (along with a few staff in attendance), not just some subset. The committees, though, must insist on this approach or intelligence managers will sidestep the full-briefing rule.[13] Certainly the oversight committees have demonstrated their trustworthiness over the years, with virtually no major leaks from them and far fewer minor ones than the executive branch. Further, during its long history Congress has never had any "plumbers in the basement" – unlike the executive branch during the Nixon administration, with its Watergate conspirators.[14]

THE ROLES PLAYED BY INTELLIGENCE OVERSEERS ON CAPITOL HILL

These years of experimentation in the United States from 1974 until now about how to maintain a proper balance between efficient spy agencies, on the one hand, and the sanctity of civil liberties, on the other hand, has been turbulent,

---

[13] The current DCIA, Leon E. Panetta, has said: "I do not want to just do a Gang of Four briefing – in other words, just inform the leaders of the party. My view is, and I said this at my confirmation hearings, I think it's very important to inform all the members of the Intelligence Committees about what's going on when we have to provide notification." See Leon E. Panetta, remarks at Pacific Council on International Policy, California, May 18, 2009.

[14] Remark by constitutional scholar Raoul Berger, American Political Science Association, Annual Meeting, Chicago, Illinois (September 4, 1987), in reference to the secret Nixon White House group that attempted to stop leaks by using extralegal surveillance methods against political opponents – part of the Watergate conspiracy.

Responsibility for Intelligence Support

		Low	High
		1	2
Responsibility for	Low	The Ostrich	The Cheerleader
Intelligence Evaluation	High	3	4
		The Lemon-Sucker	The Guardian

FIGURE 6.2. A Typology of roles assumed by intelligence overseers in the U.S. Congress.

see-sawing between intensive oversight at times (in reaction to major alarms) and, more often, a lackadaisical approach to standing guard against the abuses of secret power. In dealing with their intelligence oversight duties since 1974, members of Congress have adopted one of four major roles: that of the ostrich, the cheerleader, the lemon-sucker, or the guardian, with fluctuations by some lawmakers between the different roles according to the circumstances and personalities of the time.

The Ostrich

The first type of intelligence overseer is the "ostrich." Here is the lawmaker who embraces a philosophy of benign neglect toward the intelligence agencies (see Figure 6.2). This view characterized almost all members of Congress before the domestic spy scandal of 1974–75. A classic illustration of the ostrich is Senator Barry Goldwater (R-AZ), who became chairman of SSCI in 1981. He had previously served as a member of the Church Committee. Ironically, while on that committee in 1976, Goldwater voted against the creation of the SSCI, the very panel he would come to lead. He also opposed most of the other 98 reforms recommended by the Church Committee, including closer judicial scrutiny of wiretapping operations inside the United States and more extensive congressional hearings on CIA covert actions. Goldwater was content with the system of oversight that existed before 1975: an occasional review of secret activities by a few subcommittees on intelligence housed within the Armed Services and the Appropriations committees (Barrett 2007; Johnson 1989; Ransom 1970).

The Cheerleader

The second type of intelligence overseer is the "cheerleader." In this instance, the member of Congress has removed his or her head from the sand, but only for the purpose of cheering more loudly on behalf of the intelligence agencies. The cheerleader is interested primarily in the advocacy of spies, the support of intelligence budgets, and the advancement of clandestine operations at home and abroad against suspected enemies of the United States. During hearings, the cheerleader specializes in "softball" pitches – easy questions gently tossed so that intelligence managers called as witnesses can slug them over the centerfield fence (Johnson 1994b). In press conferences, the cheerleader acts as a defense attorney for America's secret agencies, hinting at their behind-the-scenes, "if you only knew" successes; lauding the heroism of intelligence officers and agents; castigating journalists for printing leaked secrets that imperil the nation; and warning of threats at home and abroad that could lead to another 9/11 if the intelligence agencies are hamstrung by kibitzing lawmakers. Such statements by cheerleaders are often true: intelligence officers do have successes, they are occasionally heroes, sometimes they do prevent terrorist attacks. Yet the cheerleaders are one-sided in their perspective, lacking a critical eye for the intelligence inadequacies that cry out for reform.

Representative Boland assumed the role of cheerleader when he became the first chair of HPSCI in 1977. He often swallowed his personal skepticism about specific covert operations and expressed his support for the government's secret bureaucracy, determined to show that his committee could be trusted as a responsible Hill supervisor of intelligence operations.

The Lemon-Sucker

A third role type is the "lemon-sucker" – a term used by President Clinton to describe economists who display a sour disposition toward a government policy. This type is as one-sided as the cheerleader, only at the opposite extreme. For the lemon-sucker, nothing the intelligence agencies undertake is likely to be worthwhile. The secret agencies are inherently immoral: opening and reading other people's mail, eavesdropping on telephone conversations, stealing documents, overthrowing governments, perhaps killing people. The skeptical lemon-suckers also charge the spy agencies with incompetence, pointing to the CIA's inability to dispatch foreign leaders on its hit list (despite many attempts), the absence of predicted WMDs weaponry in Iraq in 2002, and the failure to anticipate either the fall of the Soviet Union or the 9/11 attacks.

For the most extreme skeptic, there is but one solution: shut down Langley and the other secret agencies. In 1996, for example, a well-regarded member of SSCI, Senator Daniel Patrick Moynihan (D-NY), who was dismayed by the CIA's inability to anticipate the collapse of the Soviet empire, called for the agency's abolition (Moynihan 1991, E17).

The Guardian

The fourth type of intelligence overseer is the "guardian." This role conforms best with the hopes of legislative reformers in 1975. Representative Hamilton (R-IN), HPSCI chair from 1985 to 1987, has argued that the ideal intelligence overseers are both "partners and critics" of the secret agencies (Davies 2002, A1). Another HPSCI member, Representative Norman D. Dicks (D-WA), has said that "overseeing the intelligence community is like being a good parent: you have to encourage and discipline" (Nolan 2005, 126–27).

As intelligence "partners," lawmakers must educate the American people on the virtues of maintaining an effective intelligence capability. Without defenders on Capitol Hill, the spy agencies are at a major disadvantage in gaining public support for their secret activities and sizable budgets. Yet, to be an effective overseer, a lawmaker must also be a critic: someone who searches for, acknowledges, and corrects programmatic flaws. This challenging role requires the ability, above all, to be objective, to speak out against questionable activities (in closed hearings on those occasions when operations are too sensitive for public review). Representative Hamilton has come as close to this ideal as any member of SSCI or HPSCI. When he was head of HPSCI, he regularly convened committee meetings, paid close attention to memos and reports from his staff and the intelligence agencies, followed up on media allegations of intelligence wrongdoing or mistakes, and spent long hours reviewing budgets and talking to intelligence professionals. Even Representative Hamilton faltered during the Iran-*contra* scandal in the mid-1980s. When staffers on the NSC assured him that they were not involved in these illegal operations, Hamilton, along with other SSCI and HPSCI leaders, accepted these assurances at face value (Johnson 2009) – always a mistake when rumors to the contrary are rampant and underscore the need for a more formal probe.

THE DYNAMIC NATURE OF INTELLIGENCE ACCOUNTABILITY

During their tenures, individual members of SSCI and HPSCI have sometimes displayed more than one approach to intelligence supervision. Representative Boland, for instance, felt it necessary to be a strong partner of the intelligence agencies in 1977–80, thereby offsetting the bad impression left by the Pike Committee's strident criticism of the CIA. As the 1980s progressed, however, Boland began to drift away from the posture of cheerleading to assume a more balanced stance as a guardian in 1981. By 1982, he had become increasingly skeptical of DCI Casey and his use of covert action to advance the *contras* against the Sandinista Marxist regime in Nicaragua. Boland, joined by a majority in the Democratically controlled Congress at the time, concluded that the mining of Nicaraguan harbors and the blowing up of power lines (along with other extreme paramilitary operations) were excessive responses to the minimal threat posed by the Sandinista regime. Boland introduced and guided to passage seven eponymous amendments, each further restraining the use of covert action in Nicaragua.

By the time his tenure had come to an end in 1985, Boland's relations with DCI Casey had substantially deteriorated, as the HPSCI chairman metamorphosed from cheerleader to guardian to full-fledged lemon-sucker. In Boland's case, the stimuli for these changes were twofold: first, what he perceived as the Reagan administration's overheated response to events in Central America; and second, a new, aggressive, and arrogant DCI (Casey) who did nothing to hide his disdain toward the notion of congressional intelligence oversight. Casey once explained his "theory" of intelligence oversight in this manner: "The job of Congress is to stay the f – – out of my business" (quoted in Johnson 1984). First, policy (paramilitary operations in Nicaragua), and then, personality (Casey's irascibility) transformed Chairman Boland's approach to intelligence accountability dramatically from cheerleader to sharp skeptic (Johnson 2011a).

IN SEARCH OF GUARDIANS

The time and study required to become an effective legislative supervisor for intelligence, plus the lack of credit back home for engaging in oversight, sums to an unattractive formula for lawmakers concerned about reelection. They usually conclude that their time is better spent raising campaign funds and pursuing legislative goals that are more closely reported on by the media – especially in their home state. Yet what about future intelligence failures that could lead to even more drastic attacks against the United States than experienced on 9/11? What if lawmakers could have prevented the failures of 9/11, or the invasion of Iraq based on the faulty assumption that Saddam Hussein had WMDs, by way of a more robust review of intelligence procedures, the effectiveness of information-sharing arrangements among the agencies (especially between the CIA and the FBI), and the quality of intelligence collection and analysis on such topics as Al Qaeda and Iraq? What member of Congress wants to explain to constituents why he or she was too busy fund-raising to improve, through serious hearings and budget reviews, the readiness of America's intelligence agencies?

The role of guardian was widely accepted by reformers in 1975 as the ideal, because it balanced support for intelligence with a determination through persistent program review to avoid future agency failures and scandals. In pursuit of this objective, how can members of Congress be encouraged to spend more time on serious program evaluation? What incentives can be introduced into the culture of Capitol Hill to make intelligence accountability a more valued pursuit?

Some initiatives to encourage better intelligence oversight could include greater recognition for lawmakers who perform with distinction as overseers. This recognition could take the form of increased perks (improved office space and parking opportunities, along with augmented funds for travel and staff support) dispensed by party leaders to lawmakers known for their oversight tenacity and fairness. Closer media coverage of oversight activities would help, too, as well as the bestowing of "Overseer of the Year" rewards by civic groups to acknowledge the hard work of lawmakers who devote time and energy to oversight intelligence hearings and budget reviews. Front-page stories on oversight in leading newspapers are rare; but when they occur, they help boost the public's appreciation of this important government function.[15] Further, academic researchers, teachers, and journalists could pay more attention to this neglected responsibility of Congress, explaining more effectively the importance of accountability to the American people.

One might think that enough oversight incentives already exist. In the first instance, the quality of intelligence accountability could well determine the degree of protection afforded the American people against domestic spy scandals. Moreover, another powerful incentive should be the desire of lawmakers to improve America's intelligence defenses, thereby helping to ward off future terrorist attacks against the United States; or to avoid further faulty conclusions about unconventional weapons abroad of the kind that helped draw the United States into war with Iraq in 2003 and could lead the nation into war again. Former DCI Robert M. Gates has stated well the case for intelligence oversight on Capitol Hill:

> [S]ome awfully crazy schemes might well have been approved had everyone present [in the White House] not known and expected hard questions, debate, and criticism from the Hill. And when, on a few occasions, Congress was left in the dark, and such schemes did proceed, it was nearly always to the lasting regret of the presidents involved. (Gates 1996, 559)

---

15   For example, see Eric Schmitt and David Rohde, "2 Reports Assail State Dept. Role on Iraq Security: Oversight Is Faulted," *New York Times*, October 23, 2007, A1.

Regardless of these compelling reasons for a lawmaker to assume the guardian role of a dedicated intelligence overseer, most observers agree that members of Congress continue to perform far below their potential when it comes to the supervision of the nation's spy agencies. As former senator Gary W. Hart (D-CO), a member of the Church Committee, emphasized: "public interest and insistence is necessary for reform" (Hart 1993, 144). Intelligence oversight is a neglected responsibility on Capitol Hill and will remain so, until the citizens of the United States demand otherwise.

7

Foreign Aid Oversight Challenges for Congress

Susan B. Epstein

U.S. foreign aid is a subset of U.S. foreign policy. It represents the largest component of the international affairs budget and is generally supported by foreign policy experts as an instrument, along with others, such as public diplomacy, defense, and the U.S. diplomatic corps, to support U.S. foreign policy interests. Primarily implemented by the U.S. Agency for International Development (USAID) and the Departments of State and Defense, among many others, the United States provides five major categories of foreign aid: bilateral development assistance, economic assistance to support strategic goals, humanitarian assistance, military assistance, and multilateral assistance.

For decades, foreign aid has been viewed as an essential foreign policy tool that contributes to U.S. national security interests. In 1947, the United States government provided aid to vulnerable populations and governments for reconstruction and economic development to postwar Europe, in part to counteract the potential spread of communism. The next year, Congress passed the Economic Cooperation Act (Title I of the Foreign Assistance Act of 1948) to authorize the Marshall Plan and provide $5.3 billion in aid to Europe for one year. By restricting funding to one year, Congress was able to retain its input in the implementation, modification, and funding of the program. For the next three years, Congress held hearings, debated, and amended the program. The Marshall Plan, which operated from 1948 to 1951, provided more than $13 billion for economic recovery to 16 Western European countries to bolster their governments, stem the spread of communism to those countries, and strengthen potential trade capabilities.[1]

Primary goals for U.S. foreign aid have shifted over the years from rebuilding postwar Europe, to advancing freedom and economic cooperation in Latin

---

[1] For more on the Marshall Plan, see CRS report 97–62, *The Marshall Plan: Design, Accomplishments, and Relevance to the Present*, by Curt Tarnoff, January 6, 1997.

America during the Kennedy administration under the Alliance for Progress Program, to supporting Southeast Asia's ability to counter Soviet and Chinese influence, to rewarding participating governments in the Middle East peace initiatives, to responding to insurgencies in Central America in the 1980s. All these foreign aid themes had U.S. national security implications.

Soon after the September 11, 2001, terrorist attacks, the George W. Bush administration explicitly linked development to national security interests of the United States and stated the importance of elevating development to be more on par with defense as a foreign policy tool. In its 2002 National Security Strategy, the Bush administration stated, "We will actively work to bring hope of democracy, development, free markets, and free trade to every corner of the world" (*The National Security Strategy of the United States of America* 2002, introductory statement).

Continuing that theme in the 2006 National Security Strategy, the Bush administration said, "Development reinforces diplomacy and defense, reducing long-term threats to our national security by helping to build stable, prosperous, and peaceful societies. Improving the way we use foreign assistance will make it more effective in strengthening responsible governments, responding to suffering, and improving people's lives" (*National Security Strategy of the United States of America* 2006, 33). In the FY2007 Foreign Affairs budget request, President Bush stated, "There are no hard lines between our security interests, our development interests, and our democratic goals" (*The Budget in Brief, Fiscal Year 2007*, 1).

President Barack Obama's FY2010 budget request reinforced the idea that U.S. foreign aid is a crucial element of U.S. national security when it said it would put funding on track to double aid within five years, and elevate diplomacy and development to be more on par with defense. In the introduction of President Obama's first National Security Strategy (NSS), the White House stated, "Our Armed Forces will always be a cornerstone of our security, but they must be complemented. Our security also depends upon diplomats who can act in every corner of the world, from grand capitals to dangerous outposts; development experts who can strengthen governance and support human dignity; and intelligence and law enforcement that can unravel plots, strengthen justice systems, and work seamlessly with other countries." Further on the NSS stated: "taken together, these efforts will position our nation for success in the global marketplace, while also supporting our national security capacity – the strength of our military, intelligence, diplomacy and development, and the security and resilience of our homeland" (*The National Security Strategy*, May 2010, 10). And, "We are focusing on assisting developing countries and their people to manage security threats, reap the benefits of global economic expansion, and set in place accountable and democratic institutions that serve basic human needs" (ibid., 15).

Throughout the post-9/11 years, Congress has recognized foreign aid as a foreign policy tool. Members have debated and funded increases in foreign aid, within regular and supplemental appropriations, largely because of national security objectives.

CONGRESSIONAL VIEWS ON FOREIGN AID AND NATIONAL SECURITY

Congress does not speak with one voice on foreign aid, but rather with 535 voices. A wide range of opinions exists. Many members of Congress favor expanding nearly all types of U.S. overseas aid – humanitarian, economic development, strategic, and military – saying not only that it is the right thing to do, but also that it promotes U.S. national interests around the world by stabilizing countries or regions, promoting democracy, and engendering good will toward the American people. Others support foreign aid for Israel and certain other recipient countries for security purposes but oppose aid for alleviating poverty or improving development. A number of members view foreign aid as a drain on the U.S. budget that marginally, if at all, benefits the American taxpayer. And some oppose foreign aid unless it expands U.S. trade. Most members of Congress, however, support providing at least some U.S. foreign aid in certain instances and to address specific concerns.

Congress changes every two years when the entire House of Representatives and one-third of senators are up for reelection. Often, with these elections comes a change in the majority party of either the House or the Senate or both. With each new Congress comes the potential for a change in the policy agenda from the previous Congress, including where U.S. foreign aid ranks among new congressional priorities. The change from the 111th to the 112th Congress (2009–2011 and 2011–2013), for example, could not be more stark regarding foreign aid. The majority party in the 111th Congress was on track to introduce, debate, and pass a major reform of foreign aid authorities; it also supported President Obama's intention to double the resources committed to foreign aid.

In contrast, early signs of the 112th Congress (2011–2013) suggest that brakes may be applied to both reform and doubling of aid funds. Campaigning on fixing the large U.S. deficit, poor economy, high unemployment, and strained budget, the 112th Congress is expected to focus on reducing spending that could result in cutting the foreign aid budget. With many Republican lawmakers routinely voting against foreign aid, but supporting aid to Israel, Representative

Eric Cantor (R-VA), the Majority Leader in the House of Representatives, proposed that the 112th Congress separate aid to Israel from the rest of foreign aid. He suggested redesignating U.S. aid to Israel (which is all military assistance) as defense funding to allow members to vote for aid to Israel but against other foreign aid. Similarly, Representative Kay Granger (R-TX), the chairwoman of the House State-Foreign Operations Appropriations Subcommittee, has expressed caution about recent increases in foreign aid saying, "We also face the continued concern in our own country about our economy and the devastating effects of skyrocketing deficits and debt." She went on to say, "I want to be sure that we aren't increasing foreign aid at the expense of our troops." And when opposing aid to a specific country she said, "We can't just give out money and say we will put up with whatever [that government] is doing."

These statements differ from the bipartisan foreign aid tenor established by some foreign relations leaders in the 111th Congress. Senator John F. Kerry (D-MA), chairman of the Senate Foreign Relations Committee, stated in a Senate report, for instance, that "development is a third pillar of U.S. national security, but in resources and stature, our assistance programs are poor cousins to diplomacy and defense." Senator Richard E. Lugar (R-IN), ranking minority member of the Senate Foreign Relations Committee, stated, "Development is critical for U.S. national security; alleviation of poverty and hunger is a key component.... Poverty denies opportunity to the world's young people and breeds extremism and instability that spills over borders" (www.usaid.gov/press/frontlines/fl_mar10/p05_lugar100309.html). And Representative Howard Berman (D-CA), then chairman of the House Foreign Affairs Committee, spoke of the importance of foreign aid, "Development assistance not only helps people to meet their basic needs and provide for their families, but also creates opportunities to expand markets for U.S. goods and services. It strengthens our national security by ameliorating the conditions under which conflict, lawlessness and extremism often flourish" (House Committee on Foreign Affairs 2010, http://www.modernizingforeignassistance.org/blog/2010/09/page/4/).

Even in a Republican paper that expressed a more cautious approach to a complete overhaul of foreign aid, the minority party expressed support of foreign aid as a national security tool by stating: "Hopefully, by creating opportunity and stability in impoverished countries, it is also a support for our national security in other ways. [Poverty reduction] should be part of the whole of our national security and diplomacy planning process." Representative Ileana Ros-Lehtinen (R-FL), at that time the ranking minority member of the House Foreign Affairs Committee and now chairwoman in the 112th Congress (2011–2013), introduced a measure that would require aid to be a part of the U.S. national security planning process (House Committee on Foreign Affairs 2009).

ROLE OF CONGRESS ON FOREIGN AID

The Constitution provides several ways for Congress to influence U.S. foreign policy, including appropriating or denying funds; passing authorizations, legislative directives, and resolutions; conducting committee oversight hearings; and providing advice and consent in the Senate for presidential appointments and approving treaties. All members and many committees can be involved in sponsoring legislation or making resolutions and policy statements that can affect foreign policy and foreign aid. Certain members and committees, however, have greater roles to play in the authorization, appropriation, and confirmation process in foreign aid policy.

Appropriations

Article I, Section 9, of the Constitution provides that "No money shall be drawn from the treasury, but in consequence of appropriations made by law." And by precedent, all appropriations originate in the House of Representatives. For the most part, most foreign aid funding is enacted within the State Department-Foreign Operations and Related Agencies Appropriations, legislated by the House and Senate State-Foreign Operations Appropriations Subcommittees and the full House and Senate Appropriations Committees. Other funding and direction comes from House and Senate appropriations committees that deal with the Department of Defense, Agriculture, Health and Human Services, and Financial Services appropriations, among others.

Authorization and Oversight

According to the Constitution, Congress has oversight power to review, monitor, and supervise U.S. government foreign aid activities, programs, and agencies. Statutes require that Congress authorize the activities and expenditure of appropriations prior to the executive branch spending the funds. The congressional committees with primary jurisdiction over most foreign aid authorization and oversight include the House Foreign Affairs Committee and the Senate Foreign Relations Committee. The House and Senate Agriculture Committees also have jurisdiction on food aid issues. Other committees such as the Armed Services, Government Reform, among others, are involved with certain issues that overlap with foreign assistance, such as military assistance, and interagency cooperation having to do with aid, organizational or program structure, and reorganization of aid agencies.

Advice and Consent

Section 2 of Article II of the Constitution gives the president the power to appoint U.S. government officials and to make treaties "by and with the Advice and Consent of the Senate." For the positions of secretary of state, USAID administrator, ambassador, and other high-level officials tasked with administering foreign aid, the Senate Foreign Relations Committee fulfills the primary role in the nomination process by conducting investigations and hearings. Investigations and hearings give committee members a chance to voice their opinions on the views of the nominee or on the administration's foreign aid agenda overall. Committee members can use their time asking the nominee questions to make a particular point on foreign aid policy. After the hearing, the committee can report the nominee favorably, unfavorably, or without recommendation to the Senate, or it can take no action. It is more common for a committee to take no action on a nomination than to reject a nominee outright. Preceded by debate, a nominee's name is then sent to the floor of the Senate for a vote. A majority of senators must be present for a vote to be called. If a member filibusters voting on the nominee, 60 votes would be required to invoke cloture, thereby ending debate and bringing the nomination to a vote. Senators can place a hold on a nominee and prevent the nominee from being voted on in the Senate. A hold can be placed on a nominee because a senator needs more time to review the nominee, because a senator disagrees with the views of a nominee, or for unrelated matters. A hold can be used to prevent a nominee from ever coming to the Senate floor for a vote.[2]

For advice and consent on treaties, the Senate Foreign Relations Committee receives the treaty in question, holds hearings, and prepares a committee report. The committee reports the treaty to the full Senate after receiving comments from the public and, at times, subject to conditions incorporated by the committee into the treaty. (The Senate does not change the treaty, but it might add conditions or understandings to accompany it.) According to the Constitution, the full Senate must approve a treaty by a two-thirds vote before sending it to the executive branch for ratification. The Senate can approve a treaty as written, with conditions, reject it and return it, or prevent action by withholding approval.

---

[2] For more information on presidential nominations, see CRS Report RL31980, *Senate Consideration of Presidential Nominations: Committee and Floor Procedure*, by Elizabeth Rybicki, May 8, 2009.

CONGRESSIONAL CHALLENGES REGARDING FOREIGN AID

Congress faces several challenges that can undermine its effective oversight of foreign aid. Overcoming some challenges requires the cooperation of the administration, nongovernmental and multilateral organizations, and Congress. For example, the 111th Congress (2009–2011) and the Obama administration worked together and informed each other on foreign aid reform. Though Congress had drafted foreign aid reform legislation, that bill did not progress through Congress. The administration, however, did move forward on its own version of foreign aid reform and continued to work with key congressional staff and some members as the administration developed its own reforms presented as the Quadrennial Diplomacy and Development Review (QDDR). This likely was done because the administration knew the majority party in Congress supported the general idea of a systematic review, and also because it might need Congress to provide new authority and funding for program or structural changes. At the same time, however, the executive and legislative branch cooperation was intermittent and not completely inclusive, as the administration continued to delay reports and briefings for Hill staff.

Congressional oversight is also hindered by the lack of a stated goal for foreign aid, which is up to the administration to provide. Having no clearly stated objectives undermines congressional ability to make foreign aid more efficient and effective, since lawmakers do not know what the target goals are. Having a national strategy for foreign aid could be a critical tool to guide lawmakers, as well as the implementing agencies, in determining whether aid is accomplishing the administration's priorities. A national foreign aid strategy articulated by the president or the secretary of state might indicate what the appropriate allocation of human and budgetary resources would be from year to year, and help to evaluate foreign aid programs and activities, possibly eliminating the less successful ones. This could result in budget savings in the long run. Some might argue that aid cannot be adjusted frequently or haphazardly because aid recipient countries and nongovernmental organizations that often disburse aid in the field need to know that they can depend on resources over time. Typically, however, top U.S. aid recipient countries have more to do with U.S. strategic interests than need (i.e., Israel and Egypt). Aside from the Iraq and Afghanistan wars, the list of aid recipient countries typically does not changed drastically from one administration to the next.[3]

---

[3]   See Appendix 7A for the list of top 10 U.S. aid recipient countries in FY2008 under the
      George W. Bush administration versus FY20010 under the Obama administration.

A third broad challenge for congressional oversight of U.S. foreign aid policy is that while most top administration officials who deal with foreign aid are in the Department of State and the USAID, many are not. Having so many officials with foreign aid responsibilities scattered among numerous departments and agencies makes any lack of coordination more evident, but also means that general congressional oversight of foreign aid programs is more complicated.

Senator Kerry, chairman of the Senate Foreign Relations Committee in the 111th Congress (2009–2011), said upon introducing the Foreign Assistance Revitalization and Accountability Act of 2009:

> The issues we face today – from chronic poverty and hunger to violent acts of terrorism–require that we work seamlessly toward identifiable goals. The U.S. has increased development funding and elevated its priority. Yet the USAID has been allowed to atrophy. Many new programs are located outside of USAID in roughly two dozen departments and agencies. We don't really know whether these programs are complementary or working at cross-purposes. (Menendez 2009, http://www.politickernj.com/senatormenendez/3184/kerry-lugar-menendez-corker-introduce-legislation-reform-foreign-aid)

The following are some more specific challenges facing Congress in its oversight responsibilities of U.S. foreign aid policy.

Appropriations

Constitutional experts say that framers of the Constitution gave Congress budgetary powers because its members would be closer to the people than would the executive branch. Some would argue that the most powerful tool Congress has in influencing foreign aid and how it is used to enhance U.S. national security interests is the power of the purse. Because Congress can fund or not fund programs, policies, departments, and agencies for which the administration requests resources, it has significant leverage to get top administration officials to testify, provide data, and cooperate with Congress to set and implement foreign aid priorities. This presents a foreign aid challenge for Congress, though, because it can be politically difficult for members to commit funds to overseas programs when their constituents contend that domestic needs are more important. Members of Congress are less likely to reap much political gain for advocating foreign aid than for supporting domestic spending. To put foreign aid spending in perspective, however, the United States spends about 1 percent of its annual budget on foreign aid and about 20 percent on defense. Robert M. Gates, former secretary of defense, advocated increases in foreign aid funding, saying investing in aid may help stabilize failed states around the world and may reduce the need to send U.S. troops into combat which is more costly, both in money and human resources.

Another appropriations-related challenge is that Congress rarely passes regular stand-alone appropriations bills for foreign affairs but rather approves foreign affairs funding in omnibus or consolidated appropriations measures. In the past 10 years, Congress has passed only two Foreign Operations Appropriations bills, and those were signed into law after the start of the fiscal year for which they provided funds. In the other years, foreign aid appropriations were either continuing resolutions or placed in large multi-agency omnibus appropriations. Those in Congress who have jurisdiction over foreign aid lose their leverage to make foreign aid changes within the appropriations process when many appropriations are merged together for quick passage. In omnibus appropriations, Congress is primarily concerned with the total funding level and not the particulars of aid programs or specific accounts. Also, omnibus bills make it easier for amendments, directives, across-the-board rescissions, and earmarks to be slipped in without members understanding them or debating them before voting. Continuing Resolutions (CRs) make it easier for Congress to restrict funding since often CRs continue at the previous year's budget level.

Emergency supplemental appropriations, used intermittently in the 1980s and 1990s, nearly every year by the George W. Bush administration, and continued in FY2010 by the Obama administration, disaggregate the power of the purse that Congress has by separating certain activities, such as aid to Iraq, Afghanistan, and Pakistan during U.S. military involvement in those countries. When the president submits his budget, knowing a supplemental will also be submitted before the end of the budget cycle, Congress is unable to see the total cost of the administration's entire foreign policy agenda up front. Aid for each country and U.S. overall foreign policy are related to total international affairs expenditures. When an administration sends a supplemental request to Congress mid-budget cycle, Congress and the appropriations committees cannot create the proper balance among short-term aid needs overseas, long-term development needs, and what is in the short-term and long-term U.S. national security interest.

In recent years, appropriations bills have become the legislative vehicle to pass authorization measures in lieu of passage of reauthorization legislation. This is a problem, in part, because appropriations are in effect for only one year, whereas authorization language sets multiyear policy and tone. This, some say, further weakens the authorizers and strengthens the appropriators, giving them both the power of the purse and power to create new programs and policies. Others, however, claim that the staff of the authorizing and appropriating committees work together to get authorizing language into an appropriations bill, a back door method of passing authorizations, but at least perceived needed measures usually get passed.

A recent-year budgeting phenomenon is forward funding. Funding for the Pakistan Counterinsurgency Capability Fund (PCCF) in the Supplemental Appropriations Act, 2009, provided $700 million to assist the government of Pakistan in building and maintaining the capability of its security forces. The funding was directed by Congress not to be available for expenditure until FY2010. Congress used its power to direct when the funding would become available, but this created confusion in FY2010 and FY2011 appropriations reports and debates.

Congress is also challenged in the foreign aid appropriations process to balance multiyear funding needs with proper oversight. Many aid proponents in the NGO community seek multiyear aid; they contend it is particularly important for long-term development planning and to assure unstable regions that the money to promote stability will continue. Many believe that Congress resists providing multiyear funding because it would lose its influence over those programs and how the money gets spent.

The Foreign Assistance Act of 1961 requires the executive branch to report to Congress each year on country allocations of U.S. aid, as well as to notify Congress of any programming changes throughout the year, in order for Congress to track the use of foreign aid funds. While this and other reporting required by Congress creates tension between Congress and the aid agencies having to do the many reports, this provides Congress with more information and a closer involvement with foreign aid activities. A problem may exist when so many reports are sent to the Hill that very few get read by members or their staff. In this case, time and tax dollars are wasted, if improved oversight does not result.

Authorization

A basic role of Congress – to authorize government activities and expenditures – has not been fulfilled with regard to foreign aid in recent years. By law, Congress must authorize spending of appropriations before the foreign policy agencies can disburse funds.[4] Because Congress speaks with many voices on

---

4   Sec. 10 of the Foreign Military Sales Amendment, 1971, PL 91–672; (22 U.S.C. 2412) requires the following: "(a) Notwithstanding any provision of law enacted before the date of enactment

some controversial foreign aid issues, such as funds for international family planning, it has been unable to pass comprehensive foreign aid authorization legislation since 1985. Prior to that year, Congress typically would re-authorize foreign aid including new funding ceilings every two years, dovetailing with the annual appropriations process. Passing a foreign aid authorization and a foreign relations authorization (a biannual requirement for Congress to re-authorize every two years the expenditure of funds for the Department of State and its programs) are the primary activities of the House Foreign Affairs Committee and Senate Foreign Relations Committee. In years that Congress does not pass foreign aid authorization, Congress waives the authorization requirement in appropriations measures. The foreign aid authorization legislation was traditionally a way for members of Congress to weigh in on issues important to them as individuals, as a party, as committees, and as a whole. Being unable to pass an authorization bill in the past 25 years has weakened congressional foreign affairs authorizing committees and Congress's ability to oversee administration policies, some would say.

The difficulty for Congress to pass a foreign aid authorization package is matched by its importance. Specific contentious issues can ruin chances of passage. A case in point is U.S. policy on international family planning. The matter of funding international family planning has see-sawed as the presidency has passed from one party to the other and back again since the Reagan administration. On taking office, President Obama removed restrictions on foreign aid funding for international family planning, but Congress has been unable to voice its opinion through legislation, since it is unable to pass foreign aid authorization legislation and didn't even introduce a foreign aid bill in the 111th Congress (2009–2011). Largely due to this and other highly partisan and contentious aid issues, congressional action on re-authorizing aid, which could have included revamping the primary statutory basis for foreign aid, the Foreign Assistance Act of 1961, continues to elude Congress. As a result, the act continues to be patched and amended to the point where it is now considered to be fragmented, cumbersome, and missing the mark on addressing today's overseas aid needs or U.S. national security interests. It continues to

of this section, no money appropriated for foreign assistance (including foreign military sales) shall be available for obligation or expenditure – (1) unless the appropriation thereof has been previously authorized by law; or (2) in excess of an amount previously prescribed by law. (b) To the extent that legislation enacted after the making of an appropriation for foreign assistance (including foreign military sales) authorizes the obligation or expenditure thereof, the limitation contained in subsection (a) shall have no effect. (c) The provisions of this section shall not be superseded except by a provision of law enacted after the date of enactment of this section which specifically repeals or modifies the provisions of this section."

contain Cold War references and objectives at a time when foreign aid could be more useful in countering regional instability, poverty, and terrorism overseas to act as a stronger national security tool for the United States.

Oversight

Oversight includes holding hearings to get information through testimony on a particular aspect of foreign aid. Oversight hearings provide an opportunity for members of Congress to give their opinions on specific foreign aid programs or aid recipient countries. If the party in power in the executive branch is the same as the majority party in Congress, cooperation in these oversight hearings often, but not always, is more likely. Also, the majority party in Congress can tilt the hearing more toward one side by inviting sympathetic witnesses, or can bring in hostile witness in order to demonstrate the stark contrast of the majority party to that of the minority. Whether or not the majority party in Congress is different from the party in the White House, congressional committees may want to bring high-level officials to Congress to testify, getting their statements on the record and challenging what the administration is doing or documenting what they are doing.

It can be difficult for Congress to get the total foreign aid picture – both bilateral and multilateral. More than 24 agencies and departments implement U.S. bilateral aid and multilateral aid, but coordination among them is lacking. No one committee has jurisdiction or the leverage to get all of the departments/agencies to the table. For example, the Department of Defense, for the most part, implements all U.S. military assistance abroad, but top-level Defense Department officials typically do not testify before the foreign affairs committees. Adding to the complexity is getting the multilateral organizations to testify before the foreign affairs committees. The Department of the Treasury typically testifies on the U.S. participation in multilateral organizations, but putting the total bilateral/multilateral and country-by-country aid picture together is cumbersome.

For congressional oversight of and budgeting for foreign aid to be successful and result in optimal efficiency, Congress depends on the executive branch to be forthcoming in providing data on expenditures, and on the willingness of top officials involved with U.S. foreign programs to testify before Congress. Without this cooperation, Congress would not be able to assess aid programs to determine if they are adequately funded and properly implemented. One acknowledgment in recent years is that while foreign aid programs have been operating for decades, administrations historically have done very little monitoring or evaluation of program effectiveness. This is one area that Congress has weighed in on in hearings and with legislation to require foreign aid monitoring, evaluation, and transparency.

Table 7.1 provides the list of the government entities typically involved in U.S. foreign aid.[5]

Aid: NGOs and Contractors

Twenty years ago, in 1990, USAID total direct hires numbered 3,262; today it is a little over 2,000. Most foreign aid is implemented by contractors or nongovernmental organizations (NGOs). "I think it's fair to say that USAID, our premier aid agency, has been decimated," Secretary of State Hillary Clinton said during her hearing confirmation in 2009. "It has half the staff it used to have. It's turned into more of a contracting agency than an operational agency with the ability to deliver" (quoted in Delanian 2009).

For much of its work, USAID hires large U.S. firms, many of them private, for-profit concerns whose executive ranks include former USAID employees. Those companies in turn hire subcontractors, which sometimes hire other firms. At the end of the chain are local workers at the site. Annual contract spending rose from $479 million in 2000 to about $2 billion a year in 2009. USAID personnel have lost their connection to the aid recipients, have lost the knowledge and skills that come with being in the field, and have lost the relationships that come with personally delivering the aid. If the agency has lost much of its first-hand knowledge of its overseas activities, Congress is even more removed and has less control over private sector contractors and NGOs than it would have over federal workers. While the Obama administration sought additional funds to increase USAID's workforce in FY2011, Congress did not pass either the State-Foreign Operations Appropriations nor the Foreign Aid Reauthorization measures that could have provided the means for Congress to weigh in on federal versus private sector staffing.

Advice and Consent Process

The constitutionally delegated advice and consent role empowers the Senate to approve or reject treaties and high-level presidential appointments. Regarding treaty approval, erosion of congressional power has occurred over the years partly because the number of international agreements has greatly expanded,

---

[5] See Appendix 7B for definitions of acronyms.

TABLE 7.1. *Government entities typically involved in U.S. foreign aid*

Departments	Subcabinets	Independent agencies
State	USAID	MCC
Commerce	CDC	EPA
Defense	NIST	Peace Corps
Army	PTO	IAF
Homeland Security	NOAA	FTC
Energy	US Forest Service	ADF
HHS	HRSA	TDA
Interior	NIH	IADF
Justice	APHIS	Ex-Im Bank
Labor		OGAC
Transportation		USIP
Treasury		NSF
		NRC

Note: See Appendix 7B for definition of acronyms.

and a number of them can become executive agreements based solely on the president's authority. This undermines communication and oversight on certain international agreements.

Regarding presidential foreign aid-related appointments, the president appoints more than 30 people for top foreign aid positions that are mostly sent to the Senate Foreign Relations Committee and then the entire Senate for confirmation. However, a number of other aid nominees are confirmed by other Senate committees, such as the undersecretary and assistant secretary for international affairs in Treasury which is sent to the Senate Finance Committee; the secretary of the Department of Agriculture and the undersecretary of the Foreign Agricultural Service who have responsibilities for foreign food aid and are confirmed by the Senate Agriculture, Nutrition, and Forestry Committee; the director of NIH (who oversees the Centers for Disease Control which is involved with global health programs) is confirmed by the Senate Health, Education, Labor, and Pensions Committee. (See Appendix 7C for a list of foreign aid-related nominations.) With so many different committees involved, the majority party in Congress may find it difficult to promote a particular foreign aid perspective. In addition to committee members asking questions and expressing their opinions at nomination hearings, the confirming committees have four options in dealing with nominations: the committee can report the nomination to the full Senate favorably, unfavorably, without recommendation, or take no action at all.

At times, presidents are criticized for not appointing officials quickly to fill vacancies in their administrations. Congress cannot act if the administration does not send the nominations to Capitol Hill for confirmation. Even if Congress wants certain positions filled, they cannot force the president to act more quickly to send nominees to the Hill. The Constitution provides for the president to fill vacancies during a recess of the Senate. Experts believe the intention was to be able to keep the continuity of the government while the Senate was not in session, because in the early days of the Republic, House and Senate recesses were longer. In modern times, recess appointments have been used more for political purposes, such as appointing an individual who would not likely be confirmed by a particular Senate. When this occurs, Congress has lost one of its oversight tools of not being able to question the nominee and give advice to the nominee that typically occurs during the Senate confirmation hearing. Recess appointments also allow an appointment to go forward that may go against the priorities of the Senate, or one on which a "hold" has been placed by any senator, preventing a vote often for unrelated reasons. Recess appointments expire at the end of the Senate's next session or until another person is nominated, confirmed, and permanently appointed (Hogue 2008, 4).

The president also can avoid Congress and the nominating process altogether with "special envoy" or "special representative" appointments. While other administrations throughout history had also appointed special envoys (Grieb 2001), the Obama administration angered some in Congress, especially in the minority party, when it appointed a number of "special envoys" to positions with overseas authority but who were not required to be confirmed by the Senate, thus circumventing congressional input on issues surrounding that nominee, the agency, or the activity to be overseen.

Current Aid Reform Challenges

A number of nongovernmental organizations, development experts, and policy makers pressed the 111th Congress (2009–2011) and the administration to take steps to reform the U.S. foreign aid program. Several actions occurred: legislation was introduced to reform certain aspects of foreign aid, a rewrite of the Foreign Assistance Act of 1961 was drafted by the chairman of the House Foreign Affairs Committee, the Obama administration conducted a Quadrennial Diplomacy and Development Review (QDDR), modeled after DOD's Quadrennial Defense Review (QDR), and President Obama signed a Presidential Policy Directive (PPD) on Global Development on September 22, 2010. Since the White House and the majority in both House and Senate were of the same party, congressional majority leadership and the administration generally agreed about the direction of aid. Those in Congress who disagreed had less opportunity to make their opinions known. Senator Lugar, ranking minority member of the Senate Foreign Relations Committee, and Senator Kerry, chairman of the same committee, mostly agreed on foreign aid reform. In contrast, then ranking minority member of the House Foreign Affairs Committee, Representative Ros-Lehtinen, and minority members on the committee, differed with Representative Berman's views to completely rewrite the Foreign Assistance Act of 1961. While seeing the need for reform, they expressed a more cautious approach than a massive overhaul. They had the ability to write a report expressing their views and could raise them in hearings, but those views got little visibility.

After two years of work on foreign aid reform, a new Congress has been elected and those who were in the minority in the 111th Congress (2009–2011) are now in the majority in the 112th Congress (2011–2013). The election of a new Congress could stop the momentum that the Democrats had to greatly reform foreign aid. On the other hand, a new majority party in Congress allows other ideas to be heard. Perhaps aid reform can be accomplished to attain greater efficiency and effectiveness, thereby reducing the aid budget. The challenge of getting continuity in foreign aid policy with frequent turnovers in Congress may be counterbalanced by the elevation of new ideas on how to accomplish the same thing with different methods. Also, does a new Congress with new priorities pose a dilemma for countries receiving aid from the United States? Can aid recipient countries count on U.S. aid being there each time the majority party changes in Congress, or must they turn elsewhere for help? While all members in Congress have to balance the needs, interests, and demands of their constituents with U.S. foreign policy, national security interests, and humanitarian needs abroad, Congress may want to consider the effect changes in foreign aid policy may have and the potential consequences of those changes.

CONCLUSION

The United States is the largest international economic aid donor in dollar terms, but one of the smallest among major donors as a percentage of gross national income. Aid critics and proponents alike in Congress can choose what data to use to support their views on foreign aid. While Congress plays a key role in determining the U.S. commitment to foreign aid, there are numerous obstacles in congressional oversight of foreign aid activities. Formulating a national strategy on foreign aid, improving coordination and cooperation between the administration and Congress to convey information and data on needed resources, implementing monitoring and evaluation of aid programs, as well as full participation and communication with others such as the NGO community and multilateral institutions all would contribute to a more effective foreign aid policy. Congress, by itself, could influence the evolution of U.S. foreign aid programs and their cost by debating and passing stand-alone foreign affairs funding and a foreign aid reauthorization bill.

While often lacking support by many U.S. constituents, and therefore, many U.S. lawmakers, Congress can meet many challenges of foreign aid oversight and funding by passing legislation and carrying out its constitutionally delegated responsibilities. Policy makers can communicate to their constituents the role foreign aid plays in U.S. foreign policy and national security. They can convey the message that foreign aid is a government activity that not only benefits people overseas but may also benefit Americans by reducing the use of our military, generating good will about America overseas, increasing trade opportunities, and stabilizing and de-radicalizing populations to reduce the attraction of terrorism worldwide.

APPENDIX 7A

TOP U.S. FOREIGN AID RECIPIENTS, FY2008 AND FY2010

Top 10 foreign aid recipients, FY2008	Top 10 aid recipients, FY2010
(Bush administration)	(Obama administration)
Israel	Afghanistan
Afghanistan	Israel
Egypt	Pakistan
Jordan	Egypt
Pakistan	Haiti
Iraq	Iraq
Kenya	Jordan
South Africa	Mexico
Colombia	Kenya
Nigeria	Nigeria

APPENDIX 7B

Agency Acronyms

ADF = African Development Foundation
APHIS = Animal and Plant Health Inspection Service
CDC = Centers for Disease Control and Prevention
EPA = U.S. Environmental Protection Agency
Ex-Im Bank = Export-Import Bank
FTC = Federal Trade Commission
HHS = Health and Human Services
HRSA = Health Resources and Services Administration
IADF = Inter-American Development Foundation
IAF = Inter-American Foundation
MCC = Millennium Challenge Corporation
NIH = National Institutes of Health
NIST = National Institute of Standards and Technology
NOAA = National Oceanographic and Atmospheric Administration
NRC = Nuclear Regulatory Commission
NSF = National Science Foundation
OGAC = Office of the U.S. Global AIDS Coordinator
PTO = U.S. Patent and Trademark Office
TDA = Trade Development Agency
USAID = U.S. Agency for International Development
USIP = U.S. Institute of Peace

APPENDIX 7C

Presidential Appointments with Foreign Aid Responsibilities

Senate Committee on Foreign Relations
Department of State
Secretary
Deputy Secretary
Under Secretary – Democracy and Global Affairs
Assistant Secretary – African Affairs
Assistant Secretary – Democracy, Human Rights, and Labor
Assistant Secretary – East Asian and Pacific Affairs
Assistant Secretary – Economic, Energy and Business Affairs
Assistant Secretary – European and Eurasian Affairs
Assistant Secretary – International Narcotics and Law Enforcement Affairs

Assistant Secretary – International Organization Affairs
Assistant Secretary – International Security and Nonproliferation
Assistant Secretary – Population, Refugee, and Migration
Assistant Secretary – South and Central Asian Affairs
Assistant Secretary – Western Hemisphere Affairs
Coordinator – U.S. Global AIDS
U.S. Permanent Representative and Chief of Mission – United Nations
U.S. Deputy Permanent Representative – United Nations
U.S. Agency for International Development
Administrator
Deputy Administrator
Assistant Administrator – Sub-Saharan Africa
Assistant Administrator – Asia and Near East
Assistant Administrator – Europe and Eurasia
Assistant Administrator – Global Health
Assistant Administrator – Democracy, Conflict, and Humanitarian Assistance
Assistant Administrator – Latin America and Caribbean
Assistant Administrator – Legislative and Public Affairs
Assistant Administrator – Management
Assistant Administrator – Policy and Program Coordination
Assistant Administrator – Economic Growth, Agriculture, and Trade
Inspector General
European Bank for Reconstruction and Development
U.S. Executive Director
International Broadcasting Bureau, Broadcasting Board of Governors
Director
International Joint Commission, United States and Canada
Commissioner – 3 positions
International Monetary Fund
U.S. Executive Director (2-year term of office)
U.S. Alternate Executive Director (2-year term of office)
Inter-American Development Bank
U.S. Executive Director (3-year term of office – The incumbent of this position
  also serves as U.S. Executive Director for the Inter-American Investment
  Corporation.)
U.S. Alternate Executive Director (three-year term of office – The incumbent
  of this position also serves as U.S. Alternate Executive Director for the Inter-
  American Investment Corporation.)
U.S. Trade and Development Agency
Director

Organizations with Full- and Part-Time Positions

African Development Bank

U.S. Executive Director (5-year term of office; full-time)

Governor and Alternate Governor (5-year terms of office; part-time)

Asian Development Bank

U.S. Executive Director (full-time)

Governor and Alternate Governor (part-time)

International Bank for Reconstruction and Development

U.S. Executive Director (2-year term of office; full-time – The incumbent also serves as U.S. Executive Director for the International Finance Corporation and the International Development Association.)

U.S. Alternate Executive Director (two-year term of office; full-time – The incumbent also serves as U.S. Alternate Executive Director for the International Finance Corporation and the International Development Association.)

Governor (same individual as the International Monetary Fund Governor; 5-year term of office; part-time – The incumbent also serves as Governor for the International Finance Corporation and the International Development Association.)

Alternate Governor (5-year term of office; part-time – The incumbent also serves as Alternate Governor for the International Finance Corporation and the International Development Association.)

Millennium Challenge Corporation

Chief Executive Officer (full-time)

Member, Board of Directors – 4 (of 9 total) positions (part-time; 3-year terms of office)

Overseas Private Investment Corporation

President/Chief Executive Officer (full-time)

Executive Vice President (full-time)

Member, Board of Directors – 8 (of 15 total) positions (part-time; 3-year terms of office)

Peace Corps

Director (full-time)

Deputy Director (full-time)

Member, Peace Corps National Advisory Council – 15 positions (part-time; political balance required; 2-year terms of office)

Advisory Board for Cuba Broadcasting (political balance required)

Member – nine positions (3-year terms of office)

African Development Foundation, Board of Directors (political balance required)

Member – 7 positions (6-year terms of office)

African Development Fund

Governor and Alternate Governor

Broadcasting Board of Governors (political balance required)

Member – 8 (of 9 total) positions (3-year terms of office)

Inter-American Foundation, Board of Directors (political balance required)

Member – 9 positions (6-year terms of office)

U.S. Advisory Commission on Public Diplomacy (political balance required)

Commissioner – seven positions (3-year terms of office)

Senate Committee on Finance

Department of the Treasury

Under Secretary – International Affairs

Assistant Secretary (Deputy Under Secretary) – International Affairs

Senate Committee on Agriculture, Nutrition, and Forestry

Department of Agriculture

Secretary

Deputy Secretary

Senate Committee on Armed Services

Department of Defense

Secretary

Deputy Secretary

Assistant Secretary – Global Security Affairs

PART THREE

Policy Challenges: Contours of Debate

8

Enemy Combatant Detainees

Bernard Horowitz and Harvey Rishikof

Detention policy for the global war on terrorism (GWOT) has proven to be one of the most nettlesome instruments of state policy for the administrations of both George W. Bush and Barack Obama. Even to seasoned observers of politics, it was a mystery how this contorted legal process had come about after ten years of executive orders, congressional intervention, legal decisions, and public debates. This chapter will explore the reasons that detention policy has been such a difficult instrument for our strategic approach to combating terrorism.

Detention policy is paradoxical unto itself and further paradoxical in its relationship with targeted killing. How much due process is required to authorize targeting and how much due process is owed to detainees once captured? These legal questions potentially affect battlefield decisions. Intelligence is required to counteract terrorism, but if detainees have a right not to talk, the detention is of less value. On the other hand, targeting results in no new intelligence unless other documents are part of the targeting process. This chapter will focus on the issue of detention, but surveillance, detention, interrogation, and targeting are all part of the same continuum. The tensions within this paradox are a function of varying interpretations of constitutional power, as well as of shifting classifications of terrorism as either a domestic criminal act or a form of military asymmetric power by a non-state actor under international law.

At this writing, a Congress partly controlled by the president's own party recently passed an appropriations bill, effectively denying the Obama administration the power either to try detainees in federal court in New York City

The views expressed in this article are those of the authors (Bernard Horowitz and Harvey Rishikof) and do not reflect the official policy or position of the National Defense University, the National War College, the Department of Defense, or the U.S. Government.

or to transfer detainees to third countries, effectively challenging the president's Article II constitutional authority as commander in chief. This action, affecting all detainees, would be the third bill passed by Congress in fewer than 10 years, joining the Detainee Treatment Act of 2005 (PL 109–148) and the Military Commissions Act of 2006 (PL 109–366, updated in 2009).

President Obama responded to the December 2010 bill with a signing statement on January 7, 2011, which stated:

> Despite my strong objection to these provisions, which my Administration has consistently opposed, I have signed this Act because of the importance of authorizing appropriations for … our military activities in 2011. Nevertheless, my Administration will work with the Congress to seek repeal of these restrictions, will seek to mitigate their effects, and will oppose any attempt to extend or expand them in the future. (Office of the President of the United States, *Statement by the President on H.R. 6523*, January 7, 2011)

Two months later, on March 7, 2011, Obama issued Executive Order 13567 restarting military commission trials and detainee case review proceedings at Guantanamo Bay.[1] Finally, in early April, U.S. Attorney General Eric Holder held a press conference announcing the commencement of military commission proceedings for five Guantanamo detainees relating to their roles in the 9/11 attacks. The Obama administration, at this date, appears to have abandoned its intention to use Article III courts and will be using military commissions for the current detainees in custody, largely because of congressional objections to trying accused terrorists in U.S. courts.

These objections notwithstanding, Congress has remained relatively supine over the last 10 years regarding detainees, incapable of adequately confronting vital policy questions left unresolved by the 2001 Authorization of Military Force (AUMF). As detailed in this chapter, the debate has played out like a tragic drama over five acts, with the result that policy solutions have fallen to the executive who must formulate institutional paths and to the judiciary who must regulate those choices.

---

[1] Military commissions had been suspended and amended three times since their initiation in 2004. As of March 16, 2011, the Department of Defense website lists 25 total terrorist defendants in military commission proceedings. By the count of the authors, nine of this group have had their charges dropped (but remain in custody), seven face ongoing commission proceedings (though one of this group has won a federal habeas case), four have been charged and pleaded guilty, three have been convicted (two by commission and another in federal court), and two have been transferred to their country of citizenship. See http://www.defense.gov/news/commissions.html.

ACT I: THE AUMF AND THE PATRIOT ACT

Before beginning, we should point out that this chapter does not focus on the torture debate, even though much of the legislation addressing detention policy pertains to the physical treatment of detainees. "Torture," per se, was banned by the Detainee Treatment Act of 2005, which prohibited "cruel, inhuman and degrading treatment or punishment of persons under the detention, custody or control of the United States Government," regardless of geographic location; this prohibition applied to the Central Intelligence Agency (CIA) as well as to the military. Concerning the treatment of detainees, the Detainee Treatment Act and the Military Commissions Act of 2006 left some "wiggle-room" for CIA interrogations, a group of roughly six "enhanced interrogation techniques."[2] These methods were authorized by President Bush in Executive Order 13440, through interpreting their permissibility under the Geneva Conventions, and the Convention against Torture and Other Cruel, Inhuman or Degrading Treatment. Upon taking office, President Obama rescinded Bush's order, in effect banning these practices. There is still a legal question concerning whether any such activity is forever banned, based on the legal doctrine of necessity. While the issue of "torture" has therefore been settled at least for the moment, detainee policy continues to bedevil the political process. Why? Like most mysteries, the story starts with a single act that sets in motion a series of actions that prove to be paradoxical, opaque, and interconnected—and that avoid the key issues.

The Authorization for the Use of Military Force:

The original action commencing the detention morass was part of the congressional response in the wake of the 9/11 terrorist attacks – the Authorization for the Use of Military Force (PL 107–40) (AUMF), passed on September 18, 2001. The AUMF is a unique piece of legislation, often quoted but rarely discussed or analyzed. It has created troublesome ambiguities for both administrations. It reads in full:

Joint Resolution

To authorize the use of United States Armed Forces against those responsible for the recent attacks launched against the United States.

---

[2]   These included dietary manipulation (not starvation), sleep deprivation, "facial holds," "attention grasps," and slapping. See Michael John Garcia, *Interrogation of Detainees: Requirements of the Detainee Treatment Act*, August 26, 2009 (Washington, D.C.: Congressional Research Service, Report RL33655), 9–10.

Whereas, on September 11, 2001, acts of treacherous violence were committed against the United States and its citizens; and

Whereas, such acts render it both necessary and appropriate that the United States exercise its rights to self-defense and to protect United States citizens both at home and abroad; and

Whereas, in light of the threat to the national security and foreign policy of the United States posed by these grave acts of violence; and

Whereas, such acts continue to pose an unusual and extraordinary threat to the national security and foreign policy of the United States; and

Whereas, the President has authority under the Constitution to take action to deter and prevent acts of international terrorism against the United States: Now, therefore, be it

Resolved by the Senate and House of Representatives of the United States of America in Congress assembled,

Section 1 – Short Title

This joint resolution may be cited as the 'Authorization for Use of Military Force'.

Section 2 – Authorization For Use of United States Armed Forces

(a) IN GENERAL- That the President is authorized to use all necessary and appropriate force against those nations, organizations, or persons he determines planned, authorized, committed, or aided the terrorist attacks that occurred on September 11, 2001, or harbored such organizations or persons, in order to prevent any future acts of international terrorism against the United States by such nations, organizations or persons.

(b) War Powers Resolution Requirements-

(1) SPECIFIC STATUTORY AUTHORIZATION- Consistent with section 8(a)(1) of the War Powers Resolution, the Congress declares that this section is intended to constitute specific statutory authorization within the meaning of section 5(b) of the War Powers Resolution.

(2) APPLICABILITY OF OTHER REQUIREMENTS- Nothing in this resolution supersedes any requirement of the War Powers Resolution.

Striking about the "whereas" language are three concepts – the attacks are characterized as "treacherous violence" or "grave acts of violence" and therefore outside the law of armed conflict; the right of self-defense is invoked both at home and abroad, thereby eroding the distinction between the domestic and the international spheres; and finally, the threat "continue[s] to pose an unusual and extraordinary threat to ... national security" so the unparalleled danger is enduring, and therefore past military engagement solely with Al-Qaeda. The "whereas" language recognizes the unique phenomenon that "terrorism" entails unusual treachery since civilians, not combatants, are the victims, and U.S. civilians are being targeted both at home and abroad. The erosion of the distinction between civilian and combatant is married to the reality that the continental United States has become the battlefield. There are only a few instances in United States history when this has occurred – the War of 1812, the attacks by Pancho Villa in the early 1900s, and Pearl Harbor.

But it is Section 2 of the AUMF that is the most extraordinary. The authorizing of the president by Congress to use all military force "necessary and appropriate" against those "nations, organizations, or persons" he determines "planned, authorized, committed, or aided the terrorist attacks that occurred on September 11, 2001" is unprecedented. For all intents and purposes Congress has declared war on "individuals" and "organizations" in addition to an "undisclosed number of nations." This resolution is a form of congressional blank check with the executive alone having the power and discretion to "fill in" the "individual" or "group" or "country" as the facts unfold.

President Bush's address on 9/11 concluded that there would be "no distinction between the terrorists who committed these acts and those who harbor them" (American Rhetoric 2011, http://www.americanrhetoric.com/ speeches/gwbush911addresstothenation.htm). Hence, the AUMF states that if any of the "undisclosed nations" had "harbored such organizations or persons" the president was authorized to project military force against them. The sweeping effect of this broad authorization is still being debated 10 years later.

Never had Congress granted any president such unrestricted power involving individuals and organizations, nor had there ever been such a "fill in the blank" for military power. Depending on the executive interpretation, the AUMF potentially conflates the law of armed conflict, international law, and domestic criminal law while simultaneously treating the globe as a worldwide battlefield upon which individuals and groups can become "lawful" objects of "targeted killing" – potentially jeopardizing the sovereignty of nations. To this day, the AUMF remains the basic "domestic" law legitimizing the War on Terrorism, including detainment policy.

USA Patriot Act

The 9/11 attacks created an unusual legislative environment transcending a national security policy gridlock that was in effect long before 2001. The *9/11 Commission Report* notes:

> Congress had a distinct tendency to push questions of emerging national security threats off its own plate, leaving them for others to consider. Congress asked outside commissions to do the work that arguably was at the heart of its own oversight responsibilities. Beginning in 1999, the reports of these commissions made scores of recommendations to address terrorism and homeland security but drew little attention from Congress. Most of their impact came after 9/11 (Kean and Hamilton 2003, 107).

The Uniting and Strengthening America, Providing Appropriate Tools Required to Intercept and Obstruct Terrorism Act (USA PATRIOT), passed on October 26, 2001, was designed to restructure the United States defense apparatus and transition from a Cold War paradigm to that of the War on Terrorism. Notwithstanding conventional wisdom to the contrary, its passage required extensive collaboration between Congress and the executive. A decade later, most of the PATRIOT Act is permanent and no longer controversial. Only two sections remain subject to debate; both were recently renewed until June 1, 2015 (Ramonas 2011). But however far-sighted the PATRIOT Act may have been, detainee policy was one area it did not cover:

> In the Patriot Act, Congress amended the Immigration and Nationality Act to authorize the Attorney General or his designee to certify that an alien was engaged in activity that endangered the security of the United States and to detain such alien for seven days before bringing immigration or criminal charges. This provision was never used. (Wald and Onek 2005, 128–129)

Neither the PATRIOT Act nor the AUMF comprehensively addressed detainment. National security policy gridlock resumed soon thereafter. Accordingly, it was the executive branch that first formulated detainee policy for the War on Terrorism.

President Bush's Military Order of November 13, 2001

In accordance with the AUMF's application of an "irregular" war paradigm, those captured during the execution of Operation Enduring Freedom would not be treated as conventional prisoners of war (POWs), nor would they be subject to the protections of Common Article 3 of the Geneva Conventions.[3] It therefore fell to the United States to draft a policy for captured opposition forces designated as "enemy combatants." Congress deferred to the executive branch to draft that policy. The resulting policy was issued as the Military Order of November 13, 2001.

The Order applied to non-U.S. citizens determined to have (1) been members of Al-Qaeda, or who (2) "engaged in, aided or abetted, or conspired to commit, acts of international terrorism, or acts in preparation therefore, that have caused, threatened to cause, or have as their aim to cause, injury to or adverse effects on the United States, its citizens, national security, foreign policy, or economy" or (3) "knowingly harbored one or more individuals described in subparagraphs 1 or 2." These individuals would be detained "to protect the United States and its citizens, and for the effective conduct of military operations and prevention of terrorist attacks" (Office of the President, *Military Order of November 13, 2001*).

---

[3] The Geneva Conventions are part of the Law of Armed Conflict (LOAC). For the purposes of detainee policy, they are interpreted "weakly," as a text through which judges may elect to flesh out the language of the AUMF. Common Article III ("common" because it applies to all the Geneva Conventions) applies to "armed conflicts not of an international character occurring in the territory of one of the High Contracting Parties." It reads: "Persons taking no part in the hostilities, including members of armed forces who have laid down their arms and those placed hors de combat by sickness, wounds, detention, or any other cause, shall in all circumstances be treated humanely, without any adverse distinction founded on race, colour, religion or faith, sex, birth, or wealth, or any other similar criteria. To this end, the following acts are and shall remain prohibited at any time and in any place whatsoever with respect to the above-mentioned persons:
 Violence to life and person, in particular murder of all kinds, mutilation, cruel treatment and torture;
 Taking of hostages;
 Outrages upon personal dignity, in particular humiliating and degrading treatment."
 It is a common misconception that the Conventions preclude (non-POW) military detention in time of war. Such detainment may be invoked by an occupying power if "security requirements make such a course absolutely necessary" (Article 42). Article 5 explains further: "Where in occupied territory an individual protected person is detained as a spy or saboteur, or as a person under definite suspicion of activity hostile to the security of the Occupying Power, such person shall, in those cases where absolutely military security so requires, be regarded as having forfeited rights of communication under the present Convention." Article 41.1 establishes that internment or assigned residence is the most severe measure authorized in cases of a definite security threat, and mandates that such measures are to be reviewed by a court or administrative board annually. Finally, it should also be noted that the Conventions do directly address the treatment of non-POW detainees, and require "In each case, such person shall nevertheless be treated with humanity and, in case of trial, shall not be deprived of the rights of fair and regular trial prescribed by the present Convention. They shall be granted the full rights and privileges of a protected person under the present Convention at the earliest date consistent with the security of the State or Occupying Power, as the case may be."

Next, the Order laid out guidelines for military detainment, authorizing the secretary of defense to imprison the detainees anywhere in or outside of the United States. Detainees were to be treated "humanely" and were to be provided with "adequate food, drinking water, shelter, clothing, and medical treatment," but would also be handled "in accordance with such other conditions as the Secretary of Defense may prescribe." Significantly, the executive order also reserved the right to transfer detainees to the United States.

Hence, detainees would face trial in either federal Article III courts or military courts. If the latter were selected, they would be charged with "violations of the laws of war and other applicable laws" by military commissions:

> Given the danger to the safety of the United States and the nature of international terrorism … it is not practicable to apply in military commissions under this order the principles of law and the rules of evidence generally recognized in the trial of criminal cases in the United States district courts. (Ibid)

These commissions, composed of military officers, were given "exclusive jurisdiction." Detainees were barred from seeking relief with any court of the United States or abroad. The officers were to conduct a "full and fair trial," and address both the facts of the case and matters of law; in addition, a variety of other procedures and guidelines were also included. The executive itself would conduct judicial review: "submission of the record of the trial, including any conviction or sentence, for review and final decision by [the President] or by the Secretary of Defense."

The Military Order foretells subsequent developments in the realm of detainee policy: the executive branch would lead, the judiciary would regulate the policy in time, and Congress would observe from the sidelines.

Activity Following President Bush's 2001 Military Order

Before continuing this narrative beyond President Bush's November 2001 Military Order, it is useful to distinguish two areas of the detainment policy debate. First, there is disagreement over the use of military commissions to try detainees. The commissions – originally initiated by the Military Order – did not commence until July 2004 (which is when they first incurred public and judicial scrutiny). Since that time, they have been used on only a handful of occasions and were revised several times, primarily by the Military Commissions Act (MCA) in 2006.

While President Bush's "Military Order No.1" expresses the intent and inclination to prosecute through the commissions, there is no guarantee the cases will go beyond the "discovery" phase. Hence, "combatant status" determinations (governmental verifications deeming detention necessary) and the corresponding legal battles have been a far more dominant issue than have military commissions till this date.

In the process of evaluating those held at Guantanamo Bay and other detention facilities, the Bush administration in July 2004 created Combatant Status Review Tribunals (CSRTs). These were held only once for each detainee to determine whether incarceration was warranted. The process also provided for an annual review of each detainee using an appellate process called Administrative Review Boards (ARBs). Some critics fault U.S. detainee policy during the Bush administration because they confuse CSRTs – which did not allow detainees some of the courtesies accorded in ordinary trials – with military commissions, assuming incorrectly that CSRTs had judicial power and could sentence detainees to prison or execution. In fact, CSRTs were administrative rather than adversarial. On January 20, 2009, President Obama ordered military prosecutors to halt all legal proceedings in Guantanamo until further notice (Finn 2009). On March 7, 2011, President Obama signed an executive order 13567 replacing ARBs with a similar process called Periodic Review Boards (PRBs) which were to convene for every detainee on a semi-annual basis.

ACT II: THE COURT ENTERS THE FRAY WITH DOCTRINE

Detainees incarcerated at Guantanamo filed habeas petitions as early as 2002, but were rejected.[4] In these cases, the Bush administration cited three sources of detainment authority: (1) the president's "inherent Article II power" as commander in chief, (2) the fact that the detainees were technically held outside the United States, and finally, (3) the broad powers authorized by the AUMF.[5]

Two Supreme Court cases – *Rasul v. Bush* and *Hamdi v. Rumsfeld*, both resolved on June 28, 2004 – changed the legal landscape.[6] In short, the cases held that detainees had the right to challenge their detention before

---

[4] See *Al Odah v. United States*, 321 F.3d 1134 (D.C. Cir 2003), rev'd sub nom *Rasul v. Bush* 124 S.Ct. 2686 (2004); and Jennifer K. Elsea, 2005. *Treatment of "Battlefield Detainees" in the War on Terrorism* (Washington, D.C.: Congressional Research Service), 1.

[5] Eventually, the two former assertions of power were ruled invalid, and even as we enter 2011, the AUMF, despite its lack of detail, remains the primary legal authority on which the Obama administration relies for detainment powers.

[6] *Rasul v. Bush*, 542 U.S. 466 (2004), is a U.S. Supreme Court decision establishing that the U.S. court system has the authority to decide whether foreign nationals (non-U.S. citizens) held in Guantanamo Bay were wrongfully imprisoned. *Hamdi v. Rumsfeld* 542 U.S. 507, (2004) was a U.S. Supreme Court decision reversing the dismissal of a habeas corpus petition brought on behalf of Yaser Esam Hamdi, a U.S. citizen being detained indefinitely as an "illegal enemy combatant."

a "neutral decisionmaker" – by petitioning U.S. courts with writs of habeas corpus. Additionally, the two cases held that although AUMF-covered detainees (including Hamdi, who had dual United States and Saudi citizenship) *were* subject to Common Article III of the Geneva Conventions, but they did *not* qualify for ordinary POW status. The Court directed the Department of Defense (DOD) to adopt procedures for determining whether detainees were indeed "enemy combatants" under the AUMF (i.e., whether they belonged to Al-Qaeda, the Taliban, or associated forces). The Court left open the question of how long the detainees could be held under the AUMF authority.

Ordinarily, one might have expected a legislative response to the *Rasul* and *Hamdi* rulings, which mandated the creation of a system for reviewing all the detainees held at Guantanamo. However, Congress remained silent, and it was the Bush administration that constructed a system to evaluate detainees both initially and for the foreseeable future should new evidence or circumstances arise. This plan took the form of three Department of Defense directives in 2004 – two in July and one in September (Department of Defense, *Orders Establishing Combatant Status Review Tribunal*).

The first directive established the CSRTs (review panels consisting of three commissioned U.S. military officers), which conducted one-time evaluations to determine "combatant status." The order defined "enemy combatant" as follows:

> An individual who was part of or supporting Taliban or al Qaeda forces, or associated forces that are engaged in hostilities against the United States or its coalition partners. This includes any person who has committed a belligerent act or has directly supported hostilities in aid of enemy forces.

Detainees determined not to be "enemy combatants" were to be "transferred to their country of citizenship or other disposition consistent with domestic and international obligations and US foreign policy."

The CSRT hearings gave detainees an opportunity to present "reasonably available" evidence and witnesses to aid in their defense. The government was required to present all relevant evidence, incriminating or exculpatory. The detainee was assigned a military officer (not a judge advocate general)[7] to act as a "personal representative." If the government sought to determine the status of the detainee with classified evidence, the representative could review the evidence. The CSRTs were instructed to make their rulings based on a "preponderance" standard (Elsea 2005, 2).

---

7 A judge advocate general (JAG) is a member of the legal branch of one of the U.S. armed services and handles matters of military law or jurisdiction.

The second DOD directive of July 2004 – "Implementation of Combatant Status Review Tribunal Procedures for Enemy Combatants detained at Guantanamo Bay Naval Base, Cuba" – commenced the CSRTs. It also established a more detailed structure and process for the tribunals, specifying the qualifications and responsibilities of the "personal representative," and resolving further details such as dictating how the "Recorder" (court stenographer) should transcribe the proceedings. The CSRTs were completed within a year; 520 detainees were designated "enemy combatants" and remained at Guantanamo and 38 were released (ibid).

Finally, the third directive, issued in September, created an administrative review office at Guantanamo Bay for the purpose of annually reevaluating detainees to ascertain whether they could be released. These "Administrative Review Boards" in many ways resembled the CSRTs, differing primarily in that they revisited prior rulings rather than issuing primary assessments since reviews of each case were conducted annually. The first group of ARBs was conducted between December 14, 2004, and December 23, 2005. Resulting from the 463 hearings (accounting for every detainee), 14 detainees were released (3 percent), 120 were transferred (26 percent), and 329 detainees had their status upheld (71 percent; Department of Defense, *Guantanamo Bay Detainee Administrative Review Board Decisions* 2006).

At the conclusion of the CSRT process, nearly four years into the War on Terrorism, the mechanisms for handling detainees were still under the exclusive control of the executive; Congress still had not passed any pertinent detention legislation since the AUMF. While the CSRTs and ARBs had established guidelines, they had done little to address the central question of what constituted legitimate grounds for detainment. Detainees continued to file habeas petitions but were not being recognized by the courts.

ACT III: CONGRESS RESPONDS WITH LEGISLATION

The Detainee Treatment Act of 2005

As an eventual response to the Court's *Rasul* and *Hamdi* rulings in July 2004, as well as to the Abu Ghraib prisoner abuse scandal, Congress was ultimately forced to address the detainee issue after having remained on the sidelines for four years. The result was the Detainee Treatment Act (DTA) of October 2005.

The DTA presented an excellent opportunity to finally codify anti-terrorism detention authority. Four years following the passage of the AUMF, the central questions were these: What sort of judicial review would detainees be granted? What would be the standard of review for upholding the detentions? How long could detainees be held or when would the war on terrorism end? What were standards for "repatriating" detainees to third party countries? Retrospectively, it seems only logical that these questions should have been addressed clearly and decisively (Bellinger and Padmanabhan 2011). As long as the AUMF remained the primary authority, the system would remain murky and unstable.

Ironically, the DTA left the substance of detention authority completely untouched, instead adding an ill-fitting tourniquet. The bill took pains neither to authorize nor require the ARB process. Instead, it merely stipulated that if the executive branch wished to change the system, Congress should be notified 30 days in advance.

The DTA also contained another reform to restrain court interference: the *Hamdi* and *Rasul* cases had mandated that detainees have an opportunity to review their incarceration before a "neutral decisionmaker." Therefore, Congress created a special route (different from habeas petitions) by which detainees could appeal the CSRT decisions. United States federal courts were stripped of jurisdiction to hear habeas petitions from Guantanamo detainees. As stated in the legislation, an "enemy combatant" status could be appealed on a limited basis to the Washington, D.C., Circuit Court of Appeals "to the extent the Constitution and law of the United States are applicable, whether the use of such standards and procedures to make the [enemy combatant] determination is consistent with the Constitution and laws of the United States."

The DTA created a limited review of the military commissions system and established by fiat an executive national security adjudication system. As two congressional observers explain:

> The DTA also provided for an appeal to the Court of Appeals for the District of Columbia Circuit of final sentences rendered by a military commission.... The scope of review was limited to considering whether the decision applied the correct standards consistent with Military Commission Order No. 1 (implementing President Bush's Military Order) and whether those standards were consistent with the Constitution and laws of the United States, to the extent applicable. (Elsea and Garcia 2010, 21)

As in the case of the DOD directives, which established CSRTs and Administrative Review Boards, the DTA declined to actually ratify military commissions. Instead, the DTA merely acknowledged their existence.

In summary, aside from creating new guidelines for the physical treatment of detainees, the DTA established a substitute process to habeas petitions through which detainees could appeal their "combatant status" designations, and an additional route to appeal verdicts from military commissions. In the case of the "combatant status" appeals, Congress failed to issue proper guidance by declining to create standards for validating or overturning detainment. More significantly, on both counts, Congress was reforming mechanisms created exclusively by the executive. In effect, in passing the DTA, Congress certified its deference to the presidency.

The Military Commissions Act of 2006

The *Hamdan* case constituted one of the earliest military commission trials. However, while being tried by the commission, Hamdan also filed for habeas. His petition finally rose to the Supreme Court in 2006. The Court overturned the detainee review system set up by "Military Order No.1" and the DOD directives on the basis that they had been merely acknowledged, not ratified, by Congress. In response, Congress passed the Military Commissions Act (MCA), signed into law on October 17, 2006. It explicitly authorized both the military commissions as well as the "substitute" habeas system, Section 7A, which was eventually held not to be the same as habeas, which ran directly through the Washington, D.C., District Court of Appeals as the appellate forum.

The 2006 MCA was more successful than the DTA in that it finally provided the military commissions with full constitutional authority, along with the other mechanisms which had lacked explicit congressional approval. To comply with *Hamdan*, the rules of the commissions were amended to comply with the Uniform Code of Military Justice, meaning that the commissions would now much more resemble U.S. courts martial.[8] The reform established a finite group of available charges (all constituting violations of the Laws of War), and solidified the rules concerning coerced statements, hearsay, and classified information both in the discovery process and in the courtroom.

The MCA clarified the military commission appellate system: petitioners could contest rulings first with the Court of Military Commission Review (CMCR), but only on matters of law. Cases could then be appealed to the Washington, D.C., appeals circuit, which would conduct a *de novo* review (Elsea 2010, 30–31). In essence, Congress had begun establishing a "national

---

[8] This is slightly misleading. In order to maintain certain procedures for classified information and to account for the inevitable delay of military commissions, a new statute was added to the Uniform Code of Military Justice (UCMJ) providing an exemption from several of its articles.

security court system" by making the D.C. courts and D.C. court of appeals the exclusive jurisdiction for detainee issues.

Finally, while the MCA clarified the system by taking pains to specify which violations of the LOAC would qualify a suspect to face a commission, there remained a serious flaw: in conceiving the MCA for the second time in as many years, Congress neglected to create a basis for *detainment*. At the rate military commissions were progressing (only a few detainees had been charged, and the commissions had been suspended by the *Hamdi* and *Rasul* rulings in 2004, and again by *Hamdan* in 2006), it was unlikely that more than a small fraction of Guantanamo detainees would be prosecuted. Hence, it was only a matter of time before criteria for detainment would become the central legal-policy question.

Congress had proven supine once again: like the DTA, the MCA fell short when it reestablished the federal court habeas-stripping rule. Congress had upheld the habeas-stripping provision, but it also neglected to address the substantive scope of detainment authority, merely citing the broad power of the AUMF. If judges ever had to address the intricacies of detention cases via habeas petitions, they would have very little congressional guidance in reaching a decision.

ACT IV: THE JUDICIAL AND EXECUTIVE BRANCHES REFINE DETAINEE DOCTRINE

In 2008, the Supreme Court took action to fill the void left by Congress. The *Boumediene v. Bush*[9] ruling held that those detained at Guantanamo – though non-U.S. persons technically held outside the United States – had fundamental habeas rights. The principle was established that if one was under U.S. jurisdiction "the constitution would in essence follow the flag." After years of congressional prevarication, the question of detainment predicates surged to the surface. The judiciary was left with no guidance beyond the 338-word AUMF. The ramifications for policy were clear. First, the question of whether detainees held in U.S. facilities in Afghanistan had habeas rights became an open question. Second (and related), a premium was placed on transferring detainees held abroad to the jurisdiction of other countries as quickly as possible; finally, third, because *Boumediene* extended the right to habeas to enemy

---

[9] *Boumediene v. Bush*, 553 U.S. 723 (2008), was a writ of habeas corpus claim made in a civilian court of the United States on behalf of Lakhdar Boumediene, a naturalized citizen of Bosnia and Herzegovina, held in military detention by the United States in Guantanamo Bay, Cuba.

forces without a stable detention process, given this uncertainty, U.S. forces are now less likely to take prisoners.

Post-Boumediene and International Law

After *Boumediene*, federal judges faced the task of constructing their own legal standard for assessing detainment on a case-by-case basis. Neither the AUMF, DTA, nor MCA explicitly addressed the subject. The post-*Boumediene* litigation record is strewn with a variety of judicial approaches and motifs, which overlap and diverge. The first post-*Boumediene* habeas petitioners urged a "Direct Participation in Hostilities Test" (DPH), which conceded personal involvement but denied direct participation in battle (Elsea and Garcia 2010, 44). This approach was rejected on the basis that "material support" of an AUMF-covered group also constitutes sufficient grounds for detainment. An opinion in *Basardh v. Obama* (2009) suggested a "future dangerousness test," subsequently contradicted by numerous other rulings (ibid., 47).

Another proposed guideline was a "Structured Role Test" to determine whether a detainee was a part of the "chain of command" in an AUMF-covered organization, and had issued or received orders (ibid., 52). Even the standards of military commissions have been contradicted in habeas hearings. The commissions have ruled that membership in an AUMF-covered group is not a crime in its own right (Elsea 2010, 9), yet it is widely held that membership is sufficient and not even *necessary* to uphold detention alone (Chesney 2010).

In *Who May Be Held? Military Detention through the Habeas Lens*, Chesney (2010) reviewed the current consensus: membership in an AUMF-covered group is sufficient grounds for detention. The "Structured Role Test" is sufficient but not necessary. Time spent either at the training camp or guesthouse of an AUMF-covered organization is almost singularly sufficient for upholding detainment. However, there is still widespread discord in many areas, including what constitutes "membership," the significance of the location of capture, and whether independent support of an AUMF-covered group justifies detainment (ibid.).

In the end, when the language of the AUMF (which is the only body of law treated as binding since it is "domestic") is applied in habeas rulings, the result is highly unpredictable; the application of broad, unspecified war powers constitutes the only direct guidance left to judges. Hence, habeas rulings hinge solely on the approach of individual judges, and these differ wildly, sometimes on divergent sides of the same verdict, or even in concurrent opinions. When Barack Obama entered office in 2009, many anticipated a "change" in detention policy. Obama engaged in a rapid flurry of executive maneuvers and suspended both ARB proceedings, as well as military commissions. However, ultimately, the status quo would return since the Congress continued to avoid the question of whether detention was more of an executive administrative function as a function of war, or rather a criminal prosecution with the application of the bill of rights and protections associated with incarceration.

The Obama Administration

President Obama's initial optimism about closing the Guantanamo Bay detention facility presumed that detainment was not only unjust but also unwarranted. Immediately upon taking office, Obama issued three executive orders to address detainee policy commissioning three task forces.

Executive Order 13491 – "Ensuring Lawful Interrogation" – rescinded President Bush's executive order of July 20, 2007, so that "enhanced interrogation techniques" (and "cruel treatment") were banned categorically. Detainees could only be handled in total compliance with the U.S. Army Field Manual (e.g., as POWs). Obama's order established a task force to determine whether the "interrogation practices and techniques in the Army Field Manual ... when employed by departments or agencies outside the military, provide an appropriate means of acquiring the intelligence necessary to protect the Nation, and, if warranted, to recommend any additional or different guidance for other departments or agencies." Seven months later, on August 24, 2009, the task force issued its recommendations, which affirmed that the "practices and techniques identified by the Army Field Manual or currently used by law enforcement provide adequate and effective means of conducting interrogations."

The other January 22 executive orders issued by President Obama – 13492 ("Review and Disposition of Individuals Detained at the Guantanamo Bay Naval Base and Close of Detention Facilities") and 13493 ("Review of Detention Policy Options") – concerned his intention to close Guantanamo. The former created a task force to "review all Guantanamo detentions," with the goal of finding resolutions to each case, be it transferring the detainee to a different country or prosecution either by commission or federal trial. The second order created another task force to formulate a plan to close Guantanamo in one year's time. There was to be a preliminary report (after 180 days) and a final report (after the year had passed). It appears that the work of the group pursuant of order 13492 fed into the report pursuant of 13493, as only one full report was issued.

Before any reports from the task forces, President Obama gave a speech at the National Archives on May 21, 2009, previewing the results of the task force studies: it would not be possible to close Guantanamo, at least for the moment. The president (*Remarks by the President on National Security* 2009) grouped the detainees into five categories:

1. Detainees who had violated American criminal laws and could be transferred to the United States and prosecuted in federal courts.
2. Detainees who had violated the Laws of War and would be prosecuted by military commissions.
3. Detainees who had won their habeas petitions, been ordered released by courts, and would be transferred to another country.
4. Detainees who would be transferred to another country and disciplined (if necessary) there.
5. Detainees who could not be prosecuted yet also posed a clear danger to the United States.

In theory, it was primarily this fifth category that would prevent the closing of Guantanamo. President Obama went on say:

> I have to be honest here – this is the toughest issue that we will face. We're going to exhaust every avenue that we have to prosecute those at Guantanamo who pose a danger to our country. But even when this process is complete, there may be a number of people who cannot be prosecuted for past crimes, in some cases because evidence may be tainted, but who nonetheless pose a threat to the security of the United States. Examples of that threat include people who've received explosives training at al Qaeda training camps, or commanded Taliban troops in battle, or expressed their allegiance to Osama bin Laden, or otherwise made it clear that they want to kill Americans. These are people who, in effect, remain at war with the United States. (*Remarks by the President on National Security* 2009)

The 2009 Military Commissions Act

In response to *Boumediene*, on October 28, 2009, Congress passed the 2009 Military Commissions Act, which offered a small variety of amendments to that of 2006, including procedural updates for military commissions (which President Obama had halted for review upon entering office, but subsequently resumed; Elsea and Garcia 2010, 38–39).

Like the DTA and 2006 MCA, the 2009 MCA neglected to significantly address the substantive scope of detainment authority. Because detainees could petition for habeas, the central question was which sort of past activity (on the part of the detainee) constituted "membership" in an AUMF-covered organization ("membership" having been determined to be legitimate grounds for detainment). The 2009 MCA neglected to address these legal parameters, which were (and remain) the heart of the detention debate.

Task Force Reports

Following the 2009 MCA, on January 22, 2011, the two Guantanamo Task Forces reported their results jointly. A brief "Preliminary Report" had been released on July 21 (Department of Defense, *Detention Policy Task Force Issues Preliminary Report* 2009), but contained few specifics (Department of Defense, *Determination of Guantanamo Cases Referred for Prosecution*) – the actual midterm report was suspended and never materialized (Isikoff 2009). The full, final report reflected the president's May 21 speech at the National Archives and contained these specifics:

- 126 detainees had been approved for transfer to another country, and to date (1/22/10), 44 had already been sent on their way.
- 30 detainees from Yemen would be transferred there depending on the "current security environment in that country."
- 44 detainees qualified for prosecution, either by commission or in the United States.
- 48 detainees fell into the special category of "too dangerous to transfer but not feasible for prosecution."

The setback regarding the 48 special-category detainees had been public knowledge since the National Archives speech, and the Obama administration sought to build momentum by concentrating on lowering the number of Guantanamo detainees as much as possible. On November 13, 2009, Attorney General Eric Holder announced a plan to transfer five high-profile detainees, including Khalid-Sheikh Mohammed (KSM) to the United States for prosecution via the Southern District of New York.[10]

Congressional Interventionism – Power of the Purse

Attorney General Eric Holder's announcement was greeted with widespread skepticism from a diverse group of critics. Some objected on the basis that trying terrorists in downtown New York City posed an unnecessary security risk.

---

[10]   Those to be prosecuted in the Southern District were Khalid-Sheikh Mohammed, Walid Bin Attash, Ramzi Bin Al Shibh, Ali Abdul-Aziz Ali, and Mustafa Al Hawsawi.

Others found it inappropriate to grant such detainees the right to a civilian trial, or felt that a civilian trial unnecessarily heightened the risks of acquittal absent a military commission.

In June 2009, Ahmed Ghailani – charged for the 1998 African embassy bombings – became the first high-profile Guantanamo detainee to be transferred to the continental United States for prosecution. Ghailani's trial commenced on October 4, 2010. On November 17 – four days after Holder's announcement to try the five – Ghailani was convicted on one count (conspiracy) of 285 (most of which were for murder). While Ghailani was sentenced to life imprisonment, the 284 acquitted charges resulted in a bipartisan congressional reprisal against civilian trials for detainees.[11]

Reacting to the knowledge that a number of detainees released from Guantanamo had again taken up arms against the United States – at least 14 percent of those released as of April 2009 (U.S. Federal Bureau of Investigation, *FBI Fact Sheet: Former Guantanamo Detainee Trends* 2009) – Congress added a mandate to the 2011 National Defense Authorization Act, effectively withdrawing all funding for transferring Guantanamo detainees and constraining the executive. There were some few exceptions allowing transfer. Detainees could be removed from Guantanamo if so instructed by a court order. They could also be transferred if the secretaries of state and defense provided special written certification, guaranteeing that the detainee would never again take up arms against the United States, an impossible standard to meet in the end.

Congress had apparently been considering restricting the transfer of detainees via the power of the purse for some time. A *Washington Post* editorial observed, "The Guantanamo closure process and the appropriations process for the new terrorist detention facility in Illinois offer a perfect opportunity to correct this long-festering problem. The administration will have to work with Congress, if only to permit Obama to move detainees to the new site" (Goldsmith and Wittes 2009). The Ghailani verdict apparently encouraged Congress to act on a long-brewing urge to preemptively block Guantanamo transfers.

The spending blockade had been known to the executive as early as December 9, 2010, when Attorney General Holder issued a public letter of protest to Senate leaders Harry Reid (D-NV) and Mitch McConnell (R-KY), citing the obtrusive authorizations bill soon after its promulgation. Holder

---

[11] Some view the *Ghailani* trial as a positive because despite the 284 acquitted counts, he was convicted and sentenced to life in prison. However, an overwhelming majority seem to view the case as evidence that civilian trials are inappropriate for terrorism detainees.

complained that the administration had been "unable to identify any parallel ... in the history of our nation in which Congress has intervened to prohibit the prosecution of particular persons or crimes" (Office of the Attorney General, letter to Senators Reid and McConnell 2009).

President Obama decided he could not afford to veto a critical authorizations bill and signed it into law on January 7, 2011. He issued a strongly worded signing statement of compliance and disagreement:

> Despite my strong objection to these provisions, which my Administration has consistently opposed, I have signed this Act because of the importance of authorizing appropriations for ... our military activities in 2011. Nevertheless, my Administration will work with the Congress to seek repeal of these restrictions, will seek to mitigate their effects, and will oppose any attempt to extend or expand them in the future. (Office of the President of the United States, *Statement on Signing the Ike Skelton National Defense Authorization Act for Fiscal year 2011* 2011)

On March 7, 2011, President Obama issued Executive Order 13567, which announced the resumption of both military commission proceedings and review of detainees, two processes that had been suspended upon his being voted into office. The order did away with Bush's ARBs and created similar "Periodic Review Boards" (PRBs) which were to be more adversarial than ARBs, and directed to convene semi-annually. Then, in early April, Attorney General Holder announced the commencement of commission prosecutions against five Guantanamo detainees allegedly complicit in the 9/11 attacks. Holder lamented that the Justice Department had been blocked from trying the detainees in civilian court, and stated bluntly that military commission prosecutions were not his first choice and had been forced upon the executive branch.

Whatever one might think of the advisability of President Obama's plans to prosecute Guantanamo detainees, there is no denying that the congressional spending admonition fits snugly into a pattern of nominally ameliorative congressional actions that have done aggravatingly little to tackle the "substantive scope" question but have pushed the administration toward an executive-commission approach.

IMPLICATIONS OF THE PARADOX THAT ALL WANT TO AVOID

President Bush's original inclination to strip Guantanamo detainees of habeas rights was an aggressive approach denying any law of armed conflict protections; it begged for judicial review. The *Boumediene* case forced the issue. A similar expansion of court jurisdiction lies on the horizon: there exists the possibility that detainees held abroad in Iraq and Afghanistan may one day attain habeas in U.S. courts. While such petitions have already been filed in U.S. courts, federal judges are disinclined to hear such cases at this time. The Obama administration's approach to use Article III and criminal law was blocked by an energized Congress. Given Congress's stance, the Obama administration (like the previous administration) is now reluctant to seek a congressional solution for fear of the result (Wittes 2009). Benjamin Wittes (2009) described the implications of the president's apparently conscious decision not to seek legislation to address detention:

> First, while it will not stop detentions, it will ensure that the ground rules for those detentions remain murky, ever-shifting and unclear to agencies that have to conduct operations in the field. This uncertainty will encumber operations and create perverse incentives for both targeted killings and for detentions by allied proxy forces that don't have to go through eight years of litigation to neutralize a suspected enemy fighter.
>
> Second, it leaves in place a system of judicial review of Guantanamo detentions that ill-serves detainees and government alike. The current system of making policy and reviewing detentions through habeas corpus litigation serves the government badly because the standards are unstable and evidence collected one day for intelligence purposes proves useless in justifying detentions years later when the rules shift, judges grow less comfortable and that material suddenly has to serve as evidence in court. It serves detainees badly because review has been painfully slow and detainees in habeas get only one bite at the apple. If a detainee loses his habeas case, that's it.
>
> Third, the failure to go to Congress to write the rules means that the rules for detention will be written by judges. So far, the judges who have heard habeas cases have disagreed about a great many central issues – many of which the Supreme Court will ultimately have to resolve. The high court, which has not a single national security expert, may end up making good policy or bad.

Indeed, any proper resolution must necessarily come from Congress. The executive does not have the authority to set policy alone and acts with the knowledge that its policies will eventually be reviewed by the judiciary. But in the end the judiciary will be unwilling to resolve the ultimate questions of detainment authority since detainee issues will necessarily raise questions of politics and of judicial deference.

In fact, two of the most respected Washington, D.C., District Court judges, Thomas Hogan and Richard Leon (2009), have expressly rejected suggestions that the judiciary resolve detainment authority questions:

"It is unfortunate," [Hogan] said in an oral opinion from the bench, "that the Legislative Branch of our government and the Executive Branch have not moved more strongly to provide uniform, clear rules and laws for handling these cases." While allowing that the various judges were "working very hard and in good faith," he lamented that "we have different rules of evidence" and "a difference in substantive law." For Judge Hogan, it all "highlights the need for a national legislative solution with the assistance of the Executive so that these matters are handled promptly and uniformly and fairly for all concerned."

In October 2008, [Judge Leon] issued [a habeas] opinion characterizing both the petitioners and the government as having urged him to "draft" his own preferred legal standard regarding the boundaries of detention author-ity. This he refused to do, arguing that his role instead was merely to deter-mine whether the administration's position was consistent with a pair of domestic legal considerations. (Chesney 2010)

And so after 10 years of sporadic congressional legislation; Supreme Court, court of appeals and district court opinions; and executive orders and mili-tary commissions, the state of detention policy remains unresolved. The four questions raised by the process of detention – who is subject to detention; what is the appropriate due process for detention; when should detention end; and finally, what are the state responsibilities for repatriating detainees – remain unanswered (Bellinger and Padmanabhan 2011). The international legal com-munity similarly has not been able to satisfactorily address the issue of non-state actor detention that falls between international and non-international conflict. Although the issue affects a relatively small number of detainees, the problem is significant for due process purposes and affects our approach to detaining and targeting – since information is the key to preventing terrorist acts.

The paradox continues: are detainees criminals with full constitutional rights or unlawful combatants with limited rights? As they have for the past decade, the three branches of government continue to neglect to address important questions of due process and detainee policy for fear of politics and power. Congress has acted to block the latest executive initiative for Article III trials, the executive has no interest in engaging Congress on detention policy, and the courts have begun the process to establish policy on the question of "material support" (vis-à-vis detention) but are reluctant to do more. Also based on the current political landscape, the military commissions are unsure of their constitutional status as trials begin. So the world watches and waits as Congress and the executive live the paradox of detention in the service of due process and the hunt for information to prevent terrorist acts.

9

Arms Control

David P. Auerswald

There is a strong history of bipartisanship when it comes to the evaluation of international treaties, particularly arms control treaties.

— President Barack Obama, April 8, 2010

When Majority Leader Harry Reid asked me if I thought the treaty could be considered in the lame duck session, I replied that I did not think so given the combination of other work the Congress must do and the complex and unresolved issues related to START and modernization.

— Senator Jon Kyl (R-KY), November 16, 2010

This book began with the question of whether the first branch of government is adequately organized to deal with national security issues in an integrated and coordinated manner. Specifically, Chapter 1 asked whether Congress is capable of effectively influencing security policy given heightened partisanship, message politics, party-committee relationships, and bicameralism. This chapter focuses on the Senate's role in making international treaties to help answer some of those questions. I argue that the Senate has regularly and increasingly exercised authority over national security policy using the treaty advice and consent process. The recent passage of the New START treaty was just the latest example of growing Senate assertiveness when considering treaties, despite, or perhaps because of, heightened partisanship, message politics, and party-committee relationships. Rather than being a break from the past, consideration of New START was indicative of a long-term trend.

As introduced in Chapter 1, two considerations help determine the extent of congressional influence over national security policy: whether Congress

The views expressed in this chapter are those of the author and not the National Defense University, the Department of Defense, or any other entity of the United States government.

possesses the will and the capability to affect policy. On the latter point, this chapter will argue that the constitutional requirement that the Senate provide its advice and consent before a treaty can enter into force allows the Senate the means to influence national security policy. On the former point, a number of domestic political factors – some dependent on individual lawmakers' perceptions of international events and others dependent on raw political calculation – make it more and more likely that individual senators will choose to exert their will using the treaty advice and consent process.

This chapter begins by putting treaties into context within broader patterns of executive-legislative relations. The chapter then reviews the historic record associated with Senate consideration of treaties, explaining when, why, and how the Senate has used the advice and consent process to influence national security policy. I next review the Senate's 2010 consideration of the New START arms control treaty as a concrete example of Senate policy making using the advice and consent tool. I conclude with thoughts about possible future Senate national security policy making via advice and consent.

TREATIES AND EXECUTIVE-LEGISLATIVE RELATIONS

The process of treaty ratification formally begins when the president submits a treaty to the Senate for advice and consent. Treaties are automatically referred to the Senate Foreign Relations Committee once submitted. If a majority of the committee approves of the treaty, they draft a treaty ratification document pursuant to that treaty, and send that document to the Senate floor for debate, possible amendment (and/or additional reservations), and perhaps a final vote.

Article II, Section 2, of the Constitution states that all treaties must receive Senate advice and consent from a two-thirds majority of all senators present and voting before treaties can be ratified and enter into force. That requirement encompasses a wide range of possibilities. If all members of the Senate are in attendance during a vote, a treaty ratification document would need 67 votes to pass. For important or controversial treaties, debates over which tend to be well attended, the required two-thirds vote makes advice and consent a higher standard even than the 60 seats required to invoke cloture and cut off floor debate. If only the majority and minority leaders and the presiding officer are present, the requirement for passage drops to two senators. This is the norm for relatively trivial treaties, or those for which there is broad consensus support. Advice and consent in those instances is a relatively easy hurdle to overcome, with passage often done by voice vote acclamation.

Ratification documents take two general forms. All ratification documents contain a general statement of acceptance, similar to the following: "Resolved, two-thirds of the senators present concurring therein, that the Senate advise and consent to the ratification of [Treaty X], signed on [Date Y] at [Location Z] on behalf of the United States and [the other parties to the treaty]." Some ratification documents, however, contain additional provisions following this general statement. These provisions can spell out amendments to the treaty itself, limitations on the treaty's scope or duration, executive branch reporting requirements when implementing the treaty, or anything else that the Senate wants to include. Most such provisions do not require that the treaty be renegotiated internationally, at least if the provisions do not change the underlying treaty's text. Ratification provisions are not necessarily limited to the particular issues of the treaty, in that no constitutional requirement or Senate rule specifies that provisions in a ratification document be germane to a treaty's subject matter (Henkin 1972, 136). And ratification provisions are not voted on by the House, allowing for unicameral changes to policy. In sum, ratification provisions are attractive to senators as vehicles for policy making because the provisions need not be approved by the House, are very difficult for the president to reject, and have the force of law once ratified (Auerswald 2002; Henkin 1972).

Ratification provisions go by many names, including amendments, reservations, understandings, and declarations. Regardless of name, ratification provisions fall into one of three categories. Senate amendments to the treaty text itself, or reservations or understandings as to the purpose of the underlying treaty, the parties to the treaty, or declarations as to how the United States will comply with and enforce the treaty can be thought of as *crucial* ratification document provisions. Crucial provisions define for America's international treaty partners the behavior they can expect from the United States under the terms of the treaty. *Domestic* provisions, on the other hand, specify new forms of interaction between the branches of government (e.g., executive branch reports or certifications to Congress) and have little effect on international understandings of the underlying treaty. The same holds true with *non-germane* provisions, a third type of provision, which as the name implies address subjects foreign to the purpose of the treaty and different from simply specifying executive reports or certifications pursuant to the treaty.

When given the opportunity by the submission of a treaty, the Senate regularly uses these three types of provisions to influence U.S. national security policy. A ratification document's overall effect, of course, depends on the types of provisions included in that particular document and the contents of individual provisions. Including crucial provisions has the potential to alter substantially the terms of a treaty or at least U.S. obligations under that treaty.

Domestic provisions may require onerous executive reports or prevent presidents from taking action without congressional consent. Non-germane provisions have the potential to alter U.S. foreign or security policy in substantial ways, regardless of the terms of the underlying treaty. The Senate has inserted each type of provision in different patterns over time, as discussed in the next section.

From the Senate's perspective then, a document of ratification is a very attractive tool by which to influence policy. Changing policy requires only that two-thirds of the Senate present and voting agree to the change. The House of Representatives is not involved, meaning that passing a ratification document is a much easier hurdle to overcome than is passing stand-alone legislation, particularly if House and Senate majorities disagree. After all, legislation containing a Senate initiative goes nowhere if House and Senate majorities become deadlocked. The same is not true for ratification documents. Passing a document of ratification also is significantly easier than enacting legislation when Senate preferences differ significantly from those of the president. Presidents almost always accept ratification document provisions (to do otherwise is to kill the underlying treaty) but are likely to veto legislation they disagree with. In short, using ratification documents for policy making is an attractive option in the modern era of divided government, as ratification documents require few if any compromises with the House or the president.

When examined in the broader scope of executive-legislative relations over foreign policy, the treaty advice and consent process is an example of what Samuel Huntington (1961, 3–5, 124–133) and later James Lindsay (1994, 120–127, 147, 153–156) called "strategic" foreign policy, a category of foreign policy where power is shared by the executive and legislative branches. Thus we would not expect the president to so dominate the advice and consent process that the Senate never makes policy via advice and consent. Nor would we expect Congress to so dominate the process that the president would automatically incorporate every congressional concern into the treaty's text during its negotiation.

But that said, the advice and consent process empowers the Senate in numerous ways vis-à-vis the president. The president initiates the advice and consent process by negotiating and then submitting a treaty to the Senate, but the Constitution empowers the Senate to initiate a related and parallel policy process that the president no longer controls. Rather than confronting the Senate with a take-it-or-leave-it dilemma, submitting a treaty for advice and consent begins a process in which the president gets confronted with his own take-it-or-leave-it policy dilemma. If the president wants the treaty he must accept each and every additional ratification provision passed by the Senate.

Finally, the ratification process removes many of the collective action problems confronting Congress when enacting foreign affairs legislation. For instance, the advice and consent process helps alleviate the electoral disincentives associated with questioning the president's foreign policy priorities. Senators can cloak their (perhaps contrary) actions in constitutional rhetoric. They can argue that dissecting a treaty, and by extension the president's foreign policy goals, is mandated by the Constitution. As a result, there may be fewer electoral disincentives associated with the advice and consent process than with foreign affairs legislation. When the Senate is given the opportunity by the president's submission of treaties, then, ratification documents are an attractive tool for policy making.

THE RECORD OF ADVICE AND CONSENT

Most studies of the Senate's advice and consent power focus on two issues. On the one hand are studies that deconstruct Senate conduct during particular treaty debates (Auerswald 2002; Evans and Oleszek 2002; Isaacs 1999; Pitsvada 1991). On the other hand are studies that discuss the constitutional implications of treaty ratification (Spiro 2001; Baylis 1999; Yoo 1999; Trimble and Koff 1998; Sklamberg 1997; Henkin 1995; Koplow 1992; Glennon 1991; Trimble and Weiss 1991; Koh 1990b). Recently, however, a few studies (Krutz and Peake 2009; Auerswald 2006; Auerswald and Maltzman 2003) have examined broader patterns of Senate policy making via advice and consent. In this section we will review their key findings.

Auerswald and Maltzman (2003) examined all treaties considered by the Senate between 1947 and 2000 to explain the content of ratification documents. Their data showed that the characteristics of the treaty in question played an important role in determining the likelihood that the Senate will attach a reservation to a ratification document. The authors found that the Senate was more likely to add reservations to ratification documents when the treaties concerned dealt with high politics (i.e., issues of security and sovereignty) rather than low politics (i.e., economic, legal, or normative issues). Likewise, bilateral treaties were more likely than multilateral treaties to have reservations. This reflected the fact that the imposition of a reservation is a high-risk strategy internationally when there are many other treaty signatories. As more countries have to buy on to changes, the more likely it is that one will object, putting the treaty at risk.

The preferences of the Senate also affected the likelihood of reservations. After the breakdown of the Cold War consensus, treaty reservations became more common. During the Cold War, the likelihood of a reservation being included in a ratification document was 16 percent less likely than after the Cold War ended. In addition, when the median senator became more conservative, the Senate was more likely to restrict the executive branch's independent treaty-making authority. Similarly, the likelihood of the Senate imposing a reservation also increased as the Senate became more ideologically polarized, in that reservations were increasingly likely as the ideological divide grew between the president and the 67th senator on the opposite side of the aisle (i.e., the senator needed to reach the two-thirds threshold for advice and consent). Combined, the authors found that the treaty's subject matter (high politics), Senate policy preferences (median ideology and views on foreign policy), and the institutional requirements for ratification (two-thirds majority) all increased the likelihood that the Senate would add one or more additional provisions to a basic ratification document.

Auerswald (2006) conducted a more detailed examination of security treaties from the same time period to explore whether Senate behavior was different for security treaties compared to the larger universe of treaties, and to examine the types of ratification provisions added to security treaties. For security treaties, the single best predictors of Senate behavior were the weakened foreign policy consensus that began at the height of the Vietnam War and accelerated with the end of the Cold War, and the perceived importance of each individual treaty.

On the former point, examining just security treaties demonstrated that the decline and eventual demise of the Cold War foreign policy consensus affected the number of additional provisions included in ratification documents. The Senate exercised considerable restraint crafting ratification documents during the early Cold War period, less restraint in the post-Vietnam Cold War era, and very little restraint in the post–Cold War period, as expected. The Senate was relatively passive when considering treaties during the Cold War but was very active in the post–Cold War era. This was consistent with the overall findings in the earlier study (Auerswald and Maltzman 2003). On the latter point, important treaties, as measured by the number of *New York Times* editorials associated with each treaty, led to additional ratification provisions. It seems that when the country-at-large paid attention to a treaty, senators followed suit and scrutinized that treaty more closely.

Surprising, however, was that the median ideological position in the Senate did not have a significant effect on the inclusion of additional ratification provisions for security treaties, nor did the ideological position of the pivotal senator required for a successful vote to grant advice and consent. This was different from the observed behavior in the earlier study of *all* treaties during that same time period, leading Auerswald (2006) to conclude that the demise of a U.S. foreign policy consensus played a more important role in Senate consideration of security treaties than have partisan considerations or the ideological polarization of the Senate. When it comes to security treaties, politics may stop at the water's edge, but increasingly there are fundamental disagreements among senators of all political stripes as to what should be done across that water to protect the United States.

This intuition was borne out in the data on the content of ratification documents associated with security treaties. During the Cold War, the Senate concentrated on crucial provisions that clarified U.S. treaty obligations. Senators included one or at most a few such provisions in each security treaty. Senators rarely included domestic ratification provisions, and did not include any nongermane provisions until 1988. The Senate added all three types of provisions during the post–Cold War period, and did so in larger and larger numbers as time passed. And though it is difficult to directly measure the effect of those provisions on U.S. security policy, many ratifications documents included provisions that dramatically altered policy, at least in the short term.

The Senate can use the advice and consent process to influence national security policy in a final, fundamental way, and that is by holding up the treaty in the Senate and thus preventing the treaty from entering into force. In one sense this is a negative power, in that the Senate can veto or make irrelevant a presidential priority through significant delays. Prime examples are Senate delay of the Law of the Sea treaty or the convention on the International Criminal Court. In another sense, however, delay is a positive power. The Senate can foist its own priorities on the president by holding his treaty hostage absent agreement to the Senate's initiative. The most famous, recent example of this was when Senate Republicans, led by Senator Jesse Helms (R-NC), delayed the Chemical Weapons Convention until the Clinton administration agreed to a fundamental reorganization of the foreign policy establishment, to include abolishing the U.S. Information Agency (USIA) and the Arms Control and Disarmament Agency (ACDA), and subordinating the U.S. Agency for International Development (USAID) into the State Department.

Many of the same factors that determine whether the Senate will insert its policy initiatives into a ratification document also determine the amount of time it takes the Senate to consider treaties. The most complete examination of Senate delay of treaties is contained in Krutz and Peake (2009). Using essentially the same data set as Auerswald and Maltzman (2003), covering all treaties from 1947 to 2000, Krutz and Peake found that the Senate spent 239 days, on average, considering any individual treaty.

Different factors influenced the length of debate in the Senate Foreign Relations Committee and on the Senate floor. In committee, Krutz and Peake

(2009, 153) found that the largest delay in treaty consideration was the type of treaty considered. New treaties were subject to lengthy committee debates, as were treaties that sought to establish international norms. The next most influential factor was the ideological distance between the president and the pivotal 67th senator required for passage. The higher that difference, the longer was the delay at the committee stage. Other factors that contributed to lesser delays at the committee stage included the number of seats held by the president's partisans in the full Senate, though in the opposite way we would expect. The stronger was the president's party, the lengthier was the debate. The ideology of the Senate Foreign Relations Committee chair also had a comparable impact on delays at the committee stage. The more conservative was the chair, the more the treaty was delayed in committee. Factors that sped up treaty consideration in the Senate Foreign Relations Committee included the treaty's importance and the historical era in which the treaty was considered, with more important treaties and treaties during the Cold War speeding up committee consideration. Committee deliberations also sped up when the sitting president was seen favorably by at least 65 percent of the electorate.

Delay at the floor stage was influenced by fewer factors (Krutz and Peake 2009, 157), with the most significant delays caused by the Cold War. Though Cold War treaties were given speedy review in the Senate Foreign Relations Committee, they received lengthy reviews on the floor, perhaps reflecting the greater willingness of the relative experts on the committee to give presidents the benefit of the doubt during the Cold War, whereas their non-committee, non-expert colleagues on the Senate floor needed more time to get up to speed on the treaty's content. Presidential popularity did not seem to matter when the treaty hit the floor. Instead, lengthy, public, presidential statements coincided with lengthy Senate floor debates. As with the committee stage, important treaties were subject to longer floor debates. Finally, ideological dispersion between the president and the pivotal 67th senator increased treaty consideration, just as it increased the chances of the Senate inserting additional provisions in ratification documents.

In sum, these three large-scale studies provide a road map for when the Senate is likely to influence foreign and security policy through the advice and consent process. Senators can do so either by attaching their own initiatives to treaty ratification documents or delaying a treaty to thwart a president or coerce concessions on unrelated issues. The time period of a treaty seems to matter for both phenomena, as does the ideological distance between the president and the treaty pivot, and the type of treaty being considered. The ideology of the median senator and the Senate Foreign Relations Committee chair, the treaty's importance, and presidential support and public statements only mattered in particular circumstances or during different stages of Senate debate. All this leads to the following expectations regarding Senate consideration of New START.

The "Treaty with Russia on Measures for Further Reduction and Limitation of Strategic Offensive Arms," commonly known as New START, was signed in Prague on April 8, 2010, by President Barack Obama and Russian President Dmitry Medvedev. The treaty limited the United States and Russia each to 700 deployed strategic nuclear delivery vehicles, 1,550 deployed warheads on those delivery vehicles, and 800 deployed and non-deployed strategic delivery vehicles (Senate Foreign Relations Committee 2010, 12). The treaty also reinstated and updated an on-site inspection protocol from the original START treaty regime to verify that these reductions were taking place in both countries. President Obama submitted the treaty and associated protocols to the Senate on May 13, as Treaty Document 111–5, which began a formal process that would last until December 22, 2010, when the Senate provided its advice and consent to the treaty in a 71 to 26 vote.[1] Observers over the interviewing months witnessed many of the trends referenced above in terms of the content, character, and length of Senate debate on New START.

Expected Senate Behavior

Ratification Provisions: The works referenced earlier lead to the expectation of many ratification provisions being included in the New START document of ratification. In general, the Senate is most likely to add provisions when the Senate itself is ideologically divided or leaning conservative, and when considering bilateral, security treaties in the post–Cold War era. In terms of security treaties, treaties that are perceived as important and that took place after the Cold War are guaranteed to receive lengthy ratification documents. Both sets of expectations were borne out during consideration of New START.

Four explanations from previous studies would predict a large number of additional ratification provisions being added to the basic New START ratification document. First, New START took place in the post–Cold War era. This has been a period with a seeming lack of a foreign policy consensus,

---

[1] As nuclear arms control treaties went, this was a relatively close vote. Consider that the 2002 Moscow Treaty was approved unanimously; the 1996 START II treaty was approved 87 to 4; the 1991 START treaty 93 to 6; and the 1988 INF treaty by a 93 to 5 vote.

particularly when it comes to arms control with Russia, the future of the U.S. nuclear stockpile, and missile defenses. Second, New START was a bilateral, security treaty, which should increase the chances of additional ratification provisions. Third, the Senate that considered New START was ideologically polarized. Preceding Senate elections produced an increasingly polarized chamber, with moderates of both parties having a harder and harder time getting elected. This was a time of hyper-partisanship on many issues, and indeed, partisanship was on display in the year leading up to the treaty's consideration on such issues as health care, financial reform, environmental regulation, immigration policy, gays in the military and energy policy. Fourth, the Senate in late 2010 was leaning increasingly toward the conservative side of the ideological spectrum. The Democratic majority, that had as recently as 2008 held a 59 to 41 majority, seemed poised to lose seats in the 2010 elections. And indeed, by early November the Republican Party had picked up six Senate seats, moving the Senate's ideological median member back toward the conservative side.

A fifth explanation raised earlier, this one regarding the treaty's perceived importance, would not predict much in the way of Senate behavior. The administration and some Senate supporters considered the treaty important because it both symbolized the "reset" with Russia advocated by the Obama administration and would reinstate on-site verification procedures that had lapsed with the termination of the original START verification regime. In June 10 congressional testimony, for example, Brent Scowcroft, former national security advisor under presidents Gerald Ford and George H.W. Bush, argued that "the principal result of non-ratification would be to throw the whole nuclear negotiating situation into a state of chaos." Added Principal Deputy Undersecretary of Defense James Miller in congressional testimony (Global Security Newswire 2010d), "One of our dirty little secrets is, when the Berlin Wall went down, the United States reoriented a lot of intelligence capacity away from the Soviet Union and Russia. To some fair degree … the intelligence community was relying on U.S. inspectors to be on the ground."

These arguments only partially resonated with outside perceptions, however, at least if we measure the treaty's importance by the number of *New York Times* editorials written on it. New START was the subject of three *Times* editorials. For comparison's sake, the original START and ABM treaties each received three editorials, START II received four, the Conventional Forces in Europe (CFE) treaty received five, and the Intermediate Nuclear Forces (INF) treaty received six. All were a far cry from the 29 *Times* editorials devoted to the Panama Canal treaty or the 40 written about the creation of NATO. Some think tank commentators also questioned the importance of the treaty, arguing that it was only an incremental change from President Bush's earlier Washington Treaty with Russia (Kagan 2010). So a treaty like New START, of some, but not significant, perceived importance would produce only a slight increase in additional ratifications provisions.

Length of Debate: Students of treaty advice and consent would expect that New START would receive measured, but not overly lengthy consideration. And that is indeed what occurred. The Senate considered New START for a total of 223 days, very close to the median 239 days spent on debate for all treaties considered between 1947 and 2000. Senator John Kerry (D-MA), the Senate Foreign Relations Committee chairman, initially tried to expedite his committee's review of New START. Yet scholars of the advice and consent process would predict that the two most important factors impeding consideration of New START were the ideological dispersion within the Senate and the fact that New START was a new treaty.[2] On the latter point, New START was a new treaty rather than an amendment to an existing treaty, which should increase the length of debate. On the former front, remember that the greater the ideological distance between the president and the pivotal 67th senator, the more prolonged is treaty debate.

During consideration of New START, the ideological distance between President Obama and the pivotal senator was already significant before the midterm elections. Remember that this was the Congress that had held a long and rancorous debate over health care reform in addition to the confirmation fights over two Supreme Court Justices and legislation on financial reform, the economic stimulus, fair pay, and tobacco regulation. That ideological distance was only going to increase in the next Congress after moderate Democrats were replaced by more conservative Republican senators.

The Obama administration seemed to have anticipated that fact and tried to minimize its consequences by reaching out to key Republican senators. This began before the treaty was even submitted to the Senate. According to Senator Lugar (R-IN), the Senate Foreign Relations Committee's ranking Republican member, the Obama administration invited him and Senator Kerry to the White House to discuss what it would take to get bipartisan support for the treaty. In Lugar's words, "We told him it had to get verification and missile defense right. And I think the administration team did a good job in achieving that goal. President Obama knew he would have to counter

---

[2] President Obama's mid-40 percent approval ratings through most of the debate did not help speed debate. See "Gallup Daily: Obama Job Approval," http://www.gallup.com (May 19, 2011).

the objections of some lawmakers who would launch a frontal assault on the treaty" (Kitfield 2010a).

As early as July, Senator Kerry had attempted to de-link the treaty from domestic political fights. As Kerry noted in letter in the *Washington Post* (Kerry 2010a), "From the first Senate Foreign Relations Committee hearing in April, Richard Lugar of Indiana, the panel's ranking Republican, and I have made clear that there is no room in this debate for domestic politics." Kerry's plea was by and large ignored by treaty opponents. Objections to the treaty occurred, and unfortunately for the administration, got intertwined with ideological disputes on everything from the role of the federal government, tax rates and social policy, to posturing for the 2010 elections and their aftermath, to the politics of a lame-duck congressional session. As a result, the Senate debate took longer than treaty supporters and the administration had hoped.

The Senate Debate

Committee Consideration: Two large issues dominated the committee stage of the Senate debate: missile defense and the U.S. nuclear weapons infrastructure.[3] The Senate Foreign Relations Committee focused on these and other issues during two groups of hearings during the summer of 2010. The first included five separate hearings, with testimony from the secretaries of state and defense and the chairman of the Joint Chiefs of Staff, and former secretaries of state and defense. The second set comprised eight sessions, with witnesses that included testimony from the treaty negotiators, former National Security Advisors, other senior officials, past and present, of both the State Department and the Defense Department, and officials from the nuclear weapons labs. The Senate Armed Services Committee also held eight hearings on the treaty during the summer, with a similar witness list.

There were 11 Democrats and 8 Republican on the committee. With these numbers, Chairman Kerry could have passed the treaty ratification document by late July, at the conclusion of the hearings. On August 3, however, Kerry announced (Kerry 2010b) that he was delaying the committee vote until September, "in response to requests from some colleagues for more time to review materials concerning the treaty's ratification." He went on to note that "we have the votes to report the treaty out of committee now," but he was

---

[3] Penketh notes that early debate over the treaty through June 2010 also included missile silo conversion, counting rules for rail mobile missiles, and the number of verification inspections allowed by the treaty. See Anne Penketh, "Stopping New START?" *BASIC Backgrounder,* July 2, 2010.

postponing the vote "so that we can build bipartisan consensus." The delay was widely seen as an effort to woo Senator Kyl, who was a strong conservative voice on foreign policy, the Republican Whip in the Senate, and the eventual leader of the opposition to the treaty (Global Security Newswire 2010c; Matishak 2010b). The belief was that as Kyl went, so too would go a large number of Republican votes (Grossman 2010a).

Senator Kyl and other treaty skeptics were concerned that New START would limit the number of U.S. offensive weapons at a time when the president was curtailing the modernization of the country's nuclear weapons infrastructure. Combined, this would give the U.S. only a limited number of older, unreliable nuclear weapons. Their criticism was sparked by the Obama administration's Nuclear Posture Review, which prohibited the development of new nuclear weapons capabilities or nuclear testing and also ruled out the use of nuclear weapons against non-nuclear powers (Global Security Newswire 2010a; Matishak 2010a; Pollack 2010). Senator Kyl demanded that the administration increase its funding for nuclear weapons laboratories and nuclear weapons modernization in the current and future budgets to ensure that the weapons complex remained viable into the future (Global Security Newswire 2010b; Pincus and Sheridan 2010). As quoted in the press (Global Security Newswire 2010e), Kyl wanted "a more precise and higher degree of commitment so that we know that this program is not going to go for a while and peter out."

Delaying the committee markup would in theory allow the Obama administration time to convince Senator Kyl that nuclear weapons modernization and infrastructure improvements were an administration priority. Obama administration officials had repeatedly argued that the treaty would not curtail or slow U.S. modernization plans. In late July testimony before the Senate Foreign Relations Committee, Assistant Secretary of State Rose Gottemoeller noted (Gottemoeller 2010) that "Indeed, this treaty imposes no constraint on U.S. efforts to modernize its nuclear enterprise or develop and deploy the most effective missile defenses possible to protect U.S. national security and the security of our allies and friends." The administration backed up these statements with increases to the Department of Energy budget for the nuclear weapons stockpile and weapons complex by approximately $7 billion for FY2012 and $80 billion over the decade. The administration also budgeted $100 billion in Defense Department funds to modernize strategic nuclear delivery systems over 10 years (Warner 2010).

Treaty skeptics also used committee deliberations to criticize the Obama administration's missile defense policies. Criticism on this front allegedly stemmed from Russian statements that the preamble to the treaty – which specified that there was a relationship between strategic offensive and defensive systems – placed limits on U.S. missile defense programs in Europe and at home. The conservative Heritage Foundation worried that the Obama administration or future administrations would feel constrained by the Russian perspective and "impose major self-restraints in order to avoid compliance breach with the treaty" (Brookes and Graham 2010, 1; Goldsmith and Rabkin 2010). Former Massachusetts governor Mitt Romney, a 2008 Republican presidential candidate and potential candidate in 2012, wrote that "*New START* impedes missile defense. Whatever the reasons for the treaty's failings, it must not be ratified. [The Senate] must insist that any linkage between the treaty and our missile defense system be eliminated" (Romney 2010). Senator Jim DeMint (R-SC), a strong Senate advocate of missile defenses, introduced an amendment to the New START ratification document that required the U.S. "to deploy as rapidly as technology permits an effective and layered missile defense system capable of defending the territory of the United States and its allies against all ballistic missile attacks," a policy shift that went well beyond anything contemplated by the Obama administration (Global Security Newswire 2010h).

Senator Kerry tried to dispel the linkage between New START and missile defense. He wrote (Kerry 2010a) that "The treaty will have no impact on our ability to build missile defenses against Iran, North Korea or other threats from other regions." Obama administration officials reiterated that point in congressional testimony. For example, Edward Warner, a Defense Department representative to New START negotiations with the Russians, testified (Warner 2010) that "Under the treaty, the United States is free to pursue its current and planned ballistic missile defense programs, as well as any other courses of action we might choose to pursue.... Nothing in this treaty or in the Russian unilateral statement concerning U.S. missile defenses, which is not a part of the treaty and not legally binding, will constrain us from developing and deploying the most effective missile defenses possible."

On both these issues, the ideological divide between treaty supporters and opponents was fairly stark, but it did not correspond to a simple Democratic-Republican distinction. Though Senate Democrats uniformly supported the treaty, Republicans were deeply divided by it (Katulis 2010). Both within and outside the Senate, Republicans who had served in national leadership positions during the Cold War supported the treaty, such as former Secretaries of State George Schultz and Henry Kissinger, former National Security Advisors Brent Scowcroft and Colin Powell, former Secretaries of Defense Harold Brown and Frank Carlucci, the chairman of the Senate Foreign Relations Committee, Senator Dick Lugar, as well as former distinguished Republican senators including John Danforth, Chuck Hagel, Nancy Kassebaum, Warren Rudman, and Alan Simpson.[4] Republican leaders who had come to prominence since the Cold War were by and large opposed the treaty, however, to include many former senior officials in the George W. Bush administration. In the Senate, opponents included the aforementioned Jon Kyl (R-AZ), Minority Leader Mitch McConnell (R-KY), Jim DeMint (R-SC), Orin Hatch (R-UT), and James Inhofe (R-OK). Senators Lamar Alexander (R-TN), Bob Bennet (R-UT), and Bob Corker (R-TN) were guardedly opposed, but were open to persuasion if the administration adequately funded the nuclear weapons program.

Treaty opponents demanded that the administration answer more than 700 questions for the record associated with the treaty and provide senators with the classified negotiating record associated with the treaty, an unprecedented request. Many observers believed that partisan politics were at the root of the debate. Former national security advisor Brent Scowcroft opined that "Some just don't want to give Obama a victory." Others characterized this strict questioning as an attempt to "truth-squad the administration's assertions," which was ironic given that many of these same senators had not raised such questions when considering the Bush era Washington Treaty on nuclear arms control (Pincus 2010a; Sheridan and Pincus 2010). Senior administration officials obliquely chastised treaty opponents for their attempts to replicate Senator Helms's 1990s feat of using a treaty to extract concessions on unrelated issues. In the words of Secretary of State Hillary Clinton, "It [New START] is a political issue. I wish it weren't. I hope at the end of the day the Senate will say, you know, some things should just be beyond any kind of election or partisan calculation" (Global Security Newswire 2010f).[5]

The Senate Foreign Relations Committee began its markup of the ratification document in mid-September using a version drafted by Senator Lugar. The committee passed an amended version of that document on September 16, 2010. The committee included in the resolution a number of treaty opponents' concerns, particularly on missile defenses and delivery system modernization. The document passed the committee on a 14 to 4 vote, with three Republicans – Richard Lugar (IN), Bob Corker (TN) and Johnny Isakson

---

[4] For a detailed list of former officials who supported the treaty by the summer, see Senate Foreign Relations Committee, "Kerry lauds bipartisan group of former cabinet members and senators who support the New START treaty," Senate Committee on Foreign Relations Press Release, June 24, 2010, http://foreign.senate.gov.

[5] For a similar perspective from a bipartisan group of retired senior foreign policy officials, see George Schultz, Madeleine Albright, Gary Hart, and Chuck Hagel, "It's Time for the Senate to Vote on New START," *Washington Post*, September 10, 2010, http://www.washingtonpost.com (September 13, 2010).

(GA) – and all eleven Democrats voting in favor of the resolution. Voting against the committee's markup resolution were Senators John Barrasso (R-WY), James Inhofe (R-OK), Jim Risch (R-ID), and Roger Wicker (R-MS).[6] After the vote, Senator Kerry said, "The Foreign Relations Committee has bridged the partisan divide and come together in the national interest. It is time for the Senate to do the same" (Kerry, 2010C). At the same time, treaty opponents made clear that they were not satisfied. In the words of Senator DeMint, "If we are going to move ahead with the commitment not to protect the people of the United States, I think everyone in this country ought to know it" (Global Security Newswire 2010g).

Floor Consideration: The debate now shifted to the Senate floor. The timing of the debate fed into the preexisting ideological divide to affect the ratification process. The Democrats had a 59 to 40 majority when President Obama submitted the treaty to the Senate in May. This was not necessarily as strong a position as it seemed. The majority party was one vote shy of a filibuster-proof supermajority, a very strong position had the Senate been considering a normal legislative initiative. But this was a treaty, needing 67 votes for advice and consent, leaving the Democrats eight votes short. The Democrats did not have much trouble invoking cloture, given that the Senate Foreign Relations Committee ranking Republican, Senator Lugar, was a vocal supporter of the treaty. Convincing seven other Republican senators to cross party lines was not guaranteed by any means in the lead-up to or aftermath of the 2010 midterm elections.

The Obama administration's strategy through the fall was to engage in retail politics, playing to the local concerns of individual senators. Specifically, they continued to negotiate with Senator Kyl, to take concrete steps to solidify support from senators in states hosting nuclear weapons facilities, and to court the few moderate Republican senators remaining in the Senate, such as Susan Collins and Olympia Snow of Maine, whose constituencies might not oppose the treaty. For example, in early October, the administration included $624 million in additional money for the nuclear weapons complex as part of a stop-gap continuing appropriations bill (Global Security Newswire 2010i), something that appealed to the congressional delegations from South Carolina, Tennessee, and New Mexico.

The 2010 midterm congressional elections complicated the Obama administration's retail politics strategy and their hopes of winning quick passage

---

[6]   Senator Jim DeMint (R-SC) was absent for the vote. Both he and Risch did not support the resolution of ratification despite having their amendments incorporated into the final committee resolution.

on the floor. As the election approached, it seemed increasingly likely that the Democrats would lose Senate seats in the November balloting. When the November 2 election results were counted, the Democrats had lost control of the House and six seats in the Senate. Engaging in one-on-one deal-making became much more difficult. Newly empowered Senate Republicans demanded that a final vote on New START be delayed until the next Congress rather than during a lame-duck session. Ten incoming Republican senators sent a letter to that effect to Senator Reid in mid-November. But a 2011 vote was deadly for the administration, as they would need 14 Republican votes to pass the treaty in 2011 instead of eight in 2010.

The administration continued with its strategy of negotiating with Senator Kyl, upping the ante on November 12 with a further increase of $4.1 billion for the nuclear weapons complex over five years. Administration officials flew to Arizona to brief Kyl on the proposal that weekend.[7] The senator responded that regardless of new funding, he could not support a vote on New START before the next Congress (Kyl 2010). "When Majority Leader Harry Reid asked me if I thought the treaty could be considered in the lame duck session, I replied I did not think so given the combination of other work Congress must do and the complex and unresolved issues related to START and modernization."

Kyl's opposition to a near-term vote was a major blow to treaty supporters, who believed that he could sway a number of Republicans with his vote. Senator Lugar noted that Kyl's rejection of the treaty changed the whole prognosis for New START. "This is a situation of some national security peril," he said (Global Security Newswire 2010j). Senator Joe Lieberman (D-CT) agreed, saying, "Honestly, it's one of those cases where one senator, Jon Kyl, has so much influence with so many colleagues on a particular issue, that he pretty much determines whether there are enough votes" (quoted in Scully and Sorcher 2010). While it generated trepidation among some, Kyl's opposition also sparked outrage among some treaty supporters and a vow to push for ratification without him. Gary Samore, a senior National Security Council staff member, told reporters that the administration and Kyl had been negotiating for several weeks during multiple meetings, and the White House thought they had reached an agreement until Kyl's announcement (Grossman 2010c). Said President Obama, "There is enough gridlock, enough bickering. If there

---

7 An informed Senate aide was quoted in the press as asking, "The key question for Republicans now is have they leveraged enough on nuclear weapons, or should they ask for more?" See Elaine Grossman, "Offering Nuclear Plus-Ups, White House Awaits Kyl's Word on New START," *Global Security Newswire*, November 15, 2010, http://gsn.nti.org (November 15, 2010).

is one issue that should unite us – a Republicans and Democrats – it should be our national security" (Obama 2010a).

By the end of November, treaty critics, including Kyl, were stating that there was simply not enough time on the Senate calendar to adequately review the treaty. Senator Kerry made the counter-argument that "There is plenty of time to consider this treaty. A significant national security matter hangs in the balance and the Senate should be willing to work overtime to allow for a full and complete consideration of the treaty. If time is the only concern, then we should have no concerns" (Kerry 2010d). Minority Leader McConnell responded that New START should not be considered until a series of domestic issues had been addressed by the Senate first, particularly the impending demise of the Bush tax cuts at the end of the year. "A little while ago, I delivered a letter to Senator Reid signed by all 42 Senate Republicans. It says that every Republican will vote against proceeding to any legislative matter until we've funded the government and protected every taxpayer from a tax hike. Basically, first things first" (McConnell 2010a). Opponents repeatedly argued that New START needed at least two weeks of debate, something that could not occur when the Senate was also considering tax legislation, stop-gap government spending, repealing the "Don't Ask, Don't Tell" policy on gays in the military, and the "Dream Act" immigration bill. Senator Kerry eventually went public with a list of reasons explaining why he had delayed consideration of New START at each stage in the process, each one related to Republican requests for more time. He argued that it was disingenuous for the Republicans to claim now that they had no time.[8] By this point it was clear that there was a fundamental disagreement as to the wisdom of the treaty that was tied into a variety of other debates over the role of government and the Obama administration's priorities.

Through December the Senate focus was on vote counting and parliamentary maneuvering to influence the New START floor debate. Early in the month, both sides floated ideas as to linking support for extending the Bush tax cuts to passage of New START, with the tax cut extension as a prerequisite for passing the treaty (Friedman 2010; Rogin 2010a). At the same time, Senator DeMint again warned that he would filibuster the treaty into the next Congress if not provided with the negotiating record on missile

---

[8] These included a July request to delay the committee vote, as discussed earlier, a request to postpone floor consideration until after the midterm election, and a request to delay floor consideration until the next Congress. See Elaine Grossman, "Democrats Scramble to Lock in GOP Votes for Arms Treaty," *Global Security Newswire*, December 16, 2010, http://gsn.nti.org.

defenses. Though DeMint did not have the votes to sustain a filibuster, he could repeatedly delay debate with the necessity of passing repeated cloture motions. In anticipation of that tactic, the majority leader countered by bringing New START to the floor at the same time as the aforementioned legislative initiatives. They could therefore shift from the treaty to other legislation or back again anytime there was a delay in either respective debate.

As December unfolded, however, more and more Senate Republicans began voicing their support for the treaty, as displayed in Table 9.1. In September, Senator Lugar was the only Republican firmly in the yes column. Senators Corker and Isakson had voted for the ratification document in committee, but had not committed to final passage at that time. By mid-December, however, press reports listed seven Republicans as supporting New START, two votes shy of the nine needed for final passage. This could have been due to the Obama administration's funding increases, discussed earlier. It could also have been in part due to endorsements of New START by President George H.W. Bush and former Secretaries of State Colin Powell and Condoleezza Rice in mid-December, as well as a public endorsement of the treaty by five former secretaries of state in Republican administrations. Regardless of the reasons, the momentum seemed on the side of treaty supporters as debate opened over New START on December 15, 2010.

Four important things occurred at the start of the floor debate. First, the White House announced that they would risk everything on a vote in the current Congress rather than delay until the next Congress when their task would only be harder. Vice President Joe Biden was quoted as saying, "We'd rather lose now with the crowd that's done the work rather than go back and start from scratch" (Rogin 2010b). Second, the "motion to proceed" associated with the treaty passed 66 to 32, with nine Republican senators in support.[9] This was significant in that the White House had just received the Republican votes it needed to pass the treaty. Third, the administration shifted their focus from Senator Kyl to Senator John McCain as the main Republican they would work with to garner additional Republican votes. McCain's support could be vital in terms of allaying Republican fears about future missile defense policy, and he seemed willing to work with the administration on a missile defense amendment to the ratification document in a way that other missile defense

---

[9] Senator Evan Bayh (D-IN) was absent from the vote for medical reasons. Though Senator Corker voted no on the motion to proceed, he said he would eventually support the treaty. See Josh Rogin, "White House Gives Up on Getting Kyl's Support for New START," *The Cable*, December 16, 2010, http://www.foreignpolicy.com.

TABLE 9.1. *Republican Senate support for new START*

Senators	Committee vote (Sept 16)	Prelude to debate[a] (Dec 1–15)	Motion to proceed (Dec 15)	Cloture motion (Dec 21)	Final passage (Dec 22)
Lugar (IN)	X	X	X	X	X
Alexander (TN)		X		X	X
Bennet (UT)		X	X	X	X
Brown (MA)			X	X	X
Cochran (MS)				X	X
Collins (ME)		X	X	X	X
Corker (TN)	X			X	X
Graham (SC)			X		
Gregg (NH)		X			X
Isakson (GA)	X			X	X
Johanns (NE)					X
Murkowski (AK)			X	X	X
Snowe (ME)		X	X	X	X
Voinovich (OH)		X	X	X	X
TOTAL	3	7	9	11	13

[a] Names listed for this two-week period are based on a variety of press accounts cited elsewhere in this chapter.

supporters, such as Senator DeMint, would not.[10] Fourth and finally, Senator Reid announced that he would keep the Senate in session through the winter holidays, if necessary, to reach a final vote on New START. Holding Congress in session for an extended period of time, such as over a weekend, through the night, or over a holiday, is a time-tested way of focusing congressional attention on the issues at hand.

With the votes seemingly there to pass the ratification document, attention focused on preventing so-called "killer amendments" from altering the text of the treaty itself, something that would force the Obama administration to renegotiate the treaty with Russia and start the process all over again. Treaty

---

[10] Senator Kyl did not help his cause with statements that "If I announce for or against the treaty at this point, nobody will listen to me" and that the Democrats were "disrespecting one of the two holiest days for Christians" by debating the treaty right before Christmas. See Josh Rogin, "Biden to Kerry: I'd Rather See New START Fail This Year than Be Delayed Next Year," *The Cable*, December 15, 2010, http://www.foreignpolicy.com. Vice President Biden stated during a December 15 MSNBC interview, "Senator Kyl is opposed to the treaty. He's flat out opposed to the treaty." Biden went on to say, "Don't tell me about Christmas. I understand about Christmas. I hope I don't get in the way of your Christmas shopping, but this is the nation's business. This is the national security at stake." Quoted in Josh Rogin, "White House Gives Up on Getting Kyl's Support for New START," *The Cable*, December 16, 2010, http://www.foreignpolicy.com.

supporters were able to defeat amendments that would have altered the treaty's preamble on missile defenses, increased the number of weapons inspections mandated by the treaty, increased the number of deployed launchers allowed by the treaty, and included tactical nuclear weapons in the treaty (Baker 2010a; Baker 2010b; Cassata 2010; Rogin 2010d).

The other danger was that debate over unrelated legislation might sidetrack the momentum on New START or alienate Senate Republicans to the point that they would vote no just to spite the administration. And indeed, the debate over the repeal of "Don't Ask, Don't Tell" cost the administration the vote of Senator Lindsay Graham (R-SC), who said that "this lame duck has been poisoned" (Baker 2010b) and that his concerns regarding missile defenses had not been met (Rogin 2010d). Said Minority Leader McConnell,

> The Senate can do better than to have the consideration of a treaty interrupted by a series of controversial political items. So leaving aside for a moment any substantive concerns, and we have many, this is reason enough to delay a vote. Our top concern should be the safety and security of our nation, not some politician's desire to declare a political victory and host a press conference before the first of the year. Americans have had more than enough of artificial timelines set by politicians eager for attention. (McConnell 2010b)

These dangers notwithstanding, the Senate passed a cloture motion on December 21 to end debate on New START. Senators had built on the committee's draft resolution of ratification, but had avoided amendments that would have forced the treaty to be renegotiated with the Russians. Final passage occurred on Wednesday, December 22, 2010, by a vote of 71 to 26. Thirteen Republican senators supported New START, as listed in Table 9.1. Senator Kerry said after the vote, "America is most secure when we set aside partisan politics and Democrats and Republicans debate our national security on the merits. That happened today and the world is safer because the Senate did its duty" (Kerry 2010e).

What the Senate Agreed To

The final resolution of ratification focused on four big issues: increased support for U.S. nuclear weapons infrastructure, ensuring that Russia could not limit U.S. missile defense deployments, the effect of the treaty on conventionally armed strategic missiles (dubbed "prompt global strike" capabilities), and future limitations on Russian tactical nuclear weapons. The Senate included provisions in the ratification document on each of these topics and ensured that, at the least, the legislative branch was supplied with increased information to make future choices. The final New START ratification document contained 29 additional provisions above and beyond the boilerplate text included with every treaty. Ten were crucial provisions aimed at clarifying U.S. obligations under the treaty. Nine were not germane to the contents of New START, but instead focused on a variety of issues raised in the previous paragraphs. Ten were domestic provisions that required executive branch reports, certifications, and consultations.

From a policy-making perspective, the most important ratification provisions fell into the "crucial" and "non-germane" categories. The crucial provisions included four dedicated to ensuring that U.S. missile defenses were in no way limited by the treaty. Two crucial provisions did the same with regard to global strike capabilities. One other provision dealt with ensuring that Russian rail mobile missile systems were counted as ICBM launchers under the treaty, and three others were on a variety of miscellaneous topics. The administration did not seriously object to any of them.

Perhaps more interesting was what was included in the non-germane provisions. This was where the Senate had perhaps the most obvious effect on U.S. national security policy, an effect that might have been harder to achieve in 2010 via normal legislation, given that Senate Republicans did not have much chance of shepherding these initiatives through the House of Representatives controlled at that time by the Democrats. The subjects included missile defenses (1 provision), global strike (2 provisions), modernizing the nuclear stockpile (1 provision), the nuclear weapons complex (1 provision) and strategic delivery vehicles (2 provisions), tactical nuclear weapons (1 provision), and funding for the Cooperative Threat Reduction (CTR) program (1 provision). Of these, the only one that might have gotten through the House without a fight was the CTR provision, which simply stated that the president should continue the CTR program and use it to facilitate the implementation of New START, something most Democrats supported.

The missile defense provision was more controversial, particularly with skeptical Democrats. The provision specified that the United States was free under New START to construct "a layered missile defense system capable of countering missiles of all ranges," and that the United States "is committed to improving United States strategic defensive capabilities both quantitatively and qualitatively." The language in that second statement went well beyond the 1999 National Missile Defense Act's commitment that it was U.S. policy to deploy a national missile defense system, and it was certainly not a policy statement shared by all across the aisle. The ratification document also specified that the United States seek to negotiate reductions in Russian tactical nuclear weapons, but that such negotiations not include any limits on missile defenses. This provision could in theory make it much harder to convince the Russians to give up their numerical advantage in tactical weapons, as the United States could not trade limitations on U.S. missile defense (desired by the Russians) for cuts in Russian tactical weapons (desired by the United States).

On global strike, the Senate prohibited the president from sharing telemetry data with the Russians if those data were not relevant to New START and/or could undermine the effectiveness of any global strike system. By this action, the Senate was trying to ensure that the Russians could not defeat global strike (or pass telemetry data to third parties bent on defending against U.S. global strike systems) and that future presidents could not abandon global strike on the argument that its vulnerabilities were well known internationally. The Senate also specified that conventional global strike weapons do not affect strategic stability between the United States and Russia. By this language, the Senate laid down a marker that future presidents could not curtail such a program by arguing that global strike undermined strategic stability, an argument that the Clinton administration had made during the 1990s with regard to national missile defenses.

Finally, the Senate addressed concerns of adequate funding for the maintenance and modernization of the nuclear weapons stockpile and related infrastructure, to include maintaining the nuclear weapons labs. The Senate specified that the United States was committed to funding these programs, at a minimum at levels established by the Kyl-Obama administration negotiations of late 2010. The document also specified that the president accelerate the design of certain specific, new, nuclear weapons facilities and fully fund those facilities. The Senate took a similar tack with regard to nuclear delivery systems, in that the ratification document required the president to commit to modernizing and replacing the strategic nuclear triad. The Senate seemed to be saying that arms control was acceptable only so long as the remaining force was state-of-the-art and capable of being expanded quickly should international circumstances change.

CONCLUDING THOUGHTS

Article II, Section 2, of the Constitution states that all treaties must receive Senate advice and consent from a two-thirds majority of all senators present and voting before treaties can be ratified and enter into force. The Senate has regularly and increasingly exercised authority over national security policy using the treaty advice and consent process, and did so yet again when considering New START. The president initiates the advice and consent process by negotiating and then submitting a treaty to the Senate, but the Constitution empowers the Senate to initiate a related and parallel policy process that the president no longer controls. Rather than confronting the Senate with a take-it-or-leave-it dilemma, submitting a treaty for advice and consent begins a process in which the president gets confronted with his own take-it-or-leave-it policy dilemma. If the president wants the treaty he must accept each and every additional ratification provision passed by the Senate.

Consideration of New START was indicative of the long-term trend. This chapter argued that the constitutional requirement for advice and consent allowed the Senate the means to influence national security policy during the New START debate. A variety of factors – to include the time period of the treaty's consideration, the ideological distance between the president and the treaty pivot, and the type of treaty being considered – helped determine the extent to which individual senators chose to add crucial, domestic, and non-germane initiatives into the New START ratification document. In that document, the Senate included policy guidance on missile defense, the modernization of the nuclear stockpile and infrastructure, global strike capabilities, tactical nuclear weapons and mobile missiles, among others.

If the record from the past 60 years and recent debate over New START are a guide, policy making via advice and consent will continue to have an important impact on U.S. foreign policy in the years ahead. Most important, as debate over the wars in Iraq and Afghanistan have demonstrated, the United States currently lacks anything approaching a Cold War consensus on much beyond a generic opposition to terrorism. At the same time, the legislative process appears dominated by partisan concerns and ideological differences between the president and opposition parties in Congress. In such an environment, senators are likely to take advantage of the treaty advice and consent process to further their respective agendas. As a result, presidents who want the country to speak with a single voice would be wise to clear the national script with the Senate, because the Senate is likely to use the advice and consent process, when available, to shape long-term U.S. foreign policy in ways that may conflict with presidential initiatives.

National Security Surveillance

Louis Fisher

Presidential authority to engage in national security surveillance has been shaped by executive initiatives, congressional statutes, and judicial decisions. After the terrorist attacks of 9/11, the Bush administration decided to author-ize warrantless national security surveillance in violation of the Foreign Intelligence Surveillance Act (FISA). The operation remained secret until disclosed by the *New York Times* in December 2005. Pressured by the admin-istration, Congress passed legislation in 2008 to give retroactive immunity to the telecoms that assisted with the surveillance. In so doing, Congress gave a green light to executive agencies and private companies that act against the law. In defense, administration officials claimed that the president has cer-tain "inherent" powers under Article II of the Constitution that may not be limited by congressional statutes or judicial rulings. Efforts to challenge the Bush surveillance policy in court have been difficult because federal judges are reluctant to dispute national security claims by the executive branch, espe-cially when private parties seek access to information the government regards as "state secrets."

SOME EARLY PRECEDENTS

On May 21, 1940, on the eve of World War II, President Franklin D. Roosevelt sent a confidential memo to Attorney General Robert H. Jackson, authorizing and directing him to obtain information "by listening devices" to monitor the conversations or other communications "of persons suspected of subversive activities against the Government of the United States, including suspected spies." Roosevelt told Jackson to keep these investigations "to a minimum and to limit them in so far as possible to aliens" (Fisher and Harriger 2011, 740). No specific law in 1940 prohibited Roosevelt from taking this initiative.

From the 1920s forward, the Supreme Court offered unsteady guidance on surveillance by the government. In *Olmstead* v. *United States* (1928), the Court upheld the use of wiretaps by prohibition agents to monitor and intercept phone calls. Small wires had been inserted in telephone wires leading from homes and offices. Sharply divided, 5 to 4, the Court reasoned that the taps did not enter the premises of a residence, did not constitute physical entry, and were therefore not a "search" or "seizure" under the Fourth Amendment ("The right of the people to be secure in their persons, houses, papers, and effects, against unreasonable searches and seizures, shall not be violated, and no Warrants shall issue, but upon probable cause, supported by Oath or affirmation, and particularly describing the place to be searched, and the persons or things to be seized"). The warrant requirement became an issue with the national security surveillance conducted after 9/11. *Olmstead* provoked a powerful dissent from Justice Brandeis, who accurately predicted that the Court's analysis would not withstand developing technology. He also issued a warning that has stood the test of time: "The greatest dangers to liberty lurk in insidious encroachment by men of zeal, well-meaning but without understanding."

Writing for the majority, Chief Justice Taft invited Congress to establish standards for wiretapping: "Congress may of course protect the secrecy of telephone messages by making them, when intercepted, inadmissible in evidence in federal criminal trials, by direct legislation, and thus depart from the common law of evidence." In 1934, Congress passed Section 605 of the Federal Communications Act to make it a crime to intercept or to use any wire or radio communication. The statute prevented the government from introducing at trial any evidence obtained from a wiretap. This statutory policy had no application to the kind of national security surveillance that President Roosevelt had authorized, where the purpose was monitoring and not prosecution.

Olmstead was eventually overturned, but from 1928 to 1967 the Court struggled with new forms of technological intrusion, including a "detectaphone" placed against the wall of a room. Without penetrating the wall, government agents could pick up sound waves on the other side of the wall and, with the help of a receiver that amplified the sound waves, hear telephone conversations. In *Goldman* v. *United States* (1942), the Court ruled that there was neither a "communication" nor an "interception" within the meaning of Section 605 and found no violation of the Fourth Amendment.

In other cases, the ingenuity of government investigators and police easily outpaced the Court's reasoning in *Olmstead*. Using a key made by a locksmith, state police entered a suspect's home and installed a concealed microphone in the hall. They bored a hole in his roof to allow wires to transmit sounds to a neighboring garage. On subsequent visits, the police entered to move the microphone to a bedroom and later to a closet. Although a trespass and probably a burglary had occurred, the Court in *Irvine* v. *California* (1954), found no violation of Section 605 and upheld the government's action. Interestingly, in this case the Court observed: "All that was heard through the microphone was what an eavesdropper, hidden in the hall, the bedroom, or the closet, might have heard." Nothing more than that! In another case, *Silverman* v. *United States* (1961), the Court held that a "spike mike" – an electronic listening device pushed through the wall of an adjoining house until it touched the heating duct of a suspect's home – marked a physical penetration and violated the Fourth Amendment.

JUDICIAL AND CONGRESSIONAL CHECKS

In *Katz* v. *United States* (1967), the Court finally put an end to *Olmstead* and returned to basic principles. Divided 7 to 1, it declared unconstitutional the placing of electronic listening and recording devices on the outside of public telephone booths to obtain incriminating evidence. Although the government had made no physical entrance into the area occupied by the suspect, he had a legitimate expectation of privacy within the phone booth. Finally facing up to the technological sophistication of the government, the Court held that the Fourth Amendment "protects people, not places."

Because of *Katz*, Congress was under pressure to rethink its statutory policy. In 1968, it passed legislation that required law enforcement officers to obtain a judicial warrant before placing taps on phones or installing bugs (concealed microphones). In case of an "emergency" involving organized crime or national security, the government could intercept communications for up to 48 hours without a warrant. That grace period temporarily lifted the need for a judicial warrant but did not eliminate that constitutional requirement. This legislation on wiretaps and electronic surveillance in 1968 is often referred to as "Title III authority."

In a section of this statute, Congress announced that nothing in the law limited the constitutional power of the president to protect against the overthrow of the government or against "any other clear and present danger to the structure or existence of the Government." The language here is of interest. Congress by statute placed limits on the president. At the same time, it appeared to recognize that the president, pursuant to his Article II authority, might independently authorize surveillance without a judicial warrant.

When President Richard Nixon entered office in 1969, he decided to engage in warrantless domestic surveillance, particularly to monitor opponents of the Vietnam War. The National Security Agency (NSA) put together a list of these people, eventually placing names on a domestic "watch list" called the MINARET: a tracking system that allowed the agency to follow individuals and organizations involved in the anti-war movement (Bamford 2002, 428–429; Bamford 1983, 323–324). NSA agreed to use its surveillance powers to violate both the First and the Fourth Amendments. Newspaper stories in 1974 disclosed that the Central Intelligence Agency (CIA) had been extensively involved in illegal domestic surveillance, had infiltrated dissident groups, and had kept a file on approximately 10,000 American citizens. During testimony before a Senate committee, CIA Director William Colby affirmed the existence of this program (Olmsted 1996, 11–12, 35).

The Nixon administration took other steps to monitor what it considered to be radical groups and individuals in the country. Tom Charles Huston, a young aide working in the White House, drafted a 43-page, top secret memorandum that called on the capacities of several intelligence agencies. He told Nixon: "Use of this technique is clearly illegal; it amounts to burglary" (Olson 2003, 16; Emery 1995, 25; Johnson 1989, 133–156). The Huston plan directed the NSA to intercept, without judicial warrant, the domestic communications of U.S. citizens using international phone calls or telegrams (Bamford 2002, 430; Theoharis 1978, 13–39). Under pressure from FBI Director J. Edgar Hoover and Attorney General John Mitchell, Nixon withdrew the Huston Plan (Emery 1995, 26–27). However, in separate plans, called SHAMROCK, NSA entered into agreements with such U.S. companies as Western Union and RCA Global to gain access to telegrams that U.S. citizens had expected would be kept private (Bamford 2002, 438–439; Morgan 1980, 75–76).

The Nixon administration believed that the president had "inherent" power to monitor domestic organizations that planned to attack and subvert the government, justifying warrantless surveillance when necessary. In 1971, a district court held that warrantless electronic surveillance could not be justified simply because the executive branch thought some domestic organizations were trying to subvert government. The government needed to obtain judicial warrants. Rejecting the claim of a broad inherent presidential power, the court ruled that the president was "still subject to the constitutional limitations imposed upon him by the Fourth Amendment" (*United States v. Sinclair* 1971).

The Sixth Circuit affirmed, also rejecting the inherent power argument (*United States v. United States Dist. Ct. for E.D. of Mich.* 1971). Unanimously, the Supreme Court agreed. The fundamental value in the concept of a warrant issued under the Fourth Amendment "is its issuance by a 'neutral and detached magistrate'" (*United States v. United States District Court* 1972). Executive officers charged with investigative and prosecutorial duties could not be sole judges of exercising their powers. That fundamental principle would be violated repeatedly by the Bush administration after 9/11. In 1972, the Supreme Court looked to the language in the 1968 statute, which declined to specify the president's power to conduct warrantless national security surveillance. The Court concluded that the statutory language merely disclaimed congressional intent to define presidential power in the statute and did not affirmatively grant any authority to the president.

The 1972 ruling prompted Congress to adopt statutory guidelines to define the president's power to conduct surveillance over foreign powers. After years of hearings, Congress was prepared to pass the landmark Foreign Intelligence Surveillance Act (FISA) of 1978. In testimony, Attorney General Edward H. Levi recognized the need for independent review by a detached and neutral magistrate. A judicial check was essential. FISA established a special tribunal called the FISA Court to assure independent supervision on surveillance activities by the executive branch. The statutory procedures in the 1978 statute, with regard to electronic surveillance within the United States for foreign intelligence purpose, were to be "the exclusive means." The result: the president had no access to claimed inherent powers.

The 1978 statute required the government to certify that "the purpose" of surveillance was to obtain foreign intelligence information. The USA PATRIOT Act of 2001 altered that standard by allowing application for a search order if a "significant purpose" was to obtain foreign intelligence information. This legislative action made it easier to obtain permission from the FISA Court, but judicial permission was still needed. There was no freedom to skirt the FISA Court altogether. Legislation after 9/11 made other changes to FISA: increasing the number of judges from seven to 11, and authorizing the attorney general to order emergency electronic surveillance without a warrant provided that he informed a judge with jurisdiction over national security wiretaps and obtained a warrant within 24 hours. Again, the procedure for judicial warrants was relaxed somewhat but not entirely eliminated.

ELECTRONIC SURVEILLANCE AFTER 9/11

On December 16, 2005, the *New York Times* reported that President Bush in the period immediately following the 9/11 attacks, had secretly authorized the NSA to listen to Americans and others inside the United States without a court-approved warrant. As reported in the *Times*, the NSA had been monitoring the international telephone calls and international emails "of hundreds, perhaps thousands" of people over the intervening years in an effort to obtain evidence about terrorist activity (Risen and Lichtblau 2005). The administration decided it was not bound by the Supreme Court's decision in 1972 or the FISA statute passed by Congress. It would operate on what it regarded as "inherent" presidential powers, a source of authority that both the Court and Congress had repudiated.

In a weekly radio address on December 17, President Bush acknowledged that he had authorized the NSA, "consistent with U.S. law and the Constitution, to intercept the international communications of people with known links to Al Qaeda and related terrorist organizations" (Bush 2005a). In fact, his program violated the Court's 1972 decision and FISA. What did he mean by "U.S. law and the Constitution"? In the radio address, he emphasized that the authorization he gave the NSA "helped address that problem [of combating terrorism] in a way that is fully consistent with my constitutional responsibilities and authorities." With this language, he appeared to be drawing authority solely from Article II of the Constitution, even when in violation of judicial rulings and congressional statutes.

In a news conference on December 19, Bush cited specific references to constitutional authority: "As President and Commander in Chief, I have the constitutional responsibility and the constitutional authority to protect our country. Article II of the Constitution gives me that responsibility and the authority necessary to fulfill it." He also cited statutory authority, pointing out that after September 11 Congress had passed the Authorization for Use of Military Force (AUMF) to grant him "additional authority to use military force against Al Qaida" (Bush 2005b, 1876). Congress enacted the AUMF to invade Afghanistan.

On December 19, Attorney General Alberto Gonzales held a press briefing on the NSA program, claiming that "the president has the inherent authority under the Constitution, as Commander-in-Chief, to engage in this kind of activity." When asked why the administration did not seek a warrant from the FISA Court, Gonzales said the administration continued to seek warrants from this court but was not "legally required" to do so in every case if another statute granted the president additional authority. Gonzales emphasized the need for "speed and agility," claiming that the FISA process lacked those qualities: "You have to remember that FISA was passed by the Congress in 1978. There have been tremendous advances in technology" since that time.

This is a fair point about technological advances, but FISA had been amended many times over the years, including after 9/11. Why did the administration not ask Congress to amend FISA to meet its needs after the terrorist attacks? Gonzales replied that he had been advised it "would be difficult, if not impossible" (Fisher 2008, 292–293). Yet a few years later Congress amended FISA in response to recommendations from the executive branch.

On January 19, 2006, the Office of Legal Counsel in the Justice Department released a 42-page "white paper" that defended the legality of the NSA program. It concluded that the surveillance activities were supported by the president's "well-recognized inherent constitutional authority as Commander in Chief and sole organ for the Nation in foreign affairs to conduct warrantless surveillance of enemy forces for intelligence purposes to detect and disrupt armed attacks on the United States" (OLC 2006, 1). On pages two and three, the department linked "sole organ" to the 1936 Supreme Court decision of *United States* v. *Curtiss-Wright*. In addition to these constitutional arguments, the department claimed that Congress, when it passed the AUMF, "confirmed and supplemented the President's recognized authority under Article II of the Constitution to conduct such warrantless surveillance to prevent further catastrophic attacks on the homeland" (OLC 2006, 2).

THE ADMINISTRATION'S CASE

Let us first examine OLC's statutory argument. During debate on the AUMF, no member of Congress understood that the legislation modified in any way the requirements of FISA or gave the president independent authority to conduct national security wiretaps without seeking approval from the FISA Court. If lawmakers decide to amend a statute, like FISA, they know how to do it. A bill is brought up and debated to amend an existing statute. The process is direct, specific, conscious, and deliberate. Members know what they are doing. Amending a statute must always be done explicitly, with full awareness, not by implication.

With regard to the sole-organ doctrine, *Curtiss-Wright* introduced a number of grave misconceptions. First, the language about the president as sole organ of foreign affairs appears not in the decision but in dicta (extraneous matter) tucked away toward the end of the decision. Dicta have no controlling legal or constitutional effect. Second, the author of *Curtiss-Wright*, Justice George Sutherland, fundamentally misunderstood the president as sole organ. In 1800, during debate in the House of Representatives, Representative John Marshall (Federalist-VA) said that the president "is the sole organ of the nation in its external relations, and its sole representative with foreign nations" (Marshall 1800). What was the context of his remark?

This was a presidential year, with Thomas Jefferson battling John Adams to be the next president. Jeffersonians in the House threatened to censure or impeach President Adams for handing over to the British an individual charged with murder. In his floor statement, Marshall explained that there was no basis for either censure or impeachment. President Adams was implementing a provision in the Jay Treaty that authorized extradition to another country in cases of murder. He was not invoking any independent or inherent authority. He was carrying out a treaty, which was his duty under Article II to "take Care that the Laws be faithfully executed." Under Article VI, treaties "shall be the supreme Law of the Land." President Adams was not creating national policy by himself. He was carrying out *the policy of Congress*, expressed either by statute or treaty (Fisher 2006).

In his decades of federal service as member of the House, secretary of state, and chief justice of the United States, Marshall at no time advocated an independent, inherent, or exclusive power of the president in external affairs. To take but one example, in the 1804 decision of *Little* v. *Barreme*, the Supreme Court was asked to render a judgment on a wartime conflict between a statute passed by Congress and a proclamation issued by the president. Which should prevail? Writing for a unanimous Court, Chief Justice Marshall ruled that the statute necessarily established national policy, not the inconsistent presidential proclamation.

What can be said about the existence of "inherent" presidential power, especially in matters of national security? The OLC opinion referred to the president's "well-recognized inherent constitutional authority as Commander in Chief ... to conduct warrantless surveillance of enemy forces for intelligence purposes to detect and disrupt armed attacks on the United States." No doubt some attorneys in the executive branch accept the president's authority to conduct warrantless surveillance as "well-recognized," but there has been no such recognition by federal courts, members of Congress, or scholars. When it passed FISA, Congress made no specific acknowledgment of inherent presidential authority to conduct warrantless surveillance. All three branches have a mix of express and implied powers. Implied powers must be drawn reasonably from express powers. To that extent, both express and implied powers have a constitutional source.

The same cannot be said of inherent powers. Inherent is sometime used as synonymous with implied (Calabresi and Yoo 2008), but the two terms are fundamentally different. Inherent power has been defined in this manner: "An authority possessed without its being derived from another.... Powers over and beyond those explicitly granted in the Constitution or reasonably to be implied from express powers" (Black 1979, 703). The purpose of a Constitution is to specify and confine governmental powers to protect individual rights and liberties. That objective is undermined by claims of open-ended authorities that are not expressly given or reasonably implied in a constitution. Assertions of "inherent" powers usher in a range of vague and abstruse sources. What "inheres" in the president? The concept of inherent power is so nebulous that it invites political abuse and endangers individual liberties.

Presidents have invoked inherent powers on numerous occasions. Without exception, they have met defeat either in the courts or in Congress. These examples include President Harry Truman's claim that he could seize steel mills in 1952 to prosecute his war in Korea; President Nixon's claim that he could conduct warrantless domestic surveillance; his claim that he could refuse to spend appropriated funds (the impoundment dispute); and President Bush's claim after 9/11 that he could unilaterally create military commissions without seeking statutory authority from Congress. Every assertion of inherent authority has been turned back by Congress or the judiciary (Fisher 2007).

BUSH OFFICIALS TESTIFY

Several top officials of the Bush administration appeared before congressional committee to defend inherent presidential powers for national security surveillance. Their statements have a robotic and mechanical quality, as though they were carefully coached to repeat certain words even if they did not understand them. Their testimony reveals that the administration knew that what they intended to do after 9/11, with regard to surveillance, violated the statutory policy set forth in FISA.

On May 18, 2006, Michael V. Hayden appeared before the Senate Select Committee on Intelligence to testify on his nomination to be CIA director. He had previously served as NSA director when the surveillance program was initiated after 9/11. At the hearing, Hayden defended the legality of the NSA program on constitutional, not statutory, grounds. He did not cite AUMF as legal authority. In recalling his service at NSA after September 11, he told the committee that when he talked to his lawyers, "they were very comfortable with the Article II arguments and the President's inherent authorities." During their discussion on the lawfulness of the NSA program, the legal defense "anchored itself on Article II" (Hayden 2006, 31–32).

Hayden presented the constitutional question to three NSA lawyers, meeting with them separately. They "came back with a real comfort level that this was within the President's authorities." They did not put anything in writing and Hayden "did not ask for it." The attorneys "talked to me about Article II" (ibid., 54, 116–117). Simply talking to an attorney, particularly at such an abstract level as "Article II," is insufficient when seeking legal guidance. What is said orally can look very superficial in writing. Only by putting legal analysis on paper and having the draft circulated for comment by other lawyers and specialists can an agency head hope to receive useful and thoughtful legal analysis. At the hearing, Senator Evan Bayh (D-IN) said that references to Article II and inherent are "so nebulous and so broad." When describing presidential power at that level of generality, it would be difficult to locate something that "would not be authorized under Article II power" (ibid., 107).

Statements by Hayden at the hearing suggest that he knew the surveillance program desired by the administration was not legal under FISA. After 9/11, CIA Director George Tenet asked him: "Is there anything more you can do [with surveillance]?" Hayden replied: "Not within my current authorities" (ibid., 28). Again at the hearing: "I was asked by Director Tenet, 'Could you do more?' I said, 'not within current law'" (ibid., 54). Those statements suggest that Hayden knew that the proposed surveillance program violated FISA.

The administration's dependence on Article II and inherent powers reappeared when Michael McConnell, Director of National Intelligence, testified before the Senate Select Committee on Intelligence on May 1, 2007. Senior officials in the administration had begun to argue that they could no longer pledge to seek warrants from the FISA Court for each domestic surveillance. They insisted that the president possessed independent authority under the Constitution to order warrantless surveillance. McConnell referred several times to Article II as a source of inherent presidential authority. When asked by one senator whether the administration would no longer circumvent the FISA Court, McConnell replied: "Sir, the president's authority Article II is in the Constitution. So if the president chose to exercise Article II authority, that would be the president's choice." He repeated that "Article II is Article II, so in a different circumstance, I can't speak for the president what he might decide" (Risen 2007). It is remarkable to have a witness at a congressional hearing inform lawmakers that Article II is in the Constitution. The statements by McConnell suggest that he was counseled by the administration to repeat these code words, whether he understood them or not.

THE RESULTS OF LITIGATION

A number of private parties went to court to challenge the legality of the surveillance conducted by the Bush administration and the telecoms that lent their assistance. To demonstrate the injury necessary to have a case accepted in court, plaintiffs argued that the contacts they used to have with clients over the telephone were now made impossible because of NSA monitoring. To continue their contacts with clients, they had to travel and meet personally with them, including those who lived outside the United States. The government attempted to have all of these lawsuits dismissed on the ground that any litigation would necessarily disclose "state secrets" injurious to the nation. That argument, used frequently in other court proceedings, had less credibility in the surveillance cases because the administration, after the *New York Times* disclosure, had publicly acknowledged the existence of the NSA program (which the administration called the Terrorist Surveillance Program, or TSP) and had defended its legality with the OLC white paper.

In a case in California, decided on July 20, 2006, a district court held that the state secrets privilege did not block action on the lawsuit. Moreover, plaintiffs had demonstrated sufficient injury to establish standing. The government wanted the case dismissed or go to summary judgment (reaching the legal issue without the fact-finding of depositions and the disclosure process). The court denied that motion in *Hepting* v. *AT&T Corp.* 2006). This case ground on, year after year, with the government eventually blocking the right of private litigants to gain evidence through the discovery process.

On August 17, 2006, a district court in Michigan ruled that the surveillance program violated the Constitution and federal statutes. Contrary to arguments from the administration, the court found that the plaintiffs had been able to "establish a prima facie case based solely on Defendants' [the government's] public admissions regarding the TSP." This decision, *American Civil Liberties* v. *National Sec. Agency* (E.D. Mich. 2006), was reversed by the Sixth Circuit on July 6, 2007. The appellate court's analysis, announced in *ACLU* v. *National Sec. Agency* (6th Cir. 2007), made it nearly impossible for any litigant in this type of case to establish standing. On February 19, 2008, the Supreme Court declined to take this case.

A major surveillance case involved the Al-Haramain Islamic Foundation, based in Oregon. In 2004, the Treasury Department froze its U.S. assets and designated it a terrorist organization. On a routine discovery request, the company obtained from the Treasury Department a top-secret calling log that showed it was a target of warrantless surveillance. Treasury insisted that the company return the document, which it did. On November 16, 2007, the Ninth Circuit in *Al-Haramain Islamic Foundation, Inc.* v. *Bush*, ruled that although the company could not refer to the inadvertently released document, it could proceed with the case by relying on extensive public disclosures by the Bush administration concerning the TSP.

The *Al-Haramain* case moved back and forth between appellate and trial courts. On July 2, 2008, District Judge Vaughn Walker decided what should happen when there is a conflict between the FISA and the state secrets privilege. Which should prevail? If the state secrets privilege ranked higher in value, the case would come to a halt. But in a case called *In re National Sec. Agency Telecommunications Rec.* (2008), Judge Walker stated flatly that

FISA preempted the state secrets privilege. After this important ruling, the burden was on the plaintiffs to demonstrate that they were "an aggrieved person" under FISA.

On January 5, 2009, in a case by the same name as in the paragraph above, Judge Walker held that plaintiffs' allegations were sufficient for them to be "aggrieved persons" within the meaning of FISA (597 F.Supp.2d 1077). He declined to entertain any further challenges by the government to plaintiffs' standing and stated that he would review the sealed documents in camera (within the court's private chamber). To avoid the review from being entirely ex parte (done exclusively by the judge and representatives of the government), he ordered the government to give two attorneys for the plaintiffs clearance to see top secret/sensitive compartmented information (TS/SCI) documents.

Remarkably, the government on February 27 argued that even if the two attorneys had clearance they would have no "need to know." Access to classified documents always requires two steps: (1) clearance and (2) a need to need. In this case, Judge Walker determined that the two attorneys *did* have a need to know. Without their participation, the litigation would lack the adversary quality that courts depend on to bring out all available facts before deciding a case. Yet a party to the case – the federal government and the NSA – attempted to block his order. The next step was for Judge Walker, on May 22, to deny the government's third motion to dismiss the case. At the same time, he granted plaintiffs' motion for discovery. The case continued to move forward. Judge Walker threatened to apply sanctions to the government if it persisted in blocking his actions (Johnson 2009).

On December 21, 2010, Judge Walker ordered the government to pay nearly $2.6 million in lawyers' fees and damages to attorneys who represented Al-Haramain. He refused to grant punitive damages against the government because he found insufficient evidence that the NSA had shown "reckless or callous indifference" to the plaintiffs' rights. There was no immediate decision by the government on whether to appeal (Lichtblau 2010). The money award was modest, if not insignificant, for the federal government. Yet Judge Walker had issued several rulings very damaging to the government: (1) the executive branch violated FISA; (2) FISA trumps the TSP, making a significant dent in the state secrets privilege; (3) government efforts to dismiss the case were repeatedly rejected, allowing the case to move forward; and (4) the plaintiffs had satisfied the aggrieved-person standard of FISA (Al-Haramain 2010). The question is whether the principles on which the ruling rested pose a risk to the government in future litigation, particularly regarding the state secrets privilege.

IMMUNITY FOR THE TELECOMS

In October 2007, the Senate Intelligence Committee voted to give the telecoms that assisted NSA immunity from lawsuit because they had "acted in good faith" and believed the TSP was legal and presidentially authorized (Lichtblau 2007a). The logic here was strange. There could be little doubt that the TSP violated FISA by, among other things, skirting the FISA Court. How could these telecoms have possibly acted "in good faith"? Did they buy into loose arguments from the administration about "Article II" and "inherent" powers? Telecoms have sophisticated offices of general counsel whose attorneys are very familiar with FISA, its history, and its intent, and who have the capacity (and duty) to independently analyze what is, and is not, legal. The administration sent letters to the companies to request their assistance, stating "very forcefully" that the TSP was being "directed by the president, and this has been deemed lawful at the very highest levels of the government" (Lichtblau 2007b). Faced with a "forceful" letter claiming that the NSA program had been "deemed lawful," telecoms should be able to analyze the legal issues and not simply acquiesce to administration claims. Would Congress grant immunity to other private parties who helped the administration violate laws and the Constitution, such as the companies that gave the CIA assistance in transporting suspects to other countries for interrogation and torture?

On February 21, 2008, President Bush argued that "[i]f we do not give liability protection to those who are helping us, they won't help us. And if they don't help us, there will be no program. And if there's no program, America is more vulnerable" (Bush 2008). These sentences may seem to provide logic in their progression, but they all depend on the willingness of private parties to engage in illegal and unconstitutional practices. That step in itself makes America, the Constitution, and the legal system vulnerable. If the phone companies wanted protection from legal action, they could have complied with the immunity provisions already present in FISA. The statute made telecoms immune from suit if they had been provided a court order or a certification from the attorney general stating, in writing, that the order had been obtained or was unnecessary (*Congressional Record* 2008, H5760).

In July 2008, Congress debated a set of amendments to FISA. The issues were important. Telecoms objected that they were being sued but could not mount an effective defense because of the presence of state secrets. House Judiciary Chairman John Conyers (D-MI) said he "would be open to developing a set of procedures that allow both plaintiffs and defendants to make their case (*Congressional Record* 2008, H5755). House debate was brief. Only one hour was permitted for debate and no amendments were allowed (H. Rept.

No. 110–721). The House agreed to the resolution establishing those procedures, 230 to 168.

During House debate on the bill, Representative Jane Harman (D-CA)
stated: "this bill make clear that no president can ignore it ever again. FISA is
the exclusive means by which our government can conduct surveillance. In
short, no more warrantless surveillance" (*Congressional Record* 2008, H5762).
Representative James Langevin (D-RI) made a similar observation: "the bill
clarifies that FISA is the exclusive means by which the executive branch may
conduct electronic surveillance on U.S. soil. No President will have the power
to do an end-run around the legal requirements of FISA" (*Congressional
Record* 2008, H5766). The bill was not that clear. Section 102 of the 2008 legislation provided that its procedures "shall be the exclusive means by which
electronic surveillance and the interception of domestic wire, oral, or electronic communications may be conducted." The original FISA statute of 1978
contained the same restriction. Nevertheless, the Bush administration and its
supporting telecoms ignored that law and its requirement for review by the
FISA Court. Why should the statute of 2008 be any more effective in curbing
claims of "inherent" presidential power? Representative Dan Lungren (R-CA)
expressed the view that "the President did have inherent authority to conduct
warrantless searches to obtain foreign intelligence information" (*Congressional
Record*, 2008, H5766). According to his position, presidential authority would
trump the FISA statute. The bill passed the House, 293 to 129.

During Senate debate, lawmakers provided different analyses on the avail-
ability of inherent president power. To Senator Russell D. "Russ" Feingold
(D-WI), "the arguments that the President has inherent Executive authority to
violate the law are baseless" (*Congressional Record* 2008, S6454). Senator Kit
Bond (R-MO), vice chairman of the Intelligence Committee, disagreed. He
referred to a decision by the FISA Court of Review that "the President has that
[inherent] authority, and if the Congress tried to pass a law saying the President
does not have that authority, it would be found to be unlawful" (*Congressional
Record* 2008, S6468). The FISA Court is not a reliable source of authority for
constitutional law. It operates in secret and has no adversarial process to permit litigants on separate sides to make their case, a procedure followed by all
other federal courts. At another point in the debate, Senator Bond inserted
his analysis of the bill: "Section 102 of the bill will not – and cannot – preclude the President from exercising his Article II constitutional authority to
conduct warrantless foreign intelligence surveillance" (*Congressional Record*
2008, S6391). Accepting that analysis, no statutory language about "exclusive
means" could control the president when he decides to invoke "Article II" or
"inherent" authority.

The decision to extend immunity to the telecoms was exceedingly controversial. Senator Arlen Specter (R-PA) asked: "How can we intelligently grant retroactive immunity on a program that most Members of Congress do not know what we are granting retroactive immunity on?" (*Congressional Record* 2009, S6384). Few members of Congress had been briefed on the intricacies of the TSP or the role performed by the telecoms. Senator Patrick J. "Pat" Leahy (D-VT) expressed concern that the legislation would "reduce the role of the court to a rubber stamp." Once the attorney general certifies to a court that the surveillance had been "determined to be lawful," a lawsuit against a telecom "will be dismissed and everybody is off the hook" (*Congressional Record* 2008, S6406). The legality of the surveillance would not be determined by a court but by a statement from an executive official. Leahy remarked about the bill: "What it says is, if you are in charge, you can just go out and break the law, and then when they look at you, send a letter to the court saying: I have determined that when I broke the law, I did not really break the law, so you have to let me off the hook.… This bill makes our courts the handmaidens of a coverup, and it is wrong" (*Congressional Record* 2008, S6406). The bill passed the Senate, 69 to 28.

Under the immunity statute, a private party may not bring a civil action against a telecom if the attorney general certifies to a district court that the company being sued had been provided a certification in writing from the administration that its activity was "(i) authorized by the President; and (ii) determined to be lawful" (122 Stat. 2469). In other words, President Bush could have violated FISA but, at the same time, decide to "authorize" the TSP and determine that the program was "lawful." A total blank check to the president to override existing law? Not entirely. The statute provides that the written certification shall be given effect "unless the court finds that such certification is not supported by substantial evidence provided to the court pursuant to this section." A court would have to conduct some kind of inquiry to determine the quality, substance, and reliability of the evidence supporting the certification. The immunity statute had no effect on lawsuits against the government, such as *Al-Haramain* discussed in the previous section.

On June 3, 2009, Judge Vaughn Walker granted the government's motion to dismiss all charges against the telecoms (*re National Security Agency Telecommunications Records Litigation*). Judge Walker noted that the immunity statute of 2008 "appears to be *sui generis* among immunity laws: it creates a retroactive immunity for past, completed acts committed by private parties acting in concert with government entities that allegedly violated constitutional rights. The immunity can only be activated by the executive branch of government and may not be invoked by its beneficiaries."

Plaintiffs had advanced three constitutional objections to the immunity statute: Congress had usurped the judicial function, had violated a principle of law prohibiting Congress from dictating to the judiciary specific outcomes in particular cases, and had impermissibly delegated lawmaking power to the executive branch. Judge Walker ruled against the plaintiffs on each of these points. He concluded that the statute "provides a judicial role, albeit a limited one, in determining whether the Attorney General's certifications meet the criteria for the new immunity" created in the statute. The statute allowed a court to "reject the Attorney General's certification."

Plaintiffs argued that "the secrecy provisions allowing for certifications and supporting documentation to be submitted in camera and ex parte violates due process." Unlike *Al-Haramain*, where Judge Walker threatened to apply sanctions to the government unless it allowed attorneys for the plaintiffs to be in his chambers and examine classified documents, Congress had foreclosed that process with the immunity statute. If the attorney general filed a declaration that disclosure of his certification would "harm the national security of the United States," the court shall "review such certification and the supplemental materials in camera and ex parte." Plaintiffs could participate in the briefing and argument of the case, "but only to the extent that such participation does not require the disclosure of classified information to such party." To the extent that classified information is relevant to the proceeding, the court "shall review such information in camera and ex parte" (122 Stat. 2469). As Judge Walker noted in his ruling, the statute "evinces a clear congressional intent that parties not have access to classified information." After examining the attorney general's submissions, he determined that they had "met his burden" under the immunity statute.

This decision was appealed to the Ninth Circuit. The government filed its brief on May 19, 2010. The private parties filed a reply brief on July 1, 2010. However, this case remained with the district court and was decided by Judge Walker on December 21, 2010, as discussed earlier in this chapter. Other cases challenging the constitutionality of NSA surveillance (Hepting, Jewel, etc.) are before the Ninth Circuit, to be decided separately. If they return to district court they will not be before Judge Walker, who has retired.

CONCLUSION

From Franklin D. Roosevelt in 1940 to George W. Bush, presidents have invoked "inherent" powers to conduct warrantless national security surveillance, sometimes in the absence of statutory authority and sometimes in violation of it. The TSP was created to circumvent what some executive officials regarded as an outmoded FISA. If that was their concern, they should have asked Congress to amend the legislation. It has been revised many times over the years, including after 9/11. By failing to adhere to statutory authority, the administration put at risk a number of telecoms that had been recruited to implement the surveillance program. They could have refused on legal and constitutional grounds to participate, but decided to submit to executive arguments.

Claims of inherent presidential authority were developed within the Bush administration by a few attorneys within the Justice Department, often in secret memos, with little vetting by senior officials. Those analyses, now available, are shot through with shallow and incompetent constitutional interpretation (Baker 2010; Cole 2010; Bruff 2009). Decisions to violate statutory restrictions always come at the cost of checks and balances, separation of powers, and the types of structural safeguards the framers eagerly embraced to limit the danger to individual liberties that comes from a concentration of political power. To the framers that constitutional principle was bedrock. We seem to always have to relearn it.

Works Cited

Aberbach, Joel D. 2002. "What's Happened to the Watchful Eye?" *Congress & the Presidency* 29: 20–23.

———. 1990. *Keeping a Watchful Eye: The Politics of Congressional Oversight.* Washington, DC: Brookings Institution Press.

Abrams, Jim. 2010. "Partisanship's Bad Now in Washington? Think Again." *Washington Examiner*, 8 March, 15.

Accinelli, Robert. 1996. *Crisis and Containment: United States Policy toward Taiwan, 1950–1955.* Chapel Hill, NC: University of North Carolina Press.

Acheson, Dean. 1971. *The Korean War.* New York: W. W. Norton.

Adler, E. Scott. 2002. *Why Congressional Reforms Fail: Re-Election and the Committee System.* Chicago, IL: University of Chicago Press.

Adler, E. Scott and John D. Wilkerson. 2008. "Intended Consequences: Jurisdictional Reform and Issue Control in the U.S. House of Representatives." *Legislative Studies Quarterly* 33 (February): 85–112.

Advisory Panel to Assess Domestic Response Capabilities for Terrorism Involving Weapons of Mass Destruction. 2000. *II. Toward a National Strategy for Combating Terrorism, Second Annual Report to the President and the Congress.* Accessed 15 December 2010. http://www.rand.org/nsrd/terrpanel.

Ahuja, Sunil. 2008. *Congress Behaving Badly: The Rise of Partisanship and Incivility and the Death of Public Trust.* Westport, CT: Praeger.

Albion, Robert Greenhalgh, 1980. *Makers of Naval Policy, 1798–1947,* ed. Rowena Reed. Washington, DC: United States Naval Institute Press.

Allen, Admiral Thad. 2007. "Hearing on Challenges Affecting the Coast Guard's Marine Safety Program." Testimony before the House Subcommittee on Coast Guard and Maritime Transportation (August).

Alstyne, Van. 1972. "Congress, the President, and the Power to Declare War: A Requiem for Vietnam." *University of Pennsylvania Law Review* 121(1): 1–28.

Ambrosius, Lloyd. 1987. *Woodrow Wilson and the American Diplomatic Tradition.* New York: Cambridge University Press.

American Rhetoric. 2011. "The Rhetoric of 9–11: President George W. Bush—Address to the Nation on 9-11-01." http://www.americanrhetoric.com/speeches/gwbush911addresstothenation.htm.

Anderson, Jack and Drew Pearson. 1968. *The Case against Congress*. New York: Simon and Schuster.

Armario, Christine and Dorie Turner. 2010. "Nearly 1 in 4 Fails Military Entrance Exam." *Examiner*, 22 December, 16.

Aspin-Brown Commission. 1996. *Preparing for the 21st Century: An Appraisal of U.S. Intelligence*. Report of the Commission on the Roles and Capabilities of the United States Intelligence Community. Accessed 1 March 2011. http://www.gpoaccess.gov/int/index.html.

Auerswald, David P. 2006. "Senate Reservations to Security Treaties." *Foreign Policy Analysis* 2 (January): 83–100.

2002. "Advice and Consent: The Forgotten Power." In *Congress and the Politics of Foreign Policy*, ed. Colton C. Campbell, Nicol C. Rae, and John F. Stack, Jr. Upper Saddle River, NJ: Prentice-Hall.

Auerswald, David P. and Forrest Maltzman. 2003. "Policymaking through Advice and Consent: Treaty Consideration by the United States Senate." *Journal of Politics* 65 (November): 1097–1110.

Baker, Nancy V. 2010. "Who Was John Yoo's Client? The Torture Memos and Professional Misconduct." *Presidential Studies Quarterly* 40: 750–770.

Baker, Peter. 2010a. "Senate Rejects Amendment Blocking New START Treaty." *New York Times*, 19 December, A35.

2010b. "Democrats Scramble to Save Votes to Ratify Nuclear Pact." *New York Times*, 20 December, A1.

Bamford, James. 2002. *Body of Secrets*. New York: Anchor Books.

1983. *The Puzzle Palace*. New York: Penguin Books.

Banks, William and Peter Raven-Hansen. 1994. *National Security Law and the Power of the Purse*. New York: Oxford University Press.

Barabak, Mark Z. 2010. "Nation Appears Poised for Midterm Change." *Los Angeles Times*, 10 October. http://inlandpolitics.com/blog/2010/10/10/latimes-nation-appears-poised-for-midterm-change/.

Bartlett, John. 1968. *Familiar Quotations* (14th ed.). Boston: Little, Brown.

Barrett, David M. 2007. "Congressional Oversight of the CIA in the Early Cold War, 1947–1963." In *Intelligence and Accountability: Safeguards against the Abuse of Secret Power*, vol. V, ed. Loch K. Johnson. Westport, CT: Praeger.

2005. *The CIA and Congress*. Lawrence, KS: University Press of Kansas.

Barry, John and Evan Thomas. 2010. "A War Within." *Newsweek*, 20 September, 30.

Baumgartner, Frank R. and Bryan D. Jones. 1993. *Agendas and Instability in American Politics*. Chicago, IL: University of Chicago Press.

Baumgartner, Frank R., Bryan D. Jones, and Jeffrey C. Talbert. 1993. "The Destruction of Issue Monopolies in Congress." *American Political Science Review* 87 (September): 657–671.

Baumgartner, Frank R., Bryan D. Jones, and Michael C. Macleod. 2000. "The Evolution of Legislative Jurisdictions." *Journal of Politics* 62 (May): 321–349.

Baylis, Elena. 1999. "Confronting the Problem of Reservations to Human Rights Treaties." *Berkeley Journal of International Law* 17 (2): 277–329.

Bellavita, Christopher. 2008. "Changing Homeland Security: What Is Homeland Security?" *Homeland Security Affairs* 4 (June): 1–30.

Bellinger III, John B. and Vijay M. Padmanabhan. 2011. "Detention Operations in Contemporary Conflicts: Four Challenges for the Geneva Conventions and Other Existing Law." *American Journal of International Law* 105 (April): 201–243.

Bennet, Michael F. 2010. Testimony on "Legislative Proposals to Change Senate Procedure," before the Senate Committee on Rules and Administration, 28 July. Accessed 27 August 2011. http://rules.senate.gov/public/?a=Files. Serve&File_id=847ae43d-3001–4073-bbab-f10f0fde1850.

Berger, Henry W. 1975. "Bipartisanship, Senator Taft, and the Truman Administration." *Political Science Quarterly* 90 (Summer): 221–237.

Binder, Frederick. 1994. *James Buchanan and the American Empire*. Selinsgrove, PA: Susquehanna University Press.

Binder, Sarah A. 2001. "Congress, the Executive, and the Production of Public Policy: United We Govern?" In *Congress Reconsidered* (7th ed.), ed. Lawrence C. Dodd and Bruce I. Oppenheimer. Washington, DC: CQ Press.

Binder, Sarah, Thomas Mann, Norman Ornstein, and Molly Reynolds." 2009. "Mending the Broken Branch: Assessing the 110th Congress, Anticipating the 111th." Brookings Institution, January, online report.

Bingaman, Jeff. 1994. "The 12th Annual Gilbert A. Cuneo Lecture: The Origin and Development of the Federal Acquisition Streamlining Act." *Military Law Review* (Summer): 149–165.

Black, Henry Campbell. 1979. *Black's Law Dictionary* (5th ed.). St. Paul, MN: West.

Blechman, Barry. 1992. *The Politics of National Security: Congress and U.S. Defense Policy*. New York: Oxford University Press.

Bogue, Allan. 1981. *These Earnest Men: The Republicans of the Civil War Senate*. Ithaca, NY: Cornell University Press.

Bolt, Ernest. 1977. *Ballots before Bullets: The War Referendum Approach to Peace in America, 1914–1941*. Charlottesville, VA: University of Virginia Press.

Braden, Tom. 1975. "What's Wrong with the CIA?" *Saturday Review* 2 (April 5): 14.

Broder, David S. 2010. "A Test of Two Parties." *Washington Post*, 6 May, A19.

Brookes, Peter and Owen Graham. 2010. "Experts: New START Is a Non-Starter." *Webmemo No. 2951* Washington, DC: Heritage Foundation, 7 July.

Brownstein, Ronald. 2010. "Why Senators Are Falling." *National Journal*, 18 September, online edition.

2007. "Who's Watching the President?" *Los Angeles Times*, 21 March, online edition.

2006. "Treating Oversight as an Afterthought Has Its Costs." *Los Angeles Times*, 19 November, online edition.

Bruff, Harold H. 2009. *Bad Advice: Bush's Lawyers in the War on Terrorism*. Lawrence, KS: University Press of Kansas.

Buhl, Lance C. 1978. "Maintaining 'An American Navy,' 1865–1889." In *Peace and War: Interpretations of American Naval History, 1775–1978*, ed. Kenneth J. Hagan. Westport, CT: Greenwood Press.

Burgin, Eileen K. 1991. "Representatives' Decisions on Participation in Foreign Policy Issues." *Legislative Studies Quarterly* 16 (November): 521–546.

Burreilli, David F. 2001. "Military Child Care Provisions: Background and Legislation." In *The Child Care Disaster in America: Disdain and Disgrace*, ed. B. Ring. Hauppauge, NY: Nova Science.

2002. *Abortion Services and Military Medical Facilities*. Report 95-387F. Congressional Research Service. Washington, DC.

Burton, David. 2004. *William Howard Taft: Confident Peacemaker*. New York: Fordham University Press.

Bush, George W. 2008. Weekly Compilation of Presidential Papers, 44: 259.

2005a. "Bush on the Patriot Act and Eavesdropping," *News York Times*, 18 December, 30.

2005b. Public Papers of the Presidents, 2005, II: 1876.

2001. Executive Order 13228, "Establishing the Office of Homeland Security and the Homeland Security Council" (October).

Calabresi, Steven G. and Christopher S. Yoo. 2008. *The Unitary Executive: Presidential Power from Washington to Bush*. New Haven, CT: Yale University Press.

Campbell, Angus, Philip Converse, Warren Miller, and Donald Stokes. 1976. *The American Voter*. Chicago, IL: University of Chicago Press.

Caro, Robert. 2002. *Master of the Senate: The Years of Lyndon Johnson*. New York: Knopf.

Cassata, Donna. 2010. "New START Treaty: Dems Beat Back GOP Efforts to Alter Accord." *Huffington Post*. 20 December. Accessed 22 December 2010. http://www.huffingtonpost.com.

Castelli, Elsie. 2010. "Transparency, Public Input to Guide IT Policies." *Federal Times*, 11 January, 13.

Chaddock, Gail Russell. 2010. "John Boehner, Would-Be Speaker, Pitches His Roadmap to Fix Congress." *Christian Science Monitor*, 30 September. Accessed 12 August 2011. http://www.csmonitor.com/USA/Politics/2010/0930/John-Boehner-would-be-Speaker-pitches-his-roadmap-to-fix-Congress.

Chang, Gordon. 1990. *Friends and Enemies: The United States, China, and the Soviet Union, 1948–1972*. Palo Alto, CA: Stanford University Press.

Chertoff, Michael. 2007. "Department of Homeland Security Memorandum to Representative Peter King" (September).

Chesney, Robert. 2010. "Who May Be Held? Military Detention through the Habeas Lens." *Boston College Law Review* 52 (December): 769–870.

Chesney, Robert, Benjamin Wittes, and Larkin Reynolds. 2011. "The Emerging Law of Detention 2.0: The Guantanamo Habeas Cases as Lawmaking." *Brookings Institution* (May). Accessed 8 June 2011. http://www.brookings.edu/~/media/Files/rc/papers/2011/05_guantanamo_wittes/05_guantanamo_wittes.pdf.

Clark, Charles S. 2011. "Open Secrets," *Government Executive*. 1 February. Accessed 12 August 2011. http://www.govexec.com/features/0211-01/0211-01s1.htm.

Clark, Kathleen. 2010. "'A New Era of Openness?' Disclosing Intelligence to Congress under Obama." *Constitutional Commentary* 26 (February): 1–20.

Clausen, Aage R. 1973. *How Congressmen Decide*. New York: St. Martin's Press.

Clayton, Mark. 2011. "The New Cyber Arms Race." *Christian Science Monitor*, 7 March. Accessed 1 September 2011. http://www.csmonitor.com/USA/Military/2011/0307/The-new-cyber-arms-race.

Cohen, Dara K., Mariano-Florentino Cuellar, and Barry R. Weingast. 2006. "Crisis Bureaucracy: Homeland Security and the Political Design of Legal Mandates." *Stanford Law Review* 59 (Fall): 673–759.

Cohen, Richard E. 2011. "The Fixer: Upton's Oversight Far, Wide." *Politico*, 1 March, 4.

Cole, David. 2010. "The Sacrificial Yoo: Accounting for Torture in the OPR Report." *Journal of National Security Law and Policy* 4: 455–464.

Cole, Wayne. 1987. "With the Advice and Consent of the Senate: The Treaty-Making Process before the Cold War Years." In *Congress and United States Foreign Policy: Controlling the Use of Force in the Nuclear Age*, ed. Michael Barnhart. Albany, NY: State University of New York Press.

   1983. *Roosevelt and the Isolationists, 1932–1945*. Lincoln, NE: University of Nebraska Press.

Collins, Susan. 2010. "Congress Got Nasty. Here's How to Fix It." *Washington Post*, 10 October, B4.

Commager, Henry Steele. 1976. "Intelligence: The Constitution Betrayed." *New York Review of Books*, 30 September, 32.

   Congressional Quarterly. 1987. "Boland Amendments: A Review." *Weekly Online*, 23 May, 1043.

   Congressional Quarterly Weekly Report. 1954. 15 January.

   Congressional Quarterly Almanac. 1957. Vol. 13.

Conley, Richard S. 2008. "Leading a New Organization: Ridge, Chertoff, and the Department of Homeland Security." In *Leadership and Politics*, ed. Michael Genovese and Lori Cox-Han. Westport, CT: Praeger.

   2003. "The Department of Homeland Security and the Dual Politics of Reorganization: Presidential Preemption, Agency Restructuring, and Congressional Challenges." Presented at the conference "The Presidency, Congress, and the War on Terrorism: Scholarly Perspectives," University of Florida.

   2002. "The War on Terrorism and Homeland Security: Presidential and Congressional Challenges." Presented at the conference "Assessing the Presidency of George W. Bush at Midpoint: Political, Ethical, and Historical Considerations," University of Southern Mississippi.

Conyers, John. 2008. "FISA Amendment of 2008." *Congressional Record*, 154: H5755 (daily ed.), 20 June.

Cooper, Joseph and Garry Young. 2002. "Party and Preference in Congressional Decision Making: Roll Call Voting in the House of Representatives, 1889–1999." In *Party, Process, and Political Change in Congress: New Perspectives on the History of Congress*, ed. David W. Brady and Mathew D. McCubbins. Palo Alto, CA: Stanford University Press.

Crabb, Jr., Cecil V. 1995. "Foreign Policy." In *The Encyclopedia of the United States Congress*, vol. 2, ed. Donald C. Bacon, Roger H. Davidson, and Morton Keller. New York: Simon and Schuster.

   1992. *Invitation to Struggle: Congress, the President, and Foreign Policy* (4th ed.). Washington, DC: CQ Press.

Crile, George. 2007. *Charlie Wilson's War*. New York: Grove Press.

Cronin, Thomas E. 1973. "The Swelling of the Presidency and Its Impact on Congress." Invited Working Paper presented to the House Select Committee on Committees, 93rd Congress, 1st Session, Washington, DC.

Cumming, Alfred. 2010. *Sensitive Covert Action Notifications: Oversight Options for Congress*. Report R40691. Congressional Research Service. Washington, DC.

Dahl, Robert Dahl. 1950. *Congress and Foreign Policy*. New York: W. W. Norton.

Davidson, Roger. 1981. "Subcommittee Government: New Channels for Policy Making." In *The New Congress*, ed. Thomas Mann and Norman Ornstein. Washington, DC: American Enterprise Institute.

Davidson, Janine. 2009. "Making Government Work: Pragmatic Priorities for Interagency Coordination." *Orbis* (Summer): 419–438.

Davies, F. 2002. "GOP-Controlled Senate Expected to Give Less Scrutiny to War on Terror." *Miami Herald*, 7 November, A1.

Davis, Allen. 1959. "Why Jacob Collamer?" *Vermont History* 27: 41–53.

Dawson, Raymond H. 1962. "Congressional Innovation and Intervention in Defense Policy: Legislative Authorization of Weapons Systems." *American Political Science Review* 56 (1) (March): 42–57.

de Tocqueville, Alexis. 2003. *Democracy in America*, ed. Isaac Kramnick and Gerald Bevan. New York: Penguin Classics.

Deering, Christopher J. 2003. "Alarms and Patrols: Legislative Oversight in Foreign and Defense Policy." In *Congress and the Politics of Foreign Policy*, ed. Colton C. Campbell, Nicol C. Rae, and John F. Stack, Jr. Upper Saddle River, NJ: Prentice-Hall.

Delanian, Ken. 2009. "Short-staffed USAID Tries to Keep Pace." *USA Today*, 1 February.

Destler, I. M. 1985. "Executive-Legislative Conflict in Foreign Policy." In *Congress Reconsidered* (3rd ed.), ed. Lawrence C. Dodd and Bruce I. Oppenheimer. Washington DC: CQ Press.

Dingell, John. 2004. "Homeland Security Jurisdiction: The Perspectives of Committee Leaders." Testimony before House Select Committee on Homeland Security (24 March).

Dionne, Jr., E. J. 2010. "Dodd, the Happy Warrior." *Washington Post*, 9 August, A13.

Drogin, B. 2004. "Senator Says Spy Agencies Are 'in Denial.'" *Los Angeles Times*, 4 May, A1.

Earle, Geoff. 2004. "Dems Did Oversight Better, Says Grassley." *The Hill*, 13 May, 2.

Elkins, Stanley and Eric McKitrick. 1994. *The Age of Federalism: The Early American Republic, 1788–1800*. New York: Oxford University Press.

Elsea, Jennifer K. 2010. *The Military Commissions Act of 2009: Overview and Legal Issues*. Report R41163. Congressional Research Service. Washington, DC.

    2007. *Treatment of "Battlefield Detainees" in the War on Terrorism*. RL 31367. Congressional Research Service. Washington, DC.

    2005. *Detainees at Guantanamo Bay*. Report RS 22173. Congressional Research Service. Washington, DC.

Elsea, Jennifer K. and Michael John Garcia. 2010. *Enemy Combatant Detainees: Habeas Corpus Challenges in Federal Court*. Report RL 33180. Congressional Research Service. Washington, DC.

Emery, Fred. 1995. *Watergate*. New York: Touchstone.

Erickson, Robert S. and Gerald C. Wright. 2001. "Voters, Candidates, and Issues in Congressional Elections." In *Congress Reconsidered* (7th ed.), ed. Lawrence C. Dodd and Bruce I. Oppenheimer. Washington, DC: CQ Press.

Evans, Lawrence and Walter Oleszek. 2002. "A Tale of Two Treaties: The Practical Politics of Treaty Ratification in the U.S. Senate." In *Congress and the Politics of*

Foreign Policy, ed. Colton C. Campbell, Nicol C. Rae, John F. Stack, Jr. Upper Saddle River, NJ: Prentice-Hall.

Feldmann, Linda. 2010. "Obama Team Braces for Rep. Darrell Issa, Avid Investigator." *Christian Science Monitor*, 9 November, online edition.

Finn, Peter. 2009. "Obama Seeks Halt to Legal Proceedings at Guantanamo." *Washington Post*, 21 January. Accessed 26 May 2011. http://www.washingtonpost.com/wp-dyn/content/article/2009/01/20/AR2009012004743.html.

Fisher, Louis. 2008. *The Constitution and 9/11: Recurring Threats to America's Freedoms*. Lawrence, KS: University Press of Kansas.

2007. "Invoking Inherent Powers: A Primer." *Presidential Studies Quarterly* 37 (March): 1–22.

2006. "The 'Sole Organ' Doctrine." Law Library of Congress. http://www.constitutionproject.org/manage/file/441.pdf.

2000. *Congressional Abdication on War and Spending*. College Station, TX: Texas A&M University Press.

1995. *Presidential War Power*. Lawrence, KS: University Press of Kansas.

Fisher, Louis and Katy J. Harriger. 2011. *American Constitutional Law* (9th ed.). Durham, NC: Carolina Academic Press.

Fleisher, Richard and John R. Bond. 2004. "The Shrinking Middle in the U.S. Congress." *British Journal of Political Science* 34 (3): 429–451.

Forgette, Richard G. 2004. *Congress, Parties, and Puzzles: Politics as a Team Sport*. New York: Peter Lang.

Foley, Thomas. 2003. "Hearing on Perspectives on House Reform: Former House Leaders." Testimony before House Select Committee on Homeland Security (9 September).

Franck, Thomas and Edward Weisband. 1979. *Foreign Policy by Congress*. New York: Oxford University Press.

Friedman, Dan. 2010. "Kerry Expects New START Deal in Next Days." *Global Security Newswire*, 2 December. Accessed 20 December 2010. http://gsn.nti.org.

Friel, Brian. 2007. "The Watchdog Growls." *National Journal* (24 March): 20–29.

Fritz, Harry. 1976. "The War Hawks of 1812: Party Leadership in the Twelfth Congress." *Capitol Studies* 4: 25–42.

Gallup. 2011. "Gallup Daily: Obama Job Approval." 19 May. Accessed 19 May 2011. http://www.gallup.com.

Garcia, Michael John. 2009. *Interrogation of Detainees: Requirements of the Detainee Treatment Act*. Report RL 33655. Congressional Research Service. Washington, DC.

Garrett, Major. 2010. "Poll: Americans Want Their Leaders to Stand and Fight." National Journal's *CongressDailyAM*, 21 September.

Gates, Robert M. 1996. *From the Shadows*. New York: Simon and Schuster.

Gertz, Bill. 2002. *Breakdown*. Washington, DC: Regnery.

Giambastiani, Adm., Edmund P. 2010. "Childhood Obesity: A Security Issue." *Politico*, 15 July, 32.

Gibbons, William Conrad. 1984. *The U.S. Government and the Vietnam War: Executive and Legislative Roles and Relationships*, vol. 2: 1961–1964. Princeton, NJ: Princeton University Press.

Gilmore, James. 2000. *Advisory Panel to Assess Domestic Response Capabilities for Terrorism Involving Weapons of Mass Destruction*. Washington, DC: RAND Corporation.

Gleijeses, Piero. 1992. "The Limits of Sympathy: The United States and the Independence of Spanish America." *Journal of Latin American Studies* 24 (Fall): 481–505.

Glennon, Michael. 1991. "The Constitutional Power of the United States Senate to Condition Its Consent to Treaties." *Chicago-Kent Law Review* 67: 533.

Global Security Newswire (GSN). 2010a. "Obama Hopeful for New START Pact's Prospects in the Senate." 9 April. Accessed 12 April 2010. http://gsn.nti.org.

———. 2010b. "Obama Jockeys for Republican Backing on 'New START.'" 23 July. Accessed 28 July 2010. http://gsn.nti.org.

———. 2010c. "Debate on 'New START' Seen Dragging Past August." 26 July. Accessed 28 July 2010. http://gsn.nti.org.

———. 2010d. "Treaty Lapse Curbs U.S. Monitoring of Russian Nukes." 17 August. Accessed 8 September 2010. http://gsn.nti.org.

———. 2010e. "Administration Reaffirms Hope to Ratify New START in 2010." 5 August. Accessed 6 August 2010. http://gsn.nti.org.

———. 2010f. "Russia Unlikely to Violate Nuclear Pact Terms, Gates Says." 9 September. Accessed 9 September 2010. http://gsn.nti.org.

———. 2010g. "Senate Committee Passes New START." 16 September. Accessed 17 September 2010. http://gsn.nti.org.

———. 2010h. "Intel Director to Discuss New START with Senators." 29 September. Accessed 30 September 2010. http://gsn.nti.org.

———. 2010i. "Lawmakers Back Nuclear Weapons Budget Boost." 4 October. Accessed 4 October 2010. http://gsn.nti.org.

———. 2010j. "White House Pushes Ahead on New START." 18 November. Accessed 18 November 2010. http://gsn.nti.org.

Goldsmith, Jack and Jeremy Rabkin. 2010. "New START Could Erode Senate's Foreign Policy Role." *Washington Post*. 4 August, A17.

Goldsmith, Jack and Benjamin Wittes. 2009. "No Place to Write Detention Policy." *Washington Post*, 22 December. Accessed 22 December 2010. http://www.washingtonpost.com/wp-dyn/content/article/2009/12/18/AR2009121802307.html.

Gottemoeller, Rose. 2010. "Congressional Testimony on the New START Treaty before the Senate Armed Services Committee." 29 July. Accessed 6 August 2010. http://armed-services.senate.gov.

Green, Harold and Allen Rosenthal. 1963. *Government of the Atom: The Integration of Powers*. New York: Atherton Press.

Grieb, Kenneth J. 2001. "Ambassadors, Executive Agents, and Special Representatives." In *Encyclopedia of American Foreign Policy* (2nd ed.), vol. I, ed. Alexander Deconde, Fredrik Logevall, and Richard Dean Burns. New York: Charles Scribner's Sons.

Grier, Peter. 2011. "Obama Orders Guantanamo Tribunals to Resume. Is He Abandoning His Pledge?" *Christian Science Monitor*, 7 March. Accessed 7 March 2011. http://www.csmonitor.com/USA/Justice/2011/0307/Obama-orders-Guantanamo-tribunals-to-resume.-Is-he-abandoning-his-pledge.

Griffith, Robert. 1987. *Politics of Fear: Joseph McCarthy and the Senate*. Amherst, MA: University of Massachusetts Press.

Groseclose, Tim and David C. King. 2001. "Committee Theories Revisited." In *Congress Reconsidered* (7th ed.), ed. Lawrence C. Dodd and Bruce I. Oppenheimer. Washington, DC: CQ Press.

Grossman, Elaine. 2010a. "Kerry Delays Committee Vote on New START until September." *Global Security Newswire*, 4 August. Accessed 8 August 2010. http://gsn.nti.org.

2010b. "Offering Nuclear Plus-Ups, White House Awaits Kyl's word on New START." *Global Security Newswire*, 15 November. Accessed 15 November 2010. http://gsn.nti.org.

2010c. "White House Aide: Kyl Agreed to Nuclear Funds before Tripping Up Arms Treaty." *Global Security Newswire*, 19 November. Accessed 21 November 2010. http://gsn.nti.org.

2010d. "Democrats Scramble to Lock in GOP Votes for Arms Treaty." *Global Security Newswire*, 16 December. Accessed 16 December 2010. http://gsn.nti.org.

Hamilton, Lee and Thomas Kean. 2010. "There's 'Work to Be Done,' 9/11 Commission Chairs Say." *USA Today*, 11 January, 9A.

Hampson, Rick. 2011. "How Will Years of War Change Us," *USA Today*, 9 February, 2A.

Hardin, John. 1998. "Advocacy versus Certainty: The Dynamics of Committee Jurisdiction Concentration." *Journal of Politics* 60 (May): 374–397.

Hart, Gary. 1993. *The Good Fight: The Education of an American Reformer*. New York: Random House.

Hart, Gary and Rudman, Warren. 2001. *U.S. Commission on National Security*. Washington, DC: Government Printing Office.

Haviland, H. Field, Jr. 1958. "Foreign Aid the Policy Process: 1957." *American Political Science Review* 52: 689–724.

Hayden, Michael V. 2006. "Nomination of General Michael V. Hayden to be Director of the Central Intelligence Agency," Senate Select Committee on Intelligence, 109th Cong., 2nd Sess., S. Hrg. 109–808, available at http://intelligence.senate.gov/109808.pdf.

Henkin, Louis. 1995. "U.S. Ratification of Human Rights Conventions: The Ghost of Senator Bricker." *American Journal of International Law* 89 (April): 341–350.

1972. *Foreign Affairs and the Constitution*. New York: Foundation Press.

Hietala, Thomas. 1985. *Manifest Design: Anxious Aggrandizement in Jacksonian America*. Ithaca, NY: Cornell University Press.

Higgs, Robert. 2006. *Depression, War and Cold War: Studies in Political Economy*. New York: Oxford University Press.

Hilsman, Roger. 1987. *The Politics of Policy Making in Defense and Foreign Affairs*. Upper Saddle River, NJ: Prentice-Hall.

Hinckley, Barbara. 1994. *Less Than Meets the Eye: Foreign Policy Making and the Myth of the Assertive Congress*. Chicago, IL: University of Chicago Press.

Hogue, Henry. 2008. *Recess Appointments: Frequently Asked Questions*. Report RS 12308. Congressional Research Service. Washington, DC.

Holt, Michael. 2003. *The Rise and Fall of the American Whig Party: Jacksonian Politics and the Onset of the Civil War*. New York: Oxford University Press.

Holt, W. Stull. 1933. Treaties Defeated by the Senate: *A Study of the Struggle between President and Senate over the Conduct of Foreign Relations*. Baltimore, MD: Johns Hopkins University Press.

Hoskins, Harford. 1927. "The Hispanic American Policy of Henry Clay." *Hispanic American Historical Review* 7: 460–478.

Huntington, Samuel P. 1961. *The Common Defense: Strategic Programs in National Politics*. New York: Columbia University Press.

1957. *The Soldier and the State: The Theory and Politics of Civil-Military Relations*. Cambridge, MA: Belknap Press of Harvard University.

Huzar, Elias. 1950. *The Purse and the Sword: Control of the Army by Congress through Military Appropriations, 1933–1950*. Ithaca, NY: Cornell University Press.

Isaacs, John. 1999. "Test Ban Fizzles." *Bulletin of the Atomic Scientists* 55 (November/ December): 21–22.

Isikoff, Michael. 2009. "Obama's Gitmo Task Force Blows Its Deadline." *Newsweek*, 20 July. Accessed 26 May 2011. http://www.newsweek.com/2009/07/19/obama-s-gitmo-task-force-blows-its-deadline.html.

Jaffe, Greg. 2011. "One Percent of Americans Are Touched by This War." *Washington Post*, 2 March 2, A1.

Jenkins, Jeffrey. 2002. "The Gag Rule, Congressional Politics, and the Growth of Anti-Slavery Popular Politics." Presented at the Congress and History Conference, Massachusetts Institute of Technology.

Johnson, Carrie. 2009. "Showdown Looming on 'State Secrets.'" *Washington Post*, 26 May, A4.

Johnson, Charles W. 2003. "Hearing on Perspectives on House Reform: Lessons from the Past." Testimony before House Select Committee on Homeland Security (19 May).

Johnson, Loch K. 2011a. *National Security Intelligence: Secret Operations in Defense of the Democracies*. Cambridge, UK: Polity.

2011b. *The Threat on the Horizon: America's Search for Security after the Cold War*. New York: Oxford University Press.

2010. E-mail communication from former CIA officer (May 28).

2009. Remarks to the author by Lee Hamilton, University of Georgia, Athens, GA (April 9).

2004. "Presidents, Lawmakers, and Spies: Intelligence Accountability in the United States." *Presidential Studies Quarterly* 34 (December): 828–837.

2000. Interview with Walter M. Mondale, Minneapolis, MN (17 February).

1996. *Secret Agencies: U.S. Intelligence in a Hostile World*. New Haven, CT: Yale University Press.

1994b. "Playing Ball with the CIA: Congress Supervises Strategic Intelligence." In *The President, the Congress, and the Making of American Foreign Policy*, ed. Paul E. Peterson. Norman, OK: University of Oklahoma Press.

1989. *America's Secret Power: The CIA in a Democratic Society*. New York: Oxford University Press.

1988. *A Season of Inquiry: Congress and Intelligence*. Lexington, KY: University Press of Kentucky.

1985. *A Season of Inquiry: The Senate Intelligence Investigation*. Lexington, KY: University Press of Kentucky.

1984. *The Making of International Agreements: Congress Confronts the Executive*. New York: New York University Press.

Johnson, Loch K., John C. Kuzenski, and Erna Gellner. 1992. "The Study of Congressional Investigations: Research Strategies." *Congress and the Presidency* 19 (Autumn): 138–156.

Johnson, Robert David. 1998. "Congress Confronts the Cold War: The Senate Government Operations Committee and American Foreign Relations, 1953-1969." *Political Science Quarterly* 113 : 645 -671.

———. 1993. *The Peace Progressives and American Foreign Relations.* Cambridge, MA: Harvard University Press.

Jones, Charles O. and Randall Strahan. 1985. "The Effect of Energy Politics on Congressional and Executive Organization in the 1970s." *Legislative Studies Quarterly* 10 (May): 151–179.

Kaiser, Frederick M. 2010. *Congressional Oversight of Intelligence: Current Structure and Alternatives.* Report RL32525. Congressional Research Service. Washington, DC.

Kagan, Robert. "New START: Too Modest to Merit Partisan Bickering." *Washington Post.* 30 July, A19.

Katulis, Brian. 2010. "Security Is at the Root of GOP Divide." *Politico.* 28 July. Accessed 16 August 2010. http://dyn.politico.com.

Kaufmann, J.E. and H.W. Kaufman. 2004. *Fortress America: The Forts that Defended America, 1600 to the Present.* Jackson, TN: Da Capo Press.

Kean, Thomas H. and Lee H. Hamilton. 2003. The 9/11 Commission Report: Final Report of the National Commission on Terrorist Attacks upon the United States. New York: W.W. Norton.

Kellerman, Barbara and Ryan Barilleaux. 1991. *The President as World Leader.* New York: St. Martin's Press.

Kennedy, Paul. 1982. "The Kaiser and German Weltpolitik: Reflexions on Wilhelm II's Place in the Making of German Foreign Policy." In *Kaiser Wilhelm II: New Interpretations,* ed. John Rohl and Nicolaus Sombat. New York: Cambridge University Press.

Kernell, Samuel. 1986. *Going Public: New Strategies of Presidential Leadership.* Washington DC: Congressional Quarterly Press.

Kerry, John. 2010a. "How New-START Will Improve Our Nation's Security." *Washington Post.* 7 July, A15.

———. 2010b. "Vote on New START to Be Held Following the August Recess." SFRC Press Release, 3 August. Accessed 18 May 2011. http://foreign.senate.gov.

———. 2010c. "New START Wins Bipartisan Backing in Key Committee Vote." SFRC Press Release, 16 September. Accessed 18 May 2011. http://foreign.senate.gov.

———. 2010d. "Now Is the Time to Ratify New START." SFRC Press Release, 26 November. Accessed 18 May 2011. http://foreign.senate.gov.

———. 2010e. "The Historic Passage of New START." SFRC Press Release, 22 December. Accessed 18 May 2011. http://foreign.senate.gov.

Kettl, Donald F. 2003. "Contingent Coordination: Practical and Theoretical Puzzles for Homeland Security." *American Review of Public Administration* 33 (September): 253–277.

Kibbe, Jennifer. 2010. "Congressional Oversight of Intelligence: Is the Solution Part of the Problem?" *Intelligence and National Security* 25 (February): 24–49.

Kiely, Kathy and Wendy Koch. 1998. "Committee Shaped by Party Ties." *USA Today*, 5 October, 2A.

King, David C. 1997. *Turf Wars: How Congressional Committees Claim Jurisdiction*. Chicago, IL: University of Chicago Press.

1994. "The Nature of Congressional Committee Jurisdictions." *American Political Science Review* 88 (March): 48–62.

Kingdon, John. 2002. *Agendas, Alternatives and Public Policies* (2nd ed.). New York: Longmans.

Kissinger, Henry. 1999. *Years of Renewal*. New York: Simon and Schuster.

1987. "A Matter of Balance." *Los Angeles Times* 26 July, VI.

Kitfield, James. 2010a. "Lugar Calls for Passage of New START." *Global Security Newswire*, 19 July. Accessed 19 July 2010. http://gsn.nti.org.

2010b. "The 13th Crisis." *National Journal*, 7 August, 18.

2010c "Working for the Common Good." *National Journal*, 7 August, 21.

Klimas, Joshua E. 2007. *Balance Consensus, Consent, and Competence: Richard Russell, the Senate Armed Services Committee and Oversight of America's Defense, 1955–1968*. Ph.D. diss., Ohio State University.

Knott, Stephen F. 2002. "The Great Republican Transformation on Oversight." *International Journal of Intelligence and Counterintelligence* 13: 49–63.

Koempel, Michael L. 2007. Homeland Security: Compendium of Recommendations Relevant to House Committee Organization and Analysis of Consideration for the House, and 109th and 110th Congresses Epilogue. Report RL32711. Congressional Research Service. Washington, DC.

2005. *House Committees: A Framework for Considering Jurisdictional Realignment*. Report RL32661. Congressional Research Service. Washington, DC.

Koh, Harold. 1990a. *The National Security Constitution*. New Haven: Yale University Press.

1990b. "The President versus the Senate in Treaty Interpretation." *Yale Journal of International Law* 15 (Summer): 331–344.

Kolodziej, Edward A. 1966. *The Uncommon Defense and Congress, 1945–1963*. Columbus, OH: Ohio State University Press.

Koplow, David. 1992. "When Is an Amendment not an Amendment? Modification of Arms Control Agreements with the Senate." *University of Chicago Law Review* 59 (Summer): 981–1073.

Kornblut, Anne. 2010. "Obama Launches a Charm Offensive." *Washington Post*, 25 December, A1.

Kosiak, Steven M. 2008. *Analysis of the FY 2009 Defense Budget Request*. Washington, DC: Center for Strategic and Budgetary Assessments.

Krasner, Stephen. 1978. *Defending the National Interest*. Princeton, NJ: Princeton University Press.

Krehbiel, Keith.1991. *Information and Legislative Organization*. Ann Arbor, MI: University of Michigan Press.

Krutz, Glen and Jeffrey Peake. 2009. *Treaty Politics and the Rise of Executive Agreements*. Ann Arbor, MI: University of Michigan Press.

Kyl, Jon. 2010. "Kyl Statement on START." Press Release, 16 November. Accessed 18 May 2011. http://kyl.senate.gov.

Lael, Richard. 1987. *Arrogant Diplomacy: U.S. Policy toward Colombia, 1903–1922*. Wilmington, DE: Scholarly Resources.

Landler, Mark. 2010. "In a Speech on Policy, Clinton Revives a Theme of American Power." *New York Times*, 9 September, A6.

Langevin, James. 2008. "FISA Amendments of 2008." *Congressional Record*, 154: H5766 (daily ed.), June 20.

Langley, Lester. 1976. *Struggle for the American Mediterranean: United States-European Rivalry in the Gulf-Caribbean, 1776–1904*. Athens, GA: University of Georgia Press, 1976.

Laskow, Sarah. 2009. "Is Congress Failing on Homeland Security Oversight?" Center for Public Integrity. Accessed 15 July 2011. http://www.publicintegrity.org/articles/entry/1549/.

Leuchtenberg, William. 1952. "Progressivism and Imperialism: The Progressive Movement and American Foreign Policy." *Mississippi Valley Historical Review* 39 (August): 483–504.

Levy, Jack. 1989. "The Diversionary Theory of War: A Critique." In *Handbook of War Studies*, ed. Manus Midlarsky. Ann Arbor, MI: University of Michigan Press.

Lichtblau, Eric. 2007a. "Senate Deal on Immunity for Telephone Companies." *New York Times*, 18 October, A22.

2007b. "Key Senators Raise Doubts on Eavesdropping Immunity." *New York Times*, 1 November, A16.

2010. "U.S. Ordered to Pay Group of Muslims." *New York Times*, 22 December, A23.

Lindsay, James M. 1994. *Congress and the Politics of U.S. Foreign Policy*. Baltimore, MD: Johns Hopkins University Press.

1987. "Congress and Defense Policy, 1961 to 1986." *Armed Forces and Society* 13 (Spring): 371–401

Locher, James. 2002. *Victory on the Potomac: The Goldwater-Nichols Act Unifies the Pentagon*. College Station, TX: TAMU Press.

Lofgren, Charles. 1972. "War-making under the Constitution: The Original Understanding." *Yale Law Journal* 81 (July): 672–702.

Lowenthal, Mark M. 2003. *Intelligence: From Secrets to Policy* (2nd ed.). Washington, DC: CQ Press.

Lower, Richard Coke. 1993. *A Bloc of One: The Political Career of Hiram W. Johnson*. Palo Alto, CA: Stanford University Press.

Luxenberg, Steve. 2010. "Book Details Internal Struggle over Afghan Plan." *Washington Post*, 22 September, A8.

Mann, Thomas E. 2003. "Hearing on Perspectives on House Reform: Lessons from the Past." Testimony before House Select Committee on Homeland Security (19 May).

Mann, Thomas E. and Norman J. Ornstein. 2006. *The Broken Branch: How Congress Is Failing America and How to Get It Back on Track*. New York: Oxford University Press.

Manning, William R., ed. 1939. *Diplomatic Correspondence of the United States: Inter-American Affairs, 1831–1860*. Washington, DC: Carnegie Endowment for International Peace.

Margetta, Rob. 2010. "Post-Election Might Be Only Chance to Streamline DHS Oversight." *CQ.com*, 20 September.

Marshall, John. 1800. Speech in the House of Representatives. Accessed 21 September 2011. http://www.constitutionproject.org/manage/file/444.pdf.

Matishak, Martin. 2010a. "Revised Nuclear Strategy Weakens U.S. Deterrent, GOP Lawmaker Says." *Global Security Newswire*, 15 April. Accessed 19 July 2010. http://gsn.nti.org.

———. 2010b. "Senate Resolution Will Impact 'New START' Experts Say." *Global Security Newswire*, 27 July. Accessed 27 July 2010. http://gsn.nti.org.

May, Robert. 1989. *The Southern Dream of a Caribbean Empire, 1854–1861*. Athens, GA: University of Georgia Press.

May, Peter J., Joshua Sapotichne, and Samuel Workman. 2006. "Policy Coherence and Policy Domains." *Policy Studies Journal* 34 (August): 381–403.

May, Peter J., Ashley E. Jochin, and Joshua Sapotichne. 2009. "Policy Regimes and Governance: Constructing Homeland Security." Presented at the 10th Public Management Research Association Conference, Ohio State University.

Mayhew, David. 1974. *Congress: The Electoral Connection*. New Haven, CT: Yale University Press.

Mayer, Kenneth R. 1993. "Policy Disputes as a Source of Administrative Controls: Congressional Micromanagement of the Department of Defense." *Public Administration Review* 53 (July/August): 293–302.

McCain, John. 2004. Remarks, *Meet the Press*, NBC Television (21 November).

McConnell, Mitch. 2010a. "Priorities of the American People Should Come First." Press Release, 1 December. Accessed 21 May 2011. http://mcconnell.senate.gov.

———. 2010b. "A Flawed, Mishandled Treaty." Press Release, 20 December. Accessed 21 May 2011. http://mcconnell.senate.gov.

McCool, Daniel. 1990. "Subgovernments as Determinants of Political Viability." *Political Science Quarterly* 105 (2): 269–293.

McCubbins, Matthew D. and Thomas Schwartz. 1984. "Congressional Oversight Overlooked: Police Patrols versus Fire Alarms." *American Journal of Political Science* 28 (February): 165–179.

Memorandum of a Conversation with the President. 1958. *Foreign Relations of the United States, 1958–1960*. 14 July.

Menendez, Robert. 2009. "Kerry, Lugar, Menendez, Corker Introduce Legislation to Reform Foreign Aid." *PolitickerNJ*, 28 July. Accessed 21 September 2011. http://www.politickernj.com/senatormenendez/3184/kerry-lugar-menendez-corker-introduce-legislation-reform-foreign-aid.

Miller, Merle. 1973. *Plain Speaking: An Oral Biography of Harry S. Truman*. New York: Berkley.

Mink, Patsy. 1981. "Institutional Perspective: Misunderstandings, Myths, and Misperceptions." In *The Tethered Presidency: Congressional Restraints on Executive Power*, ed. Thomas M. Franck. New York: New York University Press.

Mondale, Walter F., with David Hage. 2010. *The Good Fight: A Life in Liberal Politics*. New York: Scribner.

Morgan, Richard E. 1980. *Domestic Intelligence*. Austin, TX: University of Texas Press.

Moise, Edwin. 1996. *Tonkin Gulf and the Escalation of the Vietnam War*. Chapel Hill, NC: University of North Carolina Press.

Morison, Elting, John M. Blum, et al., eds. 1951. *The Letters of Theodore Roosevelt: Volume 4*. Cambridge, MA: Harvard University Press.

Moore, John Bassett, ed. 1910. *The Works of James Buchanan: Volume X*. Philadelphia, PA: Lippincott.

Moore, John Norton. 1976. "Executive Agreements and Congressional Executive Relations." In U.S. Congress. House. Committee on International Relations, Subcommittee on International Security. *Congressional Review of International Agreements*. 94th Cong, 2d sess. Washington, DC: Government Printing Office.

Moynihan, Daniel Patrick. 1991. "Do We Still Need the C.I.A.? The State Dept. Can Do the Job." *New York Times*, 19 May, E17.

Murdock, Clark A., et al. 2004. *Beyond Goldwater-Nichols: Defense Reform for a New Strategic Era*. Washington, DC: Center for Strategic and International Studies.

Nather, David. 2004. "Congress as Watchdog: Asleep on the Job?" *CQ Weekly*, 22 May, 1190.

National Public Radio (NPR). 2010. "Who Oversees Homeland Security?" *All Things Considered* (July 20).

Nichols, Roy F. 1990. *The Disruption of American Democracy*. Brooklyn, NY: AMS Press.

Nolan, Cynthia. 2005. "More Perfect Oversight: Intelligence Oversight and Reform." In *Intelligence and Accountability: Safeguards against the Abuse of Secret Power*, vol. V, ed. Loch K. Johnson. Westport, CT: Praeger.

Obama, Barack. 2010a. "Weekly Presidential Address." 20 November. Accessed 22 May 2011. http://www.whitehouse.gov.

    2010b. "Weekly Presidential Address." 18 December. Accessed 22 May 2011. http://www.whitehouse.gov.

O'Connell, Anne Joseph. 2006. "The Architecture of Smart Intelligence: Structuring and Overseeing Agencies in the Post-9/11 World." *California Law Review* 94 (December): 1655–1744.

Ogul, Morris S. 1976. *Congress Oversees the Bureaucracy*. Pittsburgh, PA: University of Pittsburgh Press.

Oliveri, Frank. 2011a. "Gates' Budget Cuts Make GOP Squirm." *CQ Weekly*, 10 January, 123.

    2011b. "'Not Every Defense Dollar Is Sacred'." *CQ Today*, 7 January, 1.

Olmsted, Kathryn S. 1996. *Challenging the Secret Government*. Chapel Hill, NC: University of North Carolina Press.

Olson, Keith W. 2003. *Watergate: The Presidential Scandal That Shook America*. Lawrence, KS: University Press of Kansas.

Ornstein, Norman. 2003. "Hearings on Perspectives on House Reform: Lessons from the Past." Testimony before House Select Committee on Homeland Security (19 May).

Ornstein, Norman J. and Thomas E. Mann. 2006. "When Congress Checks Out." *Foreign Affairs* 85 (November/December): 67–82.

Ott, Marvin C. 2003. "Partisanship and the Decline of Intelligence Oversight." *International Journal of Intelligence and Counterintelligence* 16 (1): 69–94.

Pach, Chester. 1986. "Military Assistance and American Foreign Policy: The Role of Congress." In *Congress and United States Foreign Policy*, ed. Michael Barnhart. Albany, NY: SUNY Press.

Pach, Chester and Elmo Richardson. 1991. *The Presidency of Dwight D. Eisenhower*. Lawrence, KS: University Press of Kansas.

Page, Susan. 2003. "Bush Unscathed by Investigations: Here's Why." *USA Today*, 13 August, 1A.

Paletta, Damian. 2011. "Billions in Bloat Uncovered in Beltway." *Wall Street Journal*, 1 March, A1.

Panetta, Leon E. 2009. Remarks, Pacific Council on International Policy, Los Angeles, CA, 18 May.

Penketh, Anne. 2010. "Stopping New START?" *BASIC Backgrounder*, 2 July.

Peterson, H.F. 1942. "Edward A. Hopkins: A Pioneer Promoter in Paraguay." *Hispanic American Historical Review* 22: 245–261.

Peterson, Merrill. 1987. *The Great Triumvirate: Webster, Clay, and Calhoun*. New York: Oxford University Press.

Pierce, Emily. 2010. "Obama, McConnell: Perfect Strangers." *Roll Call*, 6 May. Accessed 21 September 2011. http://www.rollcall.com/issues/55_128/-45930–1. html.

Pincus, Walter. 2010a. "New START: A Similar Arms Reduction Pact but a Different Republican Reaction." *Washington Post*.10 August, A15.

2010b. "Intelligence Spending at Record $80.1 Billion Overall." *Washington Post*, 29 October, A2.

Pincus, Walter and Mary Beth Sheridan. 2010. "Report Findings about Russia Could Complicate Debate on New START Pact." *Washington Post*. 28 July, A9.

Pitsvada, B. 1991. *The Senate, Treaties and National Security, 1945–1974*. New York: University Press of America.

Polmar, Norman and K. J. Moore. 2003. *Cold War Submarines: The Design and Construction of U.S. and Soviet Submarines, 1945–2001*. Dulles, VA: Potomac Books.

Pollack, Joshua. 2010. "What Obama's Nuclear Posture Review Accomplishes." *Bulletin of Atomic Scientists*, 7 April. Accessed 8 April 2010. http://www.thebulletin.org.

Potter, David. 1976. *The Impending Crisis: 1848–1861*. New York: Harper and Row.

Priest, Dana and William M. Arkin. 2010a. "The Secrets Next Door." *Washington Post*. 21 July, A1.

2010b. "National Security, Inc." *Washington Post*. 20 July, A1.

2010c. "A Hidden World, Growing beyond Control." *Washington Post*, 19 July, A1.

Project on National Security Reform. 2008. *Forging a New Shield*. Accessed 18 August 2010. http://pnsr.org/data/files/pnsr_forging_a_new_shield_report.pdf.

Purvis, Hoyt. 1984. "Tracing the Congressional Role: U.S. Foreign Policy and Turkey." In *Legislating Foreign Policy*, ed. Hoyt Purvis and Steven Baker. Boulder, CO: Westview Press.

Rae, Nicol C. and Colton C. Campbell. 2001. "Party Politics and Ideology in the Contemporary Senate." In *The Contentious Senate: Partisanship, Ideology, and the Myth of Cool Judgment*, ed. Colton C. Campbell and Nicol C. Rae. Lanham, MD: Rowman and Littlefield.

Rakove, Jack. 1984. "Solving a Constitutional Puzzle: The Treatymaking Clause as a Case Study." *Perspectives in American History* 1 (Summer): 207–248.

Ramonas, Andrew. 2011. *Congressional Leaders Reach Deal on Patriot Act*. Accessed 20 May 2011. http://www.mainjustice.com/2011/05/20/congressional-leaders-reach-deal-on-patriot-act-extension/print/.

Ransom, Harry Howe. 1976. "Congress, Legitimacy and the Intelligence Community." Presented at the Annual Meeting of the Western Political Science Association, San Francisco.

1975. "Secret Intelligence Agencies and Congress." *Society* 123: 33–36.

1970. *The Intelligence Establishment.* Cambridge, MA: Harvard University Press.

Risen, James. 2007. "Administration Pulls Back on Surveillance Agreement." *New York Times*, 3 May, A16.

Risen, James and Eric Lichtblau. 2005. "Bush Lets U.S. Spy on Callers without Courts." *New York Times*, 16 December, A1.

Ritchie, Donald A. 1993. *Press Gallery: Congress and the Washington Correspondents.* Cambridge, MA: Harvard University Press.

Rogin, Josh. 2010a. "Administration and GOP Preparing for Fight over Treaty Killer Amendments for New START." *The Cable*, 9 December. Accessed 10 December 2010. http://www.foreignpolicy.com.

2010b. "Biden to Kerry: I'd Rather See New START Fail This Year than Be Delayed Next Year." *The Cable*, 15 December. Accessed 20 December 2010. http://www.foreignpolicy.com.

2010c. "White House Gives Up on Getting Kyl's Support for New START." *The Cable*, 16 December. Accessed 20 December 2010. http://www.foreign policy.com.

2010d. "New START Rolls on toward Final Vote as McConnell and Kyl Declare Opposition." *The Cable*, 19 December. Accessed 22 December 2010. http://www.foreignpolicy.com. 2.

Rohde, David W. 1991. *Parties and Leaders in the Postreform House.* Chicago, IL: University of Chicago Press.

Romney, Mitt. 2010. "Obama's Worst Foreign Policy Mistake." *Washington Post.* 6 July. Accessed 6 July 2010. http://www.washingtonpost.com/wp-dyn/content/article/2010/07/05/AR2010070502657.html.

Rosner, Jeremy. 1995. *The New Tug of War.* Washington, DC: Carnegie Endowment for International Peace.

Rudalevige, Andrew. 2006. *The New Imperial Presidency: Renewing Presidential Power after Watergate.* Ann Arbor, MI: University of Michigan Press.

Rutten, Tim. 2010. "A Post-9/11 Betrayal Endures." *Los Angeles Times*, 11 September. Accessed 11 September 2010. http://articles.latimes.com/2010/sep/11/opinion/la-oe-0911-rutten-20100911.

Rybicki, Elizabeth. 2010. "Filling the Amendment Tree in the Senate." *Extension of Remarks* 33 (January): 1–10.

2009. Senate Consideration of Presidential Nominations: Committee and Floor Procedure. Report RL31980. Congressional Research Service. Washington, DC.

Schlesinger, Arthur. 1973. *The Imperial Presidency.* New York: Popular Library.

Schlesinger, James. 2003. "Hearings on Perspectives on House Reform: Committees and the Executive Branch." Testimony before House Select Committee on Homeland Security (10 July).

Schmitt, Eric and David Rohde. 2007. "2 Reports Assail State Dept. Role on Iraq Security: Oversight Is Faulted." *New York Times*, 23 October, A1.

Schneider, Bill. 2010. "Tea Party's Real Goal: The End of Politics." *Politico*, 28 September, 35.

Schneider, Judy, Colton Campbell, Christopher Davis, and Betsy Palmer. 2003. *Reorganization of the Senate: Modern Reform Efforts.* Report RL32112. Congressional Research Service. Washington, DC.

Schoultz, Lars. 1981. *Human Rights and United States Policy toward Latin America.* Princeton, NJ: Princeton University Press.

Schroeder, John. 1973. *Mr. Polk's War: American Opposition and Dissent, 1848–1848.* Madison, WI: University of Wisconsin Press.

Schultz, George, Madeleine Albright, Gary Hart, and Chuck Hagel. 2010. "It's Time for the Senate to Vote on New START." *Washington Post.* 10 September. Accessed 13 September 2010. http://www.washingtonpost.com.

Schwarz, Frederick A. O., Jr., and Aziz Z. Huq. 2007. *Unchecked and Unbalanced: Presidential Power in a Time of Terror.* New York: New Press.

Scully, Megan and Sara Sorcher. 2010. "Clinton: White House Up on New START." *Global Security Newswire*, 17 November. Accessed 18 November 2010. http://gsn.nti.org.

Shenon, Philip. 2007. "As New 'Cop on the Beat,' Congressman Starts Patrol." *New York Times*, 6 February, A18.

Sheridan, Mary Beth and Walter Pincus. 2010. "Vote on New START Nuclear Arms Treaty Delayed in Senate." *Washington Post*, 4 August, A1.

Shipan, Charles. 2005. "Congress and the Bureaucracy." In *The Legislative Branch*, ed. Paul Quirk and Sarah Binder. New York: Oxford University Press.

Shogren, Elizabeth. 1995. "Will Welfare Go Way of Health Reform." *Los Angeles Times*, 10 August, A18.

Shor, Elena. 2007. "Rockefeller Releases Deal on Intelligence Budgets." *The Hill*, 7 March, 8.

Silberman-Robb Commission. 2005. Report of the Commission on the Intelligence Capabilities of the United States Regarding Weapons of Mass Destruction. Washington, DC: Government Printing Office.

Silbey, Joel. 1967. *The Shrine of Party: Congressional Voting Behavior, 1841–1852.* Pittsburgh, PA: Pittsburgh University Press.

Sinclair, Barbara. 2012. "Senate Parties and Party Leadership, 1960–2010." In *The U.S. Senate: From Deliberation to Dysfunction*, ed. Burdett A. Loomis. Washington, DC: CQ Press.

    2010. Testimony on "Legislative Proposals to Change Senate Procedure," before the Senate Committee on Rules and Administration. (28 July). Accessed 27 August. http://rules.senate.gov/public/index.cfm?p=CommitteeHearings&ContentRec ord_id=2208a4dd-5e20-48bd-8f82-b2f75d0cd21d&Statement_id=cc96ec80-03-dd-43ba-8e3a-ba8bef5b2aec&ContentType_id=14f995b9-dfa5-407a-9d35-56-cc7152a7ed&Group_id=1983a2a8-4fc3-4062-a50e-7997351c154b&MonthDisplay=7&YearDisplay=2010.

Sklamberg, Howard. 1997. "The Meaning of Advice and Consent: The Senate's Constitutional Role in Treaty Making." *Michigan Journal of International Law* 18: 445–474.

Smist, Frank. 1990. *Congress Oversees the Intelligence Community.* Knoxville, TN: University of Tennessee Press.

Smith, Christopher. 2009. "Interagency Reform." *Small Wars Journal* 5 (February). Accessed 17 August 2010. http://smallwarsjournal.com/blog/2009/02/print/interagency-reform/ http://smallwarsjournal.com/blog/2009/02/interagency-reform/.

Smith, Steven S. and Gerald Gamm. 2009. "The Dynamics of Party Government in Congress." In *Congress Reconsidered* (9th ed.), ed. Lawrence C. Dodd and Bruce I. Oppenheimer. Washington, DC: CQ Press.

Snider, L. Britt. 2008. *The Agency and the Hill: CIA's Relationship with Congress, 1946–2004.* Washington, DC: Center for the Study of Intelligence, Central Intelligence Agency.

    2005. "Congressional Oversight of Intelligence after September 11." In *Transforming U.S. Intelligence,* ed. Jennifer E. Sims and Burton Gerber. Washington, DC: Georgetown University Press.

Spiro, Peter. 2001. "Treaties, Executive Agreements, and Constitutional Method." *Texas Law Review* 79: 961–1035.

Sprout, Harold and Margaret Sprout. 1967. *The Rise of American Naval Power: 1776–1918* (rev. ed.). Princeton, NJ: Princeton University Press.

Starks, Tim. 2010. "Splintered Jurisdiction." *National Journal,* 27 December, 2901.

Stephens, Herbert W. 1971. "The Role of the Legislative Committees in the Appropriations Process: A Study Focused on the Armed Services Committees." *Western Political Quarterly* 24 (Spring): 146–162.

Stevenson, Charles A. 2007. *Congress at War: The Politics of Conflict since 1789.* Dulles, VA: Potomac Books.

Stone, Ralph. 1970. *The Irreconcilables: The Fight against the League of Nations.* Lexington, KY: University Press of Kentucky.

Strohm, Chris. 2010. "Post-9/11 Expansion Must End, Experts Say." *CongressDailyPM,* 20 July, 6.

    2008. "Homeland Security Authorization Bill Falls by the Wayside." *Congress Daily,* 24 September.

Stuart, Reginald. 1982. "James Madison and the Militants: Republican Disunity and Replacing the Embargo." *Diplomatic History* 6: 145–167

Sundquist, James L. 1981. *The Decline and Resurgence of Congress.* Washington, DC: Brookings Institution.

Swift, Elaine. 1996. *The Making of an American Senate: Reconstitutive Change in Congress, 1787–1841.* Ann Arbor, MI: University of Michigan Press.

Tananbaum, Duane. 1988. *The Bricker Amendment Controversy: A Test of Eisenhower's Political Leadership.* Ithaca, NY: Cornell University Press.

Tap, Bruce. 2003. "Amateurs at War: Abraham Lincoln and the Committee on the Conduct of the War." *Law and History Review* 23(2): 110–128.

Tarnoff, Curt. 1997. *The Marshall Plan: Design, Accomplishments, and Relevance to the Present.* Report 97–62. Congressional Research Service. Washington, DC.

Taylor, Andrew. 2004. "Security Plan Changes Committee Name, Little Else." *CQ Today,* 8 October, 1.

    The Economist. 2011. "Libya and the Iraq Syndrome." 5 March 5, 40.

    Washington Post, 1984. Editorial, 18 April, A26.

Theoharis, Athan. 1978. *Spying on Americans: Political Surveillance from Hoover to the Huston Plan.* Philadelphia, PA: Temple University Press.

Tierney, John T. 1993. "Interest Group Involvement in Congressional Foreign and Defense Policy." In *Congress Resurgent: Foreign and Defense Policy on Capitol Hill*, ed. Randall B. Ripley and James M. Lindsay. Ann Arbor, MI: University of Michigan Press.

Toll, Ian W. 2006. *Six Frigates: The Epic History of the Founding of the U.S. Navy*. New York: W.W. Norton.

Towell, Pat. 1985. "Defense Add-Ons Revive Senate Turf Fight." *Congressional Quarterly Weekly Report* (December 14): 2617–2618.

Treverton, Gregory F. 2009. *Intelligence in an Age of Terror*. New York: Cambridge University Press.

Trimble, Phillip and J. Weiss. 1991. "The Role of the President, the Senate and Congress with Respect to Arms Control Treaties Concluded by the United States." *Chicago-Kent Law Review* 67 (2): 645–704.

Trimble, Phillip and Alexander Koff. 1998. "All Fall Down: The Treaty Power in the Clinton Administration." *Berkeley Journal of International Law* 16 (1): 55–70.

Wald, Patricia and Joe Onek. 2005. "Detainees." In *Patriot Debates: Experts Debate the Patriot Act*, ed. Stewart A. Baker and John Kavanaugh. Washington, DC: American Bar Association

Walden, Jerrold L. 1975. "The C.I.A.: A Study in the Arrogation of Administrative Power," *George Washington Law Review* 39 (January): 66–101.

Walker, Daniel Howe. 1991. *The Political Culture of the American Whigs*. Chicago, IL: University of Chicago Press.

Warner, Edward. 2010. "Testimony to the Senate Armed Services Committee." 29 July. Accessed 6 August 2010. http://armed-services.senate.gov.

Weeks, William Earl. 1992. *John Quincy Adams and American Global Empire*. Lexington, KY: University Press of Kentucky.

Weiner, Tim. 2007. *Legacy of Ashes: The History of the CIA*. New York: Doubleday.

Wheeler, Winslow T. 2011. "The Defense Budget: Ignorance Is Not Bliss." *The Hill*, 9 March, 22.

Whitelaw, Kevin and David Kaplan. 2004. "Don't Ask, Don't Tell." *U.S. News & World Report*, 13 September, 36–37.

Widenor, William. 1980. *Henry Cabot Lodge and the Search for an American Foreign Policy*. Berkeley, CA: University of California Press.

Wilson, Woodrow. 1885. *Congressional Government*. Boston, MA: Houghton Mifflin.

Wirls, Daniel. 2008. "Lap Dogs of War: Congress and National Security Policy." Presented at the Annual Meeting of the Western Political Science Association Annual Meeting, San Diego.

Wittes, Benjamin. 2009. "Obama's Dick Cheney Moment." *Washington Post*, 29 September. Accessed 21 September 2011. http://www.washingtonpost.com/wp-dyn/content/article/2009/09/28/AR2009092802492.html.

Wittkopf, Eugene R. and James M. McCormick. 2004. *The Domestic Sources of American Foreign Policy: Insights and Evidence* (4th ed.). Lanham, MD: Rowman and Littlefield.

Ynsfran, Pablo Max. 1958. *La Expedicion Norteamericana contra El Paraguay, 1858–1859*, 2 vols. Mexico City: Editorial Guaramia.

Yoo, John. 1999. "Globalism and the Constitution: Treaties, Non-Self-Execution, and the Original Understanding." *Columbia Law Review* 99 (December): 1955–2094.

Zegart, Amy B. Forthcoming. "Domestic Politics of Irrational Intelligence Oversight." *Political Science Quarterly.*

2007. *Spying Blind: The CIA, the FBI, and the Origins of 9/11.* Princeton: Princeton University Press.

Zegart, Amy and Julie Quinn. 2010. "Congressional Intelligence Oversight: The Electoral Disconnection." *Intelligence and National Security* (December): 744–766.

Zelizer, Julian E. 2010. *Arsenal of Democracy: The Politics of National Security – From World War II to the War on Terrorism.* New York: Basic Books.

2010. "Look Who's Back: It's Obama's White House, But It's Still Bush's World." *Washington Post*, 15 August, B1.

Congressional Documents

U.S. Congress. 23 March 1818. *Annals of Congress*, 15th Cong., 1st sess., 1474–1499.

25 February 1859. *Congressional Globe*. 35th Cong., 2d sess., 1334, 1352, 1363.

21 February 1859. *Congressional Globe*, 35th Cong., 2d sess., 1187–1188.

18 February 1859. *Congressional Globe*, 35th Cong., 2d sess., 1122–1124.

26 April 1858. *Congressional Globe*, 35th Cong., 1st sess., 1783.

21 April 1858. *Congressional Globe*, 35th Cong., 1st sess., 1704, 1705, 1727–1728.

4 May 1858. *Congressional Globe*, 35th Cong., 1st sess., 1929.

11 February, 2011. *Congressional Record*. 112th Cong., 1st sess. Washington, DC: Government Printing Office, H686-H714.

29 April 2010. *Congressional Record*. 111th Cong., 2d sess. Washington, DC: Government Printing Office, E705.

29 April 2010. *Congressional Record*. 111th Cong., 2d sess. Washington, DC: Government Printing Office, S2777.

15 April 2010. *Congressional Record*. 111th Cong., 2d sess. Washington, DC: Government Printing Office, S2334.

10 March 2010. *Congressional Record*. 111th Cong., 2d sess. Washington, DC: Government Printing Office, H1251.

8 July 2009. *Congressional Record*, 111th Cong., 1st sess. Washington, DC: Government Printing Office, S6384.

25 February 2009. *Congressional Record*, 111th Cong., 1st sess. Washington, DC: Government Printing Office, E412.

20 June 2008. *Congressional Record*. 110th Cong., 2d sess. Washington, DC: Government Printing Office, H5760.

20 June, 2008. *Congressional Record*. 110th Cong., 2d sess. Washington, DC: Government Printing Office, H5766.

20 June 2008. *Congressional Record*. 110th Cong. 2d sess. Washington, DC: Government Printing Office, H5762.

9 July 2008. *Congressional Record*, 110th Cong., 2d sess. Washington, DC: Government Printing Office, S6468.

9 July 2008. *Congressional Record.* 110th Cong., 2d sess. Washington, DC: Government Printing Office, S6454.

8 July 2008. *Congressional Record.* 110th Cong., 2d sess. Washington, DC: Government Printing Office, S6406.

8 July 2008. *Congressional Record,* 110th Cong., 2d sess. Washington, DC: Government Printing Office, S6391.

13 July 2006. *Congressional Record.* 109th Cong., 2d sess. Washington, DC: Government Printing Office, H5212.

20 May 2005. *Congressional Record.* 109th Cong., 2d sess. Washington, DC: Government Printing Office, 10547–48.

1 October 2001. *Congressional Record.* 106th Cong., 1st sess. Washington, DC: Government Printing Office, S9948.

21 July 1982. *Congressional Record.* 97th Cong., 2d sess. Washington, DC: Government Printing Office, 17341–44.

22 January 1976. *Congressional Record.* 94th Cong., 2d sess., Washington, DC: Government Printing Office, 608–610.

19 December 1975. *Congressional Record.* 94th Cong., 1st sess., Washington, DC: Government Printing Office, 42217.

11 December 1974. *Congressional Record.* 93rd Cong., 2d sess. Washington, DC: Government Printing Office, 39166.

17 August 1967. *Congressional Record.* 90th Cong., 1st sess., Washington, DC: Government Printing Office, 22968.

14 November 1963. *Congressional Record.* 88th Cong., 1st sess., Washington, DC: Government Printing Office, 21840–21842.

15 July 1958. *Congressional Record.* 85th Cong., 2d sess. Washington, DC: Government Printing Office, 13978.

22 January 1928. *Congressional Record.* 70th Cong., 1st sess. Washington, DC: Government Printing Office, 1785–1790.

21 April 1914. *Congressional Record.* 63rd Cong, 2d sess. Washington, DC: Government Printing Office, 6999–7000.

U.S. Congress. House. Committee on Foreign Affairs. Press Release. 23 September 2010. 111th Cong., 2d sess., http://www.modernizingforeignassistance.org/blog/2010/09/page/4/.

House. Committee on Armed Services. Committee Print No. 10, Joint Explanatory Statement to accompany S. 3001, the FY2009 National Defense Authorization Act. 2008. 110th Cong., 2d sess. September.

2009. House. Committee on Foreign Affairs (Minority). *Republican Concept Paper: Reform of Foreign Assistance for Economic Growth and Opportunity.* 111th Cong., 2ds sess. Fall.

House. Committee on Armed Services. 2007. 110th Cong., 1st sess., H. Rept. 110–477. 6 December.

House. Committee on Armed Services. *Committee Defense Review Report.* 2006. 109th Cong., 2d sess. 6 December.

House. Committee on Armed Services. 2005. 109th Cong., 1st sess., H. Rept. 109–360. 18 December.

House. Committee on Armed Services. 2005. 109th Cong., 1st sess., H. Rept. 109–89. 20 May.

House. Permanent Select Committee on Intelligence. *Intelligence Authorization Act for Fiscal Year 2005.* 2004. 108th Cong., 2d sess. H. Rept. 108–558. 21 June.

House. Committee on Armed Services. 1990. 101st Cong., 2d sess., H. Rept. 101–665. 3 August.

House. Committee on Armed Services. 1987. 100th Cong., 1st sess., H. Rept 100–446. 17 November.

House. Committee on Armed Services. 1986. 99th Cong., 2d sess., H Rept 99–1001. 14 October.

House. Committee on Armed Services. 1983. 98th Cong., 1st sess., H. Rept. 98–107. 11 May.

House. Workshop on Congressional Oversight and Investigations. 1979. 96th Cong., 1st sess., H.Doc. No. 96–217.

House. Committee on Armed Services. 1977. 95th Cong., 1st sess., H. Rept. 95–446. 20 June.

House. Select Committee on Committees. *Committee Organization in the House.* 1973. 93rd Cong., 1st sess.

House. U.S. Foreign Operations Subcommittee. 1957. Mutual Security Act for 1958. 85th Cong., 1st sess. 19 June.

U.S. Congress. Senate. Select Committee on Intelligence. *Report on the U.S. Intelligence Community's Prewar Intelligence Assessments on Iraq.* 2003. 108th Cong., 2d sess. 7 July.

Senate. Select Committee on Secret Military Assistance to Iran and the Nicaraguan Opposition and House Select Committee to Investigate Covert Arms Transactions with Iran. *Report on the Iran-Contra Affair.* 1987. 100th Cong., 1st sess., S. Rept. 100–216 and H. Rept. 100–433.

Senate. Committee on Armed Services. 1976. 94th Cong., 2d sess., S. Rept. 94–878. 14 May.

Senate. Select Committee to Study Governmental Operations with Respect to Intelligence Activities. 1976. 94th Cong., 2d sess., S. Rept. 94–755.

Senate. Select Committee to Study Governmental Operations with Respect to Intelligence Activities. *Alleged Assassination Plots Involving Foreign Leaders: An Interim Report.* 1975a. 94th Cong., 1st sess. 20 November.

Senate. Select Committee to Study Governmental Operations with Respect to Intelligence Activities. 1975b. *Covert Action in Chile, 1963–1973.* 94th Cong., 1st sess. 18 December.

Senate. Committee on Foreign Relations. 1959. Mutual Security Act of 1959. 86th Cong., 1st sess. 21 May.

Senate. Committee on Foreign Relations. *Report.* 1858. 35th Cong., 2d sess., Serial Set, Volume 938, #60. 9 February.

Senate. Committee on Foreign Relations. 2010a. *Executive Report 111–6.* Washington, DC: Government Printing Office, 111th Congress, 2nd Session (1 October).

2010b. "Kerry lauds bipartisan group of former cabinet members and senators who support the New START treaty." Senate Committee on Foreign Relations Press Release, 24 June. Accessed 18 May 2011. http://foreign.senate.gov.

U.S. Congress. House and Senate. Senate Select Committee on Intelligence and U.S. House Permanent Select Committee on Intelligence. *Joint Inquiry into Intelligence Community Activities Before and After the Terrorist Attacks of*

September 11, 2001, Final Report. 2002. 107th Cong., 2d sess., S. Rept. 107–351 and H. Rept. 107–792. December.

U.S. Congress. Senate. U.S. Senate, Office of the Historian. "August 5, 1789: Irritating the President." http://www.senate.gov/artandhistory/history/minute/The_Senate_Irritates_President_George_Washington.htm

U.S. Congress. House. 2009. "House Resolution (H.Res.) 5: Rules of the United States House of Representatives: 111th Cong. (6 January 2009).

U.S. Congress. Senate. 2009. "Standing Rules of the U.S. Senate." 108th Cong. Accessed January 1, 2010. http://rules.senate.gov/public/index.cfm?p=RulesOfSenateHome.

"Coast Guard Authorization Act of 2010." H.R. 3619, 11th Congress. Washington, DC (28 September 2010).

"Homeland Security Act of 2002," H.R. 5005, 108th Congress. Washington, DC (2002).

"Implementing the Recommendations of the 9/11 Commission Act of 2007," H.R. 1, 110th Congress. Washington, DC (2007).

Message of the President on the Middle East. 5 January 1957. *House Document 46.* 85th Congress, 1st Session.

United States Commission on National Security/21st Century. 2001. "Road Map for National Security: Imperative for Change, The Phase III Report of the U.S. Commission on National Security/21st Century." http://govinfo.library.unt.edu/nssg/index.html (15 February).

The Budget in Brief, Fiscal Year 2007, U.S. Department of State, p. 1.

Sec. 10 of the Foreign Military Sales Amendment, 1971, PL 91–672; (22 U.S.C. 2412).

Executive Documents

Office of the President of the United States. 2011. *Statement by the President on H.R. 6523,* 7 January. accessed 26 May 2011. http://www.whitehouse.gov/the-press-office/2011/01/07/statement-president-hr-6523.

2011. *Executive Order #13567,* 7 March. Accessed 26 May. 2011http://www.gpo.gov/fdsys/pkg/FR-2011-03-10/pdf/2011-5728.pdf.

2011. Periodic Review of Individuals Detained at Guantanamo Bay Naval Station Pursuant to the Authorization for use of Military Force, 7 March. Accessed 26 May 2011. http://www.whitehouse.gov/the-press-office/2011/03/07/executive-order-periodic-review-individuals-detained-guant-namo-bay-nava.

2011. *Statement on Signing the Ike Skelton National Defense Authorization Act for Fiscal year 2011,* 7 January. Accessed 26 May 2011. http://www.whitehouse.gov/the-press-office/2011/01/07/statement-president-hr-6523.

2009. *Remarks by the President on National Security,* 21 March. http://www.whitehouse.gov/the_press_office/Remarks-by-the-President-On-National-Security-5-21-09.

2007. *Executive Order #13440,* 20 July. accessed 26 May 2011. http://edocket.access.gpo.gov/2007/pdf/07-3656.pdf.

2001. *Military Order of November 13, 2001.* Accessed 7 March 2011. http://www.fas.org/irp/offdocs/eo/mo-111301.htm.

2011. *Executive Order #13567,* 7 March. Accessed 26 May 2011. http://www.gpo.gov/fdsys/pkg/FR-2011-03-10/pdf/2011-5728.pdf.

The White House. 2010. *National Security Strategy,* May, http://www.whitehouse.gov/ sites/default/files/rss_viewer/national_security_strategy.pdf

2006. *National Security Strategy of the United States of America,* March, http:// www.comw.org/qdr/fulltext/nss2006.pdf.

2002. *National Security Strategy of the United States of America,* September, http:// www.globalsecurity.org/military/library/policy/national/nss-020920.pdf.

United States Department of Defense. 2010. *Determination of Guantanamo Cases Referred for Prosecution,* 22 January. Accessed 26 May 2011. http://www.justice. gov/opa/documents/taba-prel-rpt-dptf-072009.pdf.

2009. *Detention Policy Task Force Issues Preliminary Report,* 21 July. Accessed 26 May 2011. http://www.justice.gov/opa/pr/2009/July/09-ag-705.htm.

2006. *Guantanamo Bay Detainee Administrative Review Board Decisions Completed,* 9 February Accessed 15 March 2011. http://www.globalsecurity.org/security/ library/news/2006/02/sec-060209-dod01.htm.

2004. *Order Establishing Combatant Status Review Tribunal,* 7 July 7. Accessed 26 May 2011. http://www.defense.gov/news/jul2004/d20040707review.pdf.

United States Department of Homeland Security (DHS). 2010. *History: Department of Homeland Security.* Accessed 10 November. http://www.dhs.gov/xabout/history/ editorial_0133.shtm.

United States Department of Justice, Office of Legal Counsel (OLC). 2006. *Legal Authorities Supporting the Activities of the National Security Agency Described by the President.* Accessed 19 January 2011. http://www.justice.gov/olc/2006/nsa-white-paper.pdf.

United States Department of Justice, Office of the Attorney General of the United States. 2009. *Letter to Senators Reid and McConnell,* 9 December. Accessed 26 May 2011. http://www.lawfareblog.com/wp-content/uploads/2010/12/AG-CR-Letter-12-9-10.pdf.

United States Department of State. 1937. *Papers Relating to the Foreign Relations of the United States, 1918–1919, Russia,* vol. 4. Washington, DC: U.S. Government Printing Office.

United States Federal Bureau of Investigation. 2009. *FBI Fact Sheet: Former Guantanamo Detainee Trends,* 7 April. Accessed 4 March 2011. http://media. miamiherald.com/smedia/2009/05/27/20/recidivists.source.prod_affiliate.56.pdf.

Judicial Cases

ACLU v. National Sec. Agency, 493 F.3d 644 (6th Cir. 2007)

Al-Bihani v. Obama, 590 F.3d 866, 871, 873–74 (2010)

Al-Haramain Islamic Foundation, Inc. v. Bush, 507 F.3d 1190 (2007)

Al-Haramain Islamic Foundation v. Obama (N.D. Cal. Mar. 31, 2010)

Al-Marri v. Wright, 487 F. 3d 160 (2007)

Al Odah v. United States, 321 F.3d 1134 (D.C. Cir 2003), rev'd sub nom *Rasul v. Bush* 124 S.Ct. 2686 (2004).

American Civil Liberties v. National Sec. Agency, 438 F.Supp.2d 754 (E.D. Mich. 2006)

Bensayah v. Obama, DC Cir 08–5537, 1–04-cv-01166 (2010)

Boumediene v. Bush, 553 U.S. 723 (2008)

Ex parte Milligan, 71 U.S. 2 (1866)

Dorr v. United States, 195 U.S. 138 (1904)

Downes v. Bidwell, 182 U.S. 244 (1901)

Goldman v. United States, 316 U.S. 129 (1942)

Hamdi v. Rumsfeld 542 U.S. 507 (2004)

Hepting v. AT&T Corp., 439 F.Supp.2d 974 (N.D. Cal. 2006)

Irvine v. California, 347 U.S. 128 (1954)

Katz v. United States, 389 U.S. 347 (1967)

Little v. Barreme, 2 Cr. (6 U.S.) 170 (1804)

Myers v. United States, 272 U.S. 52 293, (1926)

In re National Sec. Agency Telecommunications Rec., 564 F.Supp.2d 1109 (2008)

National Security Agency Telecommunications Records Litigation, MDL Docket No. 06–1791 VRW (2009)

Olmstead v. United States, 277 U.S. 438 (1928)

Rasul v. Bush, 542 U.S. 466 (2004)

Silverman v. United States, 365 U.S. 505 (1961)

United States v. Curtiss-Wright Export Co. 299 U.S. 304 (1936)

United States v. Sinclair, 321 F.Supp. 1074, 1078 (E.D. Mich. 1971)

United States v. United States Dist. Ct. for E.D. of Mich., 444 F.2d 651 (6th Cir. 1971)

United States v. United States District Court, 407 U.S. 297, 316 (1972)

Authors' Interviews

John Sununu, former White House Chief of Staff, Washington, DC, 9 February 2011.

James R. Schlesinger, Director of Central Intelligence Agency, Washington, DC, 16 June 1994.

William J. Casey, Director of Central Intelligence Agency, Langley, Virginia, 11 June 1984.

Papers

Ann to Thomas Eagleton, 4 December 1977, Folder 4381, Thomas Eagleton Papers, University of Missouri.

Bob Wolthuis to Max Friedersdorf, 16 December 1975, box 3, Robert Wolthuis Files, Ford Congressional Relations Office Papers.

Dick Clark to Pam Kringler, 26 November 1975; Clark to John Haguran, 17 December 1975; both in box 44, Dick Clark Papers, University of Iowa.

Dwight Eisenhower to William Knowland, 25 January 1954, Box 6, Dwight Eisenhower Diary, Eisenhower Presidential Library, Abilene.

Harold Hughes to Robert Hart, 31 October 1974, Box S83, Harold Hughes Papers, University of Iowa.

Harold Hughes to Hubert Humphrey, 14 February 1974, Box S83, Harold Hughes Papers, University of Iowa.

Lord Napier to William Reed, 6 May 1858, Reel 54, James Buchanan Papers, Pennsylvania State Historical Society, Philadelphia.

President Lyndon B. Johnson and Larry O'Brien, 4:01 P.M., 12 December 1963, Tape K6312.08, PNO 4, Recordings of Telephone Conversations—White House Series, Recordings and Transcripts of Conversations and Meetings, Lyndon B. Johnson Library.

President Lyndon B. Johnson and Jack Brooks, 10:36 P.M., 20 December 1963, Tape K6312.13, PNO 6, Recordings of Telephone Conversations – White House Series, Recordings and Transcripts of Conversations and Meetings, Lyndon B. Johnson Library.

Tom Eagleton, "Dear Colleague," 9 September 1974, Box 35, FPD Series, Henry Jackson Papers, University of Washington.

Unsigned memo, 2 October 1974, Box 209, Robert Taft, Jr. Papers, Library of Congress.

Newspapers

The Times (London). 1960. 17 February.
New York Daily Tribune. 1860. 1 August.
New York Herald. 1859. 19 January.
    1858. 6 May.
New York Times. 1999. 30 April.
U.S. News & World Report. 1963. 26 November.
Washington Post. 1978. 9 August.
    1964. 29 June.
Washington Union. 1859. 23 February.
Wall Street Journal. 1985. 11 February.
    1981, 11 January.
    1974. 2 October.

Websites

www.usaid.gov/press/frontlines/fl_mar10/p05_lugar100309.html.

Index